The King of Kings and I

The King of Kings and I

The Greatest Story Ever Kvetched!

Jaffe Cohen

HarperSanFrancisco

An Imprint of HarperCollinsPublishers

To Stephen Ira Ball, who first taught me
the meaning of friendship.

HarperCollins Web Site: http://www.harpercollins.com
HarperCollins®, 📖®, and HarperSanFrancisco™ are trademarks of
HarperCollins Publishers Inc.

FIRST EDITION

Designed by Joseph Rutt

ISBN 0–06–251501–2 (cloth)
ISBN 0–06–251525–X (pbk.)

97 98 99 00 01 RRD(H) 10 9 8 7 6 5 4 3 2 1

Contents

Acknowledgments

This story has gone through more incarnations than Buddha. Originally conceived as an essay for John Hammond at the *New York Native*, it was later developed as the one-man show *My Life as a Christian* produced by Carol Polcovar and Raven Hall and directed by Michael Zam, who helped me piece together the narrative. It was later revived and retitled at "Highways" in Santa Monica, assisted by Tim Miller, Jordan Peimer, and Jerry Browning. More helpful friends include Ed Hall and Ken Davison in San Francisco, Maggie Casella, David Adkins, Scott McKuen and Christian Dupont in Toronto, Bob Schrock and Tom Jacobsen at Celebrations Theater in West Hollywood and Steve Kaplan at the HBO Workspace. I'm also deeply indebted to Kevin Bentley for giving me the opportunity to write this book as well as the Livingstone family, Alan, Nancy, and Chris for providing me with the daily support I needed to get the writing done. Other friends and counselors who flattered me and kept me happy along the way include Michael Stewart, Barry Gallison, Bob Smith, Vince Gatton, Leslie Harris, Lee Schweickert and Kennedy Wheatley. I'd also like to thank Mark Chimsky and David Hennessey for their editorial assistance in the home stretch. In addition, before this story could be told, it had to be suffered in real life, so I'd like to thank all the dear souls who found my life story charming long before I did. Without them this comic memoir might have been a much sadder document. Finally, to quote that great Jewish playwright, Tennessee Williamsburg, "I've come to rely on the kindness of my parents." Myron and Ruth Cohen, I think you already know that I owe it all to you.

Ira and his young lover, Joshua, were packing to move upstate, so I ambled over to their Greenwich Village apartment to make Ira feel guilty for abandoning me and to grab whatever extra household appliances they didn't want to take. I dutifully helped them empty drawers and box silverware, but all activity stopped when we discovered an envelope filled with loose photos in the bottom of the hall closet. The envelope was labeled "1973," and one picture in particular made us howl with dismay. It was me standing in my parents' suburban backyard; my hair was a long, tangled mess, most of my face was covered with beard, and my eyes were wild. It looked like I'd been raised by wolves somewhere near Levittown.

"Not a good look," Joshua decided.

"Isn't this the summer you became a Christian?" Ira asked.

"Wait a second!" Joshua exclaimed. "You're Jewish and gay. Why would you want to convert to Christianity?"

1

"It was the times," I replied hesitantly.

"It was the seventies, not the Spanish Inquisition!"

"You have to understand, we did a lot of drugs back then."

"I did a lot of drugs in college also."

"But not the right drugs. People rarely experience God on NyQuil."

"*You* experienced God?" Joshua exclaimed. "Puh-lease!"

Of the three of us, only Ira wanted to take this conversation seriously. Like me, my best friend was forty-two, with the boundless enthusiasm of a man half his age. On the other hand, Joshua was little more than half our age, with all the caution and pessimism we were so afraid we'd develop in middle age. For weeks Ira had been trying to explain seventies idealism to Joshua, and this night he seized the opportunity to teach his lover a long-overdue history lesson.

"What happened," he said softly, "is that Jaffe had a vision of Jesus. Then he went home and tried to live in a tent in his parents' backyard."

If Joshua's eyes had rolled any farther he would have snapped his optic nerve in two. "Now let me get this straight, Jaffe. You really saw Jesus?"

"Well . . . yeah."

"Really? Jesus Christ?"

"No, Jesus Santiago the superintendent. Hey, you live in New York, sooner or later you bump into everyone."

"And you really became a Christian?"

"When you see Christ you become a Christian. If I'd seen Mel Gibson I might have become an asshole."

Ira gave me a dirty look; he knew I had no patience for Joshua. Touching his lover on the shoulder, he again tried to explain: "You have to put Jaffe's experience in context. Those years were very confusing. The Vietnam War was ending. Watergate was starting. Gay Liberation was brand new." But there was only so much Joshua wanted to be reminded of about his lover's life during the years he himself was still being toilet trained. Shaking his head and snapping his fingers, he announced vehemently, "I'll never understand the seventies! A Christian? What would make a person want to become something he's not?"

Then he went to his computer to log into a chat room, where he spent the next hour introducing himself to strangers as Gryndolyn the Grand Vizier of the planet Grexyl.

L ater that night, with Joshua still at the computer, Ira walked me home down Bleecker Street, passing by the usual card shops, antique stores, and condom boutiques. This was *our* street. It sometimes seemed that, like hamsters in a habit trail, this was the only path we ever used. After we'd graduated from college our primary passion was merely to live in Greenwich Village. By the time we were thirty we'd accomplished that goal, but after that we coasted for the next ten years, often mistaking the hustle and bustle of downtown for actual changes in our lives.

But now we were over forty, in the middle of our midlife crises. Ira had already found a young lover and a new job fifty miles north, teaching theater at SUNY New Paltz. My crisis was far more disturbing: nothing was happening to me. I was still working the same old job, teaching writing at Fordham College, and trying to write hack screenplays at the rate of one page per year.

"I'll miss you so much when I move," Ira said.

"Me too," I said. "What are you doing tomorrow? Are you gonna be 'with child'?"

Ira shook his head. "Joshua thinks you're jealous of him."

"Why? Because I want your attention."

"He thinks you have boundary issues."

"No. North Korea has boundary issues. I just like to steal you away every now and then."

"Well, be kind. He's a lot brighter than you think."

Ira slipped his hand beneath my arm and squeezed it hard to communicate both affection and exasperation. This time of night, when the streets were nearly empty, was our favorite time to be together. The only guys who passed us were men in their twenties straggling home from the same bars on Christopher Street we'd stopped going to years before. Few of the faces looked familiar; ten years ago we would have recognized dozens of our friends.

"I wish there were more of us left," I sighed.

"I know what you mean," Ira said as we stepped into a Korean deli for our midnight snack.

"Everyone I meet now is at least ten years younger than me. I feel like Rip van Winkle with a bald spot."

Ira grabbed some fig bars from the counter and we got in line to pay the cashier. Exiting the deli, we crossed Carmine Street and sat down on the steps of Saint Anthony's Catholic Church. The cookies were, as usual, just a little stale.

After a few bites I announced dramatically, "Maybe I should move away from here too."

"Where would you go?" Ira asked, picking fig from between his teeth.

"I don't know. Los Angeles maybe. I might be able to get a staff job out there."

I shook my head, and Ira patted my knee to console me. Then he reached into his shirt pocket to pull out the old photograph of me; he'd stashed it there a few hours earlier.

"Here. I want you to have this."

I looked again into the wildly searching eyes of the young man I'd been at twenty.

"You were so adventurous back then," Ira said admiringly.

"Nah! I wasn't adventurous. I just moved around a lot to avoid being depressed."

"You had a lot of guts," Ira admitted. "I never told you how jealous I was that you had the nerve to drop out of school that semester and hitchhike out west."

"You were jealous of me? Why? I was totally demented."

Ira shook his head. "What you did took a lot of faith."

"You could say that again."

"That's what you should be writing about. The search for meaning. The history you and I share. The part of me I want Joshua to know better."

I looked again at the photograph of the pained young man in his parents' backyard.

"Am I still this person?"

"Absolutely."

"To write about how I came to see Jesus," I sighed, "I'd *really* have to start from the beginning."

CHAPTER 1

The Goy Next Door

I was born in Brooklyn, the homeland of the Jewish people. Now, Brooklyn is actually a very small peninsula, surrounded on three sides by a very large ocean. I was shocked the first time I saw this on a map, because as a child I always felt that the ocean was a part of Brooklyn and not vice versa. Brooklyn was the whole world; it was where I toddled happily with my mother, my father, and my big brother, Bernie. One could never leave Brooklyn, especially at the ocean, where we were never far from the shadows of skyscrapers and my father's elderly relatives: Grandpa Hershel, Bubbe Manya, and Manya's two older sisters, Fanya and Adelle, who all lived on the fifteenth floor of an apartment building across the street from the beach.

The unmarried sisters, Fanya and Adelle, even though their com-bined ages, if you counted back, would probably predate the Dead Sea Scrolls, were always referred to as "the girls." Sixty years ago Hershel and the girls had been part of a young socialists' league. Originally Hershel had wanted to marry the stately Adelle, but she turned him down; he next proposed to shy Fanya, but she was simi-larly disinclined. He eventually married my grandmother and, in effect, wound up with all three. We never knew how old these four people were, but I suspect that they were quite ancient, because a few years ago my hippie cousin Sheryl, while discussing reincarnation in front of Adelle, happened to brag, "I lived in Europe in the nineteenth century," to which Adelle growled back in Yiddish, "So did I—and I couldn't wait to get out!"

Adelle was the cranky sister. At one time she'd been wed to "Poor Mendel the Gambler," who owned a dry-cleaning store during the Great Depression. According to family legend, when the business failed, Mendel wanted to turn the store into a luncheonette but he couldn't afford to buy new equipment. All my life I've imagined Poor Mendel hanging brisket off wire hangers and baking four-hundred-pound waffles in a pants presser. I would love to have met Poor Mendel, but sometime in 1948 he died alone in his car from a massive coronary while searching for a parking space in downtown Albany. The moral: the world's a dangerous place. Stay in Brooklyn!

In fact, it seemed to me that once my father's relatives schlepped here from czarist Russia, they never wanted to go anywhere ever again. I first became aware of this one year at Passover when I was six years old. As usual, we'd gone to Grandpa's apartment for the yearly seder, and at the first opportunity I turned on the television to watch Walt Disney's version of *Davy Crockett*. This was my favorite show, because the explorers were my heroes. Although I could barely read, I was already thumbing through my mother's encyclopedia and marveling at the lives of the men who'd crossed the ocean in wooden boats and rolled through Indian territory in covered wagons, and Davy Crockett was the best of all. I watched enraptured until Grandpa Hershel sat down beside me on the bed. He looked confused because, having learned his history under Nicholas II, he was truly in the dark.

"What's this?" he asked, pointing at the TV set.

"*Davy Crockett*," I answered.

"And who's this one? The one with the animal on his head."

"That's Davy Crockett."

Grandpa nodded thoughtfully.

"And what's he doing now?"

"He wants to fight at the Alamo, so he's walking to Texas."

My grandfather was taken aback. "He's walking to Texas?!" At this point Manya sidled alongside us and watched over our shoulders. Grandpa pointed to the TV and explained, "That's Davy Crockett. He's walking to Texas."

"Really?" Manya replied. "Was this an intelligent thing to do?" And then she left the room.

But like I said, my grandparents and the girls lived across the street from the ocean, and several times a year we'd escort them across the boardwalk on Coney Island. The next hour was then spent getting us to our spot on the sand, because the girls always hiked across the beach the same way they'd fled Eastern Europe, with all their belongings in tow. For one thing, Bubbe never went anywhere without at least three hundred pounds of food, which Bernie and I would schlepp in an old Coca Cola cooler the size of an industrial freezer. We also had to carry Adelle's patio furniture, Fanya's blankets, and two or three changes of clothing. Their goal, I now see, was to re-create their apartments in sight of the water, and I wouldn't have been surprised if one day they'd brought several standing lamps and an area rug.

When we finally settled on a location, Bubbe Manya would then open the cooler and pull out enough egg salad, ruglach, and hot coffee to cater the entire beach. Buying cheeseburgers from the concession stand was forbidden because they were both expensive and unkosher, so Manya personally brought enough to feed every Jew within a five-mile radius. I remember them coming at us from nearby blankets and huddling over my head, a forest of brown pants and sundresses, all holding plates in their hands and arguing in Yiddish.

Nobody went in the water. The adults had no desire, and Bernie and I weren't allowed to because we would have gotten cramps and drowned. So I'd spend hours sitting with "the girls," digesting quietly, while the other children—the Italians and the Puerto Ricans—ran screaming back and forth from their blankets to the waves. I simply sat there, year after year, not even knowing how badly I wanted to break away until our last summer in Brooklyn, the day my grandfather decided he would walk across the ocean.

It was already late in the day and the tide was unusually low. Grandpa Hershel had strolled into the surf, and the girls were whispering about someone with cancer. My mother, wanting to get rid of me, told me to go after my grandfather, which I was happy to do, because the old man usually gave me quarters for no apparent reason. I splashed up to my grandfather, whose baggy pants were rolled above his knees. The old man was looking south toward the sun, a bright orange ball on the horizon. Then he pointed. "You see that, Jaffe? It's land!"

I nodded as though I could see something.

"That's another state!" Grandpa announced proudly.

"Wow!"

"So you know what I think? If Davy Crockett could walk to Texas, we can walk to New Jersey. You and me—let's go."

So the two of us started stepping through the ripples of water. Schools of baby fish fled as we pushed forward. Baby crabs gasped in horror and bubbled into the earth. The water was so shallow that, at points, it was nothing more than a wet film over a dark mound of sand. Sometimes the water got as deep as a bathtub and my grandfather bent down, lifted me up, and held me aloft. But then the water would get shallow and he'd put me back down. When the ocean got deep in front of us we turned, sometimes to the left and sometimes to the right. We walked wherever the sand would rise up beneath us. We just kept walking until the people on the beach couldn't be heard, until they could barely be seen. And to this day I still don't know how we managed to walk as far as we did. Maybe we were walking on sandbars churned up by Hurricane Donna, because this may also have been the summer when a storm knocked down the oak tree in our backyard. Back in those days Brooklyn did have some miraculous weather, and anything could have happened. Almost.

Because we never got to New Jersey. Suddenly the water got too deep in all directions. The surface as far as we could see was now dark green, and a buoy rang its bell and laughed at our attempt to walk past it. The sun, about to dip into the ocean, was reflecting off something in the distance. My grandfather squinted and took off his glasses.

"Maybe next time," he shrugged.

I could see land in front of us. "Can't we swim?"

Grandpa Hershel looked back from where we'd come.

"No. This is good enough."

He bent over again, took off his watchband, and cooled his forearms in the water.

"Do you know who Moses was?" he asked me. "Do you know what Moses was famous for? Moses, the greatest Jew of all time, parted the Red Sea, and led the Jews to the Promised Land, but . . . he didn't go in! Moses, the greatest of all, never entered the Holy Land. He just stood there looking. So, if Moses can live without the Holy Land, we can live without New Jersey!"

Then I remember my grandfather standing quietly for a moment, rubbing his neck and contemplating. For a moment the water felt warmer, as though we'd suddenly gone to Egypt, and the air felt ancient, because we'd traveled back in time. As I look back at this long-ago afternoon, some things become clear. My old relatives not only carried their food and furniture wherever they went; they also carried a huge load of history around with them, and within those five thousand years of Judaism they were free to roam wherever they pleased. So, in all truthfulness, I can't say they never went anywhere. It just looked that way because I didn't always know when they were shuttling back and forth between biblical times and the present. Texas, I now realize, belonged to Davy Crockett, but history belonged to the Jews, and this was where Grandpa Hershel had wanted to take me. After a long moment, he broke his silence. "Do you understand, Jaffe?" I nodded as though I did, but in fact it would be nearly half a lifetime before I realized that this was the day I found my religion.

Then, without taking my hand, Hershel turned around and started walking toward land. I didn't want to follow him, but the water was too deep to swim across the ocean, so I waded after my grandfather, who took long strides without looking back. I was annoyed we hadn't achieved our goal, so I purposely kicked up the water, splashing myself until the ocean soaked through my shorts. By the time we got back to shore my father had already packed up the cooler, and my mother was upset that my clothes were soaked. "Don't worry, Roz," Adelle told her. "They'll dry as we walk."

That evening we accompanied Hershel and the girls back to their apartment and went upstairs to finish what was left of the egg salad. Some time later my grandfather, my father, and Bernie started watching wrestling on TV, so I snuck into the kitchen to listen to the girls talking about their cousin Miriam, who had just moved to Miami.

"She wants us to move too," Bubbe Manya said.

"Florida?" Fanya sniffed.

And Adelle concluded the conversation by pointing out the window to the Atlantic Ocean, which was now a dark endless slate.

"Why should we move to Florida? We have the same ocean right here in Brooklyn!"

The King of Kings and I

And everyone nodded their heads in agreement, while I stared out the kitchen window, squinting my eyes at the dark ocean and trying to catch one more glimpse of Moses pondering the Holy Land but forbidden to go any further.

My family's exodus from Brooklyn—like the Cuban Missile Crisis—came sooner and was more unpleasant than we ever thought possible. Only a month after our last trip to Coney Island, Bernie was beat up by some "Spanish boys" on his first day of fourth grade, and when my parents questioned me for details, I eagerly reported evidence of gang warfare in the neighborhood, hoping that this would encourage them to move. It also helped that my father's brother Sol, an accountant who had settled on Long Island the year before, was quite happy living in a split level in Massapequa.

At first my mother didn't want to move that far away, but my father got a map. "Look! Brooklyn is already on Long Island. We'd only be going to a nicer neighborhood." Then he pulled out our old encyclopedia, and that night we read that Long Island, shaped like a flounder, was dotted with tiny villages named after Indian chiefs and was most famous for its "resplendent views" of Long Island Sound. Unfortunately, our encyclopedia was outdated—it had been a wedding present to my grandparents, and its article about World War I was unable to tell you who won—and we soon discovered that by 1960 most of Long Island had been ruthlessly paved over, and spending money senselessly far surpassed quiet contemplation of beauty as its premier pastime.

House hunting became a nightmare. Every weekend we would gas up my father's '52 Hudson, drive east on Southern State Parkway, and spend hour after hour trudging through identical cardboard boxes with less personality than low-security prisons. If we found anything vaguely picturesque, Uncle Sol would sadly inform us that either we couldn't afford the mortgage or there was a crack in the foundation. Some afternoons, when my mother was particularly

cranky, we wouldn't even look at houses. We'd just get off the parkway at random exits and go searching for "resplendent views." After
an hour or so of being stuck in traffic we'd finally pull into a shopping
center, at which point my father would gaze at the horizon filled with
Ford Fairlanes and tacky ranch homes and state cheerfully, "This area
used to be so beautiful!"

Finally, we did find an affordable home with a solid foundation, a
modified Cape Cod on a quarter acre in Bethpage. We made several
trips to this house, and while my parents looked for support beams
and counted closets, Bernie and I just wandered around the yard.
There was one sad willow tree near the garage that we climbed in
order to survey the terrain. We listened and watched, but Bethpage
was as silent as the dark side of the moon. Unlike Brooklyn, there
were no stores, no pedestrians, and no cars driving on the streets.
Sometimes we heard faint screaming coming from a backyard.
Sometimes we heard a lawn mower several blocks away. Bernie was
bored, but I was actually filled with a dread that was exacerbated
when I heard my parents arguing through the kitchen window.

"I don't want to live here, Jack," my mother was arguing.

"Why not?" my father countered.

"For one thing—I hate to say it—there aren't enough Jews in the
neighborhood."

"Don't worry, Roz. Once the Jews move in, the goyim will move
out."

My mother must have acquiesced, because on a cold Sunday
night in December 1961, my family left Brooklyn for good. Our furniture, which had felt cozy in the old apartment, looked dark and
inadequate against the bare walls of the new house. Also, we had no
curtains for several weeks, so we kept the lights low and steered clear
of the picture window in the living room. My mother, who had lived
her entire life in rear tenement apartments, complained constantly,
"It's like living in a fishbowl, Jack!"

The King of Kings and I

As for me, I'll never forget that first night. I was kept awake for hours by blinking lights reflecting off my bedroom ceiling. Sometime after midnight I heard car doors slamming in the street below, and I sat up to investigate. There was a block party going on, and, to my complete astonishment, our neighbors' homes were in full Christmas regalia. I'd never seen anything like this; it was like I'd died and gone to Disneyland! Particularly garish was the Worcieukowskis' house next door, where their entire name was spelled out on the roof with more lightbulbs than there were on the runway at La Guardia Airport. Santa Claus and his reindeer hung from their TV antennas; and in the center of the Worcieukowskis' lawn was a strange barnyard scene, in the middle of which was a baby whose face glowed in the dark, surrounded by men wearing towels on their heads and carrying throw pillows in their hands. Music was blaring from car radios, and a staggering horde of teenagers were drinking beer and slurring something like "No well! No well!" I crouched as far back in the dark as possible to avoid being seen.

The next morning, my first day of class at Salvatore Impellitore Elementary School, I sleepily struggled across a frozen school yard and, having no idea how to find the front door, entered through the boiler room, sneaking past an irate janitor. By the time I got to my classroom Mrs. Quinn was already teaching arts and crafts. The kids were making holiday cards, and, desperate not to be singled out, I quickly fashioned my snowflake, choosing the red construction paper over the green, and I was just about to write "Merry Christmas" when Mrs. Quinn, class registry in hand, pulled me aside and suggested that my parents might prefer "a less religious message," something like "Season's Greetings." I did what she told me, although I hadn't the slightest idea why my father would want a card celebrating the onset of winter.

My father, though, got the idea and, now believing that his family would not single-handedly create a Jewish ghetto, set about preparing us for living defensively in the heart of Christendom by assuming the role of a Jewish patriarch more strenuously than

Abraham ever had. First he set out to bolster our appreciation of Hanukkah as a Christmas substitute by sitting us down and boasting that this "greatest of all Jewish holidays" had been based on a miracle: "They took lamp oil that was supposed to last one day and they made it last eight!" Bernie and I were unimpressed. Our mother had been performing that same "miracle" with pot roast. My father was undeterred. The next day he went to Pergaments Department Store, bought a cardboard menorah, cut it out, and taped it to our picture window. A half hour later the condensation made it curl up around the edges, and later that night it fell behind the couch.

Unfortunately, the more devout my father became, the more my mother showed her complete disdain for any kind of ritual. A year after we moved to Long Island my sister Rachel was born, and Mom's demeanor became increasingly harried and distant. The next year on Yom Kippur she fasted with the greatest reluctance, and she began keeping a list of items that didn't count as real food. The first year she allowed herself a cup of Sanka. The following year she munched on Stella D'Oro bread sticks. The next year she added a small bowl of cucumbers and sour cream, and by the time I left for college, her idea of fasting for Yom Kippur was leaving the cheddar cheese off a tuna melt.

But my mother's lack of interest seemed only to invigorate her husband's piousness, and our second year on Long Island my father enrolled me in Hebrew School at the Bethpage Jewish Community Center. The grades of this after-school ordeal were named after the first five letters of the Hebrew alphabet—Aleph, Beis, Gimmel, Daled, and Hai—and the classes were taught in one large all-purpose room divided by accordion walls that barely muffled the snores coming from adjacent compartments. There were no desks, only metal chairs with armrests upon which we were to balance our Hebrew prayer book, our Hebrew language primer, and our *Illustrated History of the Jewish People*. As for teachers, most of the classes were taught by antisocial zealots who weren't able to get jobs inflicting their outmoded beliefs on adults. Chief among these was the strange, black-bearded Rabbi Mintz.

I'll never forget this man. First of all, he stammered with a dreadful lateral lisp, making it impossible for him to pronounce the Hebrew letter tzade without watering the whole front row. His juicy pronunciations of biblical villains such as Achashveros and Nebuchadnezzar were legendary, along with his sour disposition. In truth, he didn't like kids any more than we liked him, because he'd always arrive late to class and then bolt from the building at 7 P.M. sharp, scampering to the train station like an Orthodox Ichabod Crane, and never once accepting the offer of a ride from a concerned parent.

In short, Rabbi Mintz was an unhappy misanthrope, one of the few men who could make five thousand years of Jewish history sound even worse than they actually were. He relished descriptions of martyrs being stripped of their skin and holy temples that were destroyed more completely than the city of Hiroshima. Worst of all, against this vast panorama of horror, his enthusiasm for the joyous holidays was nothing less than surreal. This was clear to me that first year, when Rabbi Mintz made us celebrate Sukkoth, the Jewish harvest festival. Never having met a Jewish farmer, I was less than enthused when Rabbi Mintz marched us into the woods behind the synagogue and built a ramshackle hut out of sticks and leaves called a sukkah. Then I nearly died of embarrassment when Rabbi Mintz started praying to G-d, shaking a palm branch in one hand and a lemon in the other, a ritual that would have been more at home among the Navajo than in the shadow of the Long Island Expressway.

It was Rabbi Mintz who taught me all about God. First of all, we were never allowed to write his name in full. We always had to spell it "G-dash-D," because God was so great we weren't supposed to talk about him. "Like God would be fooled by this?" I remember thinking. Even the dumbest schmuck on *Wheel of Fortune* could have bought a vowel and figured it out. Also, Rabbi Mintz taught us that G-d was invisible and thus rarely seen in pictures. He was generally portrayed as a finger pointing down from the sky. The only full-body picture I ever saw of Jehovah was on the cover of a children's Bible I'd inherited from my cousin Norman, and G-d was this very old man standing astride the creation on the first day of Genesis, wearing nothing but a striped bathrobe. I remember thinking that this garment was somewhat informal for the King of the Universe. After much pondering I finally assumed that G-d's portrait had been painted before he'd created daytime, so, sitting in the dark, he'd simply not bothered to get dressed.

In spite of all this, I did get good grades in Rabbi Mintz's class. At first, I was merely acing my history exams; my grandmother's encyclopedia was fairly accurate on events from three thousand years ago. Then Beis year, my teacher, Mrs. Shinerman, told me I had a flair for reading Hebrew; and I actually did sound somewhat authentic, especially if I faked an accent somewhere between Ben-Gurion's and Eva Gabor's. Then Gimmel year, under the rabbi Poplack, I started loving the Jewish hymns, like "Adon Olom" and "Ayn K'Elohenu," and I would sing the Mourner's Kaddish gleefully just for the chance of harmonizing on the last "Amen!"

But the real high point came the summer before my final term with Rabbi Mintz, when I asked my parents to send me to Camp Ramah, a Hebrew sleep-away camp where every morning we joyously clasped hands and prayed for rain in the Negev. This was also the first time a girl had a crush on me: the very Orthodox Mindy Sherman of Woodmere, who knitted me a yarmulke with a woolen pom-pom on top. The last day of camp we kissed in the parking lot, and Mindy told me how she really admired my commitment to Zionism. That fall I returned to Bethpage fully expecting to study at yeshiva and live the rest of my life on a kibbutz.

Looking back at this most religious year of my life, I see that I had several reasons for going gung ho for Judaism. After four years of living in a Catholic neighborhood I still had no friends, and the following year I'd be going to junior high school, where the goyim were even bigger and meaner. In fact, the Bethpage Jewish Community Center was right across the street from the varsity football field, where I'd see these wide-shouldered cossacks making animal noises and throwing themselves at each other with a force that would easily shatter eyeglasses. I needed a safe haven. Then again, I may simply have been a twelve-year-old boy with a large appetite for spirituality. In short, I needed, and have always needed, some kind of faith, and for the briefest of moments the religion of my ancestors was enough to satisfy my cravings. Then I went through puberty.

A few weeks ago, on Easter Sunday, I watched Cecil B. DeMille's *The Ten Commandments*. I paid careful attention to the climactic sequence when Moses climbs Mount Sinai, leaving the Israelites behind with Edward G. Robinson to wait patiently for his return. Within seconds those ungrateful Jews, who only moments before had seen the miracle of the Red Sea parting, disobeyed Moses and started performing what the narrator labeled "vile affections."

I'm sure Mr. DeMille wanted to shock us with scenes of lascivious debauchery, but, unfortunately, the censors in 1956 weren't ready then for those kinds of close-ups, so what we got were girls getting piggyback rides and shoving grapes in their mouths. To simulate orgasm, they tossed their hair around and let the juice dribble down their chins. For years I thought *this* was sex. In fact, the first time I made love I grabbed my partner and dripped Welch's down his back. That's how deeply affected I was by this scene. It was, after all, my only childhood memory of Jewish people in heat.

When I think about sex now, I feel like Ronald Reagan during his scandalous second term: how much did I know, and how soon did I know it? The answer is, less than the Catholic kids, who had the advantage of crotchety old nuns who lectured them constantly on the subject. I didn't even know enough about sex to feel guilty. *Portnoy's*

Jaffe Cohen

Complaint notwithstanding, Jewish guilt vis-à-vis sex is highly over-rated. You see, sex for Jews is not such a terrible sin. It's just one more physical sport we're gonna stink at. It's a whole different mind-set. Catholics believe that the body is filthy and you're not supposed to touch yourself. For Jews, a *pig's* body is filthy and you're not supposed to touch Canadian bacon, unless it's at a buffet.

Now, in my case, "vile affections" wasn't about being attracted to girls eating grapes. I was always more attracted to the humpy guys stacking cantaloupes in the produce section. Therefore, in addition to general misinformation about sex, I also had to live with Judaism's ambivalence toward homosexuality. On the one hand, we Jews tend to be pretty liberal. We don't have to worry about going to hell; we don't have one. The closest we can imagine to eternal damnation would be something like Barbra Streisand singing Christmas carols at the Republican National Convention. On the other hand, there are small pockets of ultra-Orthodox fanatics in Israel who deplore homosexuality when they're not too busy defending low-cost condominiums with machine guns. Thankfully, in America these Jews are few and far between. Most mainstream Jews are merely sorry that homosexuals are less likely to continue the race by bringing more Jews into the world. My father expressed this attitude a few years ago when he asked me, "Couldn't you get married, have children, and be gay in your spare time?"

Needless to say, I had a hard time putting my finger on just who I was. Figuring out I was gay was like putting together a jigsaw puzzle without having a picture on the front of the box. I didn't even know that the pieces were *supposed* to fit together. Looking back at what Freud would have called my latency period—which is essentially the time of your life when you're drawing conclusions about sexuality that will later have to be erased by a very expensive psychotherapist—I'm amazed I didn't realize I was queer the first time I fantasized about being Marilyn Monroe in *The River of No Return*, or the first time

The King of Kings and I

I lusted after Lee Majors wearing tight pants on *The Big Valley*, or the first time I sat behind Wayne Peterson in fourth grade just to watch his butt squeeze through the back of the chair.

I didn't know I was gay because I didn't know what gay was. I had no language to think about my future. In any event, the same summer I kissed Mindy Sherman in the parking lot of Camp Ramah, the Worcieukowskis moved out and took their garish Christmas displays with them. A week before school began, a big Catholic family named the McDermotts moved in, consisting of a single mother and a brood of glum-looking, pale-faced girls who played house on their front porch. There were also two boys in the family: a baby in a stroller named Eddie, and the eldest, a handsome, sharp-eyed boy of fourteen named Brian.

Now, Brian was nasty, the type of boy who would pull bugs apart just to see which half could still crawl away. He was precisely the type of kid I usually avoided, and yet—something chemical had happened in my brain—I couldn't resist the sight of him. Luckily, Brian's bedroom was directly across the yard from mine, and I soon discovered that if I turned off my bedroom lights and stood back from my window, I could spy on this kid in various stages of undress. In the morning when the sun streamed in his window I could stare at him while he put on his underwear. In the evening, when the gray-blue light from his TV flickered on his walls, I could see him lying on his bed with his shirt off. "Damn it!" I would mutter to myself, "I must get inside that house!"

One night in October, it finally hit me what I'd been doing. I was watching Brian watch *Monday Night Football*, and my heart started to race with terror. Though I didn't know what gay was, I did know that spying on one's neighbor might be poorly judged by the old man upstairs in the striped bathrobe. I closed my eyes to pray. I whispered to him, "G-d—if you exist—you've been watching me watch Brian so . . ." Then I pondered for a moment. "If there's anything wrong with this, let me know right now!" Then I got down on the floor of my room and pressed my forehead into the shag carpet. After a moment, nothing happened—no thunder, no voices from beyond—so I went back to the window and gazed longingly at Brian until he turned off the lights.

The next day I began my campaign to become Brian's friend. First, I noticed that Brian came home from basketball practice every afternoon at 4:30, so I needed a way to be outdoors at that precise moment. Much to my family's dismay, I took up landscaping. My mother, who'd been unable to get me to mow the lawn, suddenly saw me passionately raking and weeding like a professional. Not only did I carefully remove each dandelion, I clipped the hedges twice and built a Japanese rock garden. My efforts didn't go unrewarded, because one day Brian waved to me as he threw open his screen door, and I knew that it wouldn't be long before we'd be the best of friends.

Unfortunately, the days were getting shorter, and one evening while weeding in the dark, I accidentally defoliated my mother's patch of pachysandra. Now the only times I could see Brian were on the weekends, when I'd wipe the steam off my window and watch Brian playing curb ball in the street with an older kid named Jerry from the other side of town. Everything about Brian made me wince with desire: his thick legs, the cold sweat on his forehead. I was enthralled by his athletic abilities and yet enraged by his confidence. Secretly I hoped that Brian would lose, believing that in defeat he would turn to me for support. However, to my great disappointment, Brian just kept winning game after game, and every time he won he would thrust his fist in the air and hoot, "Yes!"

This was my predicament when, sometime in January, a new girl enrolled in my sixth-grade class. She shyly approached the teacher's desk during free reading, and I glanced up from *Wuthering Heights* to see the plainest-looking girl imaginable. She was neither pretty nor ugly, unless you took into account her extraordinary pallor: you could see blue veins draining the blood out of her face. She also wore a man's cardigan sweater, a blouse buttoned to the top, and thick socks that bagged at the knees. I don't think I would have given her a second thought except that the teacher introduced her as Debbi McDermott, and I knew that my prayers had been answered.

That afternoon at lunch I sat down at the far end of the teachers' table, where Debbi perched upright and talked to herself with her eyes closed. I pretended to take an interest in my food when, in fact, I was watching her as she slowly ate her lunch, one tasteless food group at a time. Yes!—she had the same cleft in her chin and glinty eyes as her brother. She had the same flaxen hair. In fact, she had all the same features as Brian, only, like with the Kennedys, they were features that looked much better on the male members of the family. Meanwhile, she meticulously chewed her wax beans, cut her fish sticks with a knife and fork, and was just about to take a spoonful of canned pears when I interrupted.

"Those aren't very healthy."

Debbi McDermott looked at me, completely calm except for her eyelids, which fluttered uncontrollably.

"They're pure cellulose," I continued. "They have the same nutritional value as wood."

Debbi put down her fork and daintily wiped her mouth with a napkin.

"My name is Jaffe. I live next door to you."

Debbi cleared her throat and responded almost inaudibly.

"Thank you."

Then she pushed her canned pears away and looked off to the side. I nonchalantly pulled out some homework, but again I secretly watched her as she examined her fellow students. At the next table Rosalie DiPasquale was throwing Jell-O at Jennifer Rooney. Beyond them Larry Lustig slipped on a bean and knocked over the garbage pail. At the far end of the room Mr. Disanza, the gym teacher, was throwing Keith Koslowski against the wall. I fervently prayed she was concluding that, among these cretins and protocriminals, I was her best candidate for friendship.

That afternoon I waited outside the exit so I could walk her across the school yard. She seemed pleased to see me.

"How come you didn't move in when your family moved in?" I asked.

"I was at my grandmother's house," Debbi replied, her eyelids fluttering.

Then she added, "I wanted to be closer to the hospital."

Debbi didn't look healthy, but I hadn't suspected anything serious.

"What was the matter?" I asked shyly.

Debbi smiled and answered, "My grandmother had a stroke, but she's up in heaven now."

Her look was so joyful that it took me a moment before I registered that heaven was the place you went to after you died. I responded in the way I'd seen my family react to the news of death: by looking at the ground and making a pained expression.

"I'm sorry."

"There's no need to feel sorry. She's with Jesus!"

I was surprised by Debbi's confidence, especially when I calculated the number of people who die in any given day and doubted that Jesus would have time to be with all of them. We arrived at Debbi's driveway and Debbi unfastened the second button on her blouse, sucked in her chest to make it even more concave, reached in, and pulled out a section of brown beads.

"Grandma gave me these before she died."

I examined the beads. They looked like miniature acorns and smelled like old-lady perfume.

"Aren't they beautiful!?" Debbi swooned. "I'm the luckiest girl in the world!"

Then Debbi excused herself because she had to make dinner for her siblings. Apparently, Mrs. McDermott had taken a job waitressing in an Italian restaurant and Debbi was now primarily responsible for feeding a family of seven. The next day I again joined Debbi at the lunch table. I wanted to find out about Brian, but she insisted on telling me all about her younger sisters, who had been named, in descending order, Diane, Donna, and Delores, as well as her baby brother, Eddie, whose late entrance into the clan was described as a miracle no less astounding than the Virgin Mary's appearance at Lourdes.

For a whole week I walked Debbi home from school, hung out on her porch, and chatted amiably while hoping to be invited inside. Debbi's favorite TV show was *The Farmer's Daughter* because Inger Stevens seemed to really love the Senator's children. Her favorite Beatle was George because he probably felt left out with all the attention going to John and Paul. And her favorite movie was, by far, *The Sound of Music*, although she fervently believed that Julie Andrews should have remained a nun. I also got a closer look at the other McDermotts, and I had to conclude that Debbi was positively ruddy compared with Diane and Donna. It was as though Mrs. McDermott's chromosome for melanin, like an ink pad, had gotten weaker with each pregnancy.

But one afternoon in February my patience paid off. Debbi finally invited me inside for a game of five hundred rummy. As I entered the foyer, my eyes had to adjust to the light: the living-room curtains were deep blue, and the walls were paneled in mahogany so dark they were almost charcoal. This was the first time I'd been inside a Catholic house. It smelled like cabbage, and I'd never seen so many religious tchotchkes! There was a black velvet *Last Supper* hanging over the couch and a statue of the Virgin Mary standing on the coffee table. There were various crucifixes hanging off the bookcases and a stack of prayer cards on the dining-room table. There was a china cabinet filled with saints, as well as likenesses of John F. Kennedy and Pope John XXIII. "It's a good thing Jews don't have saints," I remember thinking to myself. "My mother hates to dust. We have one G-d," I figured. "He's invisible, so you don't have to keep wiping him off."

But the most impressive icon was yet to come. After pouring me a glass of Hawaiian Punch, Debbi led me upstairs, where I was welcomed into her room by a huge painting of Jesus himself. I couldn't have been more stunned if the sky had just turned purple. Like I said, portraits of our invisible G-d were rare indeed, and we would never have hung one up on the wall between a pair of bunk beds. Also, Debbi's wall-hanging Jesus was much more appealing than an old man too lazy to put on his pants.

Debbi's G-d was young and attractive. His head was painted on a lime green background with flecks of gold that picked up what meager light there was in the room. He also had long shiny brown hair that curled under like he'd set it the night before with Hi-C cans. He also had huge vulnerable eyes, which made me think that the other Gods on his block might have made fun of him. But he wasn't a sissy, because his rouged lips were offset by a strong jaw, a muscular neck, and large hands that could have easily caught a football.

"Should I deal first?" Debbi asked as she sat down on the dusty pink shag rug.

"Did your grandmother give you that?" I asked

"No. I saved my allowance," Debbi replied as she shuffled the cards.

"Is that Jesus?" I asked. Debbi turned her head to glance at her Savior.

"Oh yes!" she said. "That's Jesus. He's the Son of God."

"The Son of God," I thought to myself. "How odd." If God were invisible, his son would have been at least translucent. My curiosity was piqued. I asked out loud, "Does God have any other kids I don't know about?"

Debbi smiled indulgently. "Don't they teach you anything about Jesus?"

This was the first time Debbi had ever indirectly acknowledged that I was Jewish, and I was embarrassed because, in my five years of Hebrew school, the name of Jesus had never been spoken.

"I'm just kidding," I replied.

Debbi then leaned into me and whispered, as though she'd been waiting for just the right moment to reveal her innermost thoughts, "The best thing about Jesus is that, when I die, Jesus is going to lift me up in his arms and carry me up to heaven."

"Oh."

And then Debbi closed her eyes and imagined herself in the arms of her Lord, after which she opened her eyes, rearranged her cards, and lay down three fours and a royal flush. Debbi also won the next round and the round after that. I was so jealous. Not only was she lucky at cards, but also she got to sleep every night with Jesus hanging right above her pillow. She had her lover nearby and she would have him forever. Me? I'd always be peeking through windows and feeling awful.

Debbi and I played cards until well past dinnertime. At one point Donna came home with her new Bobby Sherman record, and later Diane joined the game, playing Debbi's hand while her older sister baked a ham. But there was no sign of Brian, so finally at 7:30 I admitted defeat and went back to my house. Meanwhile my mother, cranky from taking Baby Rachel to the ear doctor, was furious that I'd missed dinner. She ordered me to eat cold pot roast, even though the sight of the lukewarm gristle made me gag. I couldn't swallow it, so I kept slicing it, hoping that by cutting the pieces small enough, I would make the ugly slab of meat disappear altogether.

Finally I gave up and just sat there pondering something Debbi had told me earlier— which, in its own way, was equally indigestible.

"Mom, do Jews go to heaven?"

My mother thought hard and tried to answer the question truthfully.

"I don't know," she finally said as though the subject was closed.

"So what do you think happens after you die?"

"I don't know," she replied.

"If you had to guess—"

"I wouldn't even guess. Finish your pot roast."

At this point my father walked into the kitchen eager for a chance to lecture me on the finer points of Talmudic reasoning.

"It's not that important! Heaven? Hell? What difference does it make?"

"Let me take care of this, Jack," my mother retorted.

"I'm serious," my father continued. "Is a person supposed to act good just so he can get into heaven?"

"Jack, not now," my mother warned.

"Jaffe," my father continued, "the purpose of a good life is a good life!"

"Well—"

But before I could say anything, my mother grabbed the plate of pot roast and angrily threw it in the garbage. My father threw up his hands in disgust and I quietly slipped away from the table.

That night I went to bed angry. My frustration at not seeing Brian was compounded by my frustration at not getting a straight answer from my parents. "Nobody knows anything!" I told myself. And that night I had a dream so clear that, almost thirty years later, I can remember the scene as if it were yesterday. Something is happening in the street outside our home in Bethpage, and again, I'm sitting at my bedroom window watching a game of curb ball. Only this time the two antagonists are not Brian and Jerry, but an old man in a striped bathrobe and a young man with big eyes and long shiny hair. The old man is vainly trying to field the Spaldeens that keep sailing over his head, while the young man just keeps winning game after game after game. The old man simply can't keep up, and every time the ball goes sailing over his head the young man thrusts his arms in the air and yells, "Yes!"

The King of Kings and I

*   *   *

One of the major differences between my family and my neighbors was that my neighbors actually drank their liquor. The older ones kept beer in the refrigerator, swizzle sticks near the silverware, and packages of cocktail mix next to the dry cereal. It wasn't that my father didn't own alcohol; he actually kept a liquor cabinet in the living room overflowing with bottles of scotch and vodka. The difference was that my parents never opened these bottles. What generally happened was that my dad would receive a bottle of booze from a coworker brightly labeled "Season's Greetings," stick it in the cabinet, and then, the following year, give it away to someone else. Alcohol was merely a convenient gift idea, like a savings bond or a gift certificate at Macy's.

Now, I first became aware of my neighbors' drinking habits a few weeks after first seeing Jesus at Debbi McDermott's house. Nearly every day Debbi invited me to her house to play five hundred rummy, and I always went hoping I'd see Brian. Sadly, this never happened, because basketball season had begun and most evenings Brian was in another town playing his heart out for the Bethpage Beavers. I did eventually get an eyeful of the elder Mr. McDermott, though—an unemployed union electrician, who turned up unexpectedly in February and started making his presence known by the sound of ice cubes clanking in a tumbler of vodka and some loud bumps on the wall as he stumbled up the stairs.

Mr. McDermott didn't always live with his family, and when he did, the house was usually in an uproar. Brian now made himself scarce by staying over at Jerry's house after basketball games, and by March he seemed to have stopped coming home altogether. As for Debbi, she reacted to her father's presence by volunteering for a local Catholic charity. By April Debbi was spending most of her afternoons around the corner helping a certain arthritic Mrs. Potts by cleaning the woman's house and buying her groceries. Soon I hardly saw

Debbi unless she was running to the store to purchase Campbell's tomato soup or hobbling off to church with Mrs. Potts. As for me, I tried to forget about the McDermotts altogether, so I started watching more TV, eating more Pop-Tarts, and occasionally shoplifting a Hardy Boys book from the discount store.

But everything changed in May. Mr. McDermott started a new job in Texas installing air conditioners. With the old boozer gone, Brian returned home, which meant that I again started clipping and reclipping the hedges between our two houses until there was nothing separating our yards but pathetic little stubs. On May 14, all my pruning paid off: Brian and I had our first conversation. It was amazing! Of all possible scenarios I'd never pictured him simply coming to our house, but that's what happened. One afternoon, I was alone in the kitchen making a grilled cheese sandwich when there was a knock on the door and Brian was standing on our patio in a slight drizzle, tiny beads of water on his thick blond hair. I tried not to let him see how my heart was bursting through my rib cage.

"Those big hedge clippers I always see you with . . ." he said to me without introducing himself, "can I borrow them?"

"Sure," I said. "Come on in. They're in the garage."

We could have walked through the yard to the garage, but I wanted the thrill of having Brian inside my home. I wanted him to breathe the air I breathed, to touch the furniture I touched, to leave his heavenly footprints on our linoleum. Very deliberately, I led him the long way through our house, from the kitchen to the den, around the dining-room table, dawdling in the vestibule, and into the garage, where my father stored all the tools. It was quite a display. That winter my dad had pounded six-inch spikes into the plasterboard and outlined the shapes of all the implements, labeling their respective spots with a black Magic Marker so that each shovel, wrench, and hammer would always be returned to its proper nail.

"Whatcha got here?" Brian asked, obviously impressed.

"It's kind of stupid. My dad's idea—"

"Yeah. My dad's a jerk too."

"He seems like a nice guy."

"My dad—*pfft*. I mean, I like to drink . . . but him—jeez!"

Brian did a little imitation of his dad staggering about with a blot-toed look on his face. I laughed and pulled the manual clippers off the wall, leaving an outline that looked like either Mickey Mouse's head or an erect penis and scrotum.

"Thanks," Brian said.

Then Brian went back to his house, and I went into the bathroom and masturbated. Later that night there was a knock on the door, and when I answered it I found the hedge clippers leaning against the wall and a note saying, "Thanks for clipers. May need them tomorrow." I kissed the note and hid it between my mattress and bedsprings.

The next day, I made another grilled cheese sandwich and prayed that lightning would strike twice. Sure enough, as I was washing the dishes, Brian knocked on the door and I answered it, trying to hide my heart, which was now trying to force its way out of my mouth.

"I need 'em again," he said.

"Sure . . . fine."

Again I led Brian through the house, maneuvering him to walk ahead of me so I could check him out from behind. He had the most wonderful neck, and his jawbone was broad enough to be seen from the back of his head. This time I noticed he was glancing from side to side as he walked through our living room, and I saw our house as I'd never seen it before: our Chagall prints, our lithographs of Hasids at the Wailing Wall, our cast album of *Fiddler on the Roof*. It suddenly occurred to me that Brian may have thought me as exotic as I thought him. Later, when I gave him the hedge clippers, Brian seemed a little apologetic.

"I may just need 'em another day or two. I should buy my own fuckin' pair."

"Don't worry about it," I reassured him.

As Brian left I suddenly thought to ask, "You clipping hedges?"

Brian shrugged his shoulders as if to say, "Why else would I be borrowing hedge clippers?"

"I never see you doing it."

"In the backyard," Brian responded.

"Oh," I said.

Now I knew he was lying! This time, when Brian left I ran to my upstairs window to see Brian slinging a knapsack on his back and riding away on his bicycle. The McDermotts didn't have any hedges in their backyard, and I was dying to find out where he was going. That night Brian again returned the clippers, with another note saying, "May need clipers tomorrow to."

The next day I was thrilled to get home from school and find that my mother had gone shopping and my brother had stayed after school. Knowing that Brian would come over at the usual time, I made a few adjustments in the decor of our house. A few minutes later Brian tapped on the screen door and again I led him through our living room, but this time I'd cleverly left my father's liquor cabinet wide open and pulled a few bottles forward to catch Brian's attention. Pretending to go to the bathroom, I purposely left Brian alone in the room for a few moments, and when I returned Brian was—just as I'd hoped—nonchalantly examining a box of booze wrapped in a picture of Frosty the Snowman.

"Whatcha got here?" he asked.

"Just a couple of bottles. I don't even know what they are." I picked up a bottle of J&B and held it up to Brian. "Is this a good brand?"

Brian nodded his head. "It's the best, man."

I reached behind the J&B and pulled out an identical bottle.

"My dad's got seconds of this one. So he probably wouldn't miss it."

Brian nodded his head as he examined a bottle of Kahlúa.

"We should go drinking sometime," I suggested.

"Anytime," Brian replied. Then suddenly I got scared. It had all happened so easily. "Come on," I said. "I'll get you the clippers." I led Brian into the garage and pulled the tool off the wall. Just then, in a moment beyond my wildest expectations, Brian suggested, "You want to go hang out in the woods?"

"Sure."

"Get that bottle of J&B. I'll show you something cool."

The next thing I knew I was shoving the clippers and the "extra" bottle of scotch into a knapsack. Brian brought his bicycle up to our front door.

"Jump on the back," he said.

I climbed onto the back of Brian's banana seat and grabbed his hips as Brian's beautiful thighs powered us onto the street.

"You OK back there?" he asked me as he screeched around a corner.

"Yeah."

As Brian's legs churned I could see every striation in his big hard butt. At that moment I could have been an octopus, but even eight hands wouldn't have been enough for how much I wanted to squeeze every square millimeter of Brian's gorgeous heinie, which was only inches from my face.

"Hold tight!" Brian ordered.

"OK," I replied, grasping on to his belt and praying that the ride would never end.

A few minutes later we bounced off the side streets and onto a dirt path that led into "the woods." Now, I don't want to give the impression that Brian and I were going into any kind of rustic Garden of Eden. "The woods" was nothing more than a narrow strip of real estate owned by the Long Island Lighting Company through which they ran hundreds of miles of high-tension wires suspended on radio towers. Though this timberland did contain a few unspoiled glens and thickets of trees, one was never more than fifty yards from a gigantic steel monolith and the constant buzzing of electric cables. Still, on that day I felt like I was entering paradise.

We rode the bicycle along the path as far as we could and then dismounted, and Brian lifted it over his head and heaved it into some thornbushes where nobody would find it. Then we pushed farther along the path on foot. Brian was like some great bwana on safari and I his honored guest as he courteously held the branches aside for me. Enduring stickers and poison ivy, I gladly followed Brian a few hundred feet into this wilderness until we got to a small clearing surrounded by elms, in the middle of which was a large mound covered with twigs and leaves.

"Thanks for the clippers, man. I been cuttin' some of these bushes here. Tryin' to camouflage this thing."

"What thing?"

"This, man."

Then Brian reached into the pile of brush and pulled out a short length of rope.

"You ready for this?"

Brian peered around us to make sure we hadn't been followed. Then he pulled on the rope, and the bushes seemed to rise. Underneath them was some kind of old cellar door built at a forty-five-degree angle to the ground, and through the door I could see something like a cave. Brian pointed to it with pride.

"Somebody dug it before I got here, but I fixed it up."

Then Brian disappeared into the hole, and I followed him into a small underground room about eight feet long and eight feet across. The light from the doorway illuminated the walls, which were covered with mismatched bits of paneling, and the floor was covered with rugs and carpet fragments. The ceiling, constructed with various hunks of discarded lumber, was about five feet high, just low enough so Brian and I had to stoop slightly.

"It's a hellhole, but—fuck it—it's all mine!"

"Wow."

"Jerry dug this out a couple of years ago, and nobody knows it's here now except for me and him."

The King of Kings and I

I sat on the floor and examined the tiny room, which I realized right away was a bizarre parody of a suburban den. In addition to the wood paneling there was a Naugahyde easy chair with its legs removed, a vase with plastic flowers, and, proving that the decorator had a sense of humor, a few dusty bowling trophies and a TV set without a picture tube.

"This thing work?" I joked.

"You shittin' me? Nope. But I got a lamp here."

Brian reached behind the TV and pulled out a battery-powered searchlight, which he turned on and set next to the vase. Then he threw himself into the broken easy chair while I leaned up against the wall.

"Pretty cool, huh?"

Brian reached into the seat cushion and pulled out a pack of Marlboros.

"Still dry," he boasted.

He lit up a cigarette and offered one to me. I'd never smoked before, but I grabbed it eagerly, because I wanted anything in my mouth that had been in Brian's hand.

"Do you ever sleep here?" I asked, wondering how to keep my cigarette lit.

"When I can't go home," Brian replied. "Not too often. It's spooky shit by myself; but sometimes I'll come out with my sleeping bag." Then he sat back in the chair and threw his muscular legs up over the armrests. "Next year I'll be too old for this place, so I might as well enjoy it now." Brian took another deep drag and shook his head thoughtfully. His philosophical mood was making me unbelievably horny, especially because for Brian, thinking hard seemed to automatically make his leg twitch. Actually, Brian was never completely still; he was always cracking his neck or scratching his chest. He had the most eloquent physique imaginable, like a cricket who could send out mating signals just by rubbing his knees together.

Just then the cigarette smoke got in my eye and I started to cough.

"Whatcha doin'?" Brian pulled the cigarette out of my mouth. "You don't smoke! Jeez."

"I'm OK."

Brian looked me over. "How old are you?" he asked me.

"Twelve," I said.

Brian went into mock spasms of disbelief. "Twelve? I thought you were younger! You're only two years younger than me?"

"Debbi's in my class—"

"Debbi? I thought you were Donna's friend!"

"No, Debbi."

"Debbi? That weirdo!" Brian laughed out loud. "She's my sister, man, but she's like a nun. I don't go for that shit!" Brian shook his head and took another drag.

"So you're not religious?" I asked, not that I ever thought for a moment that he was.

"Church? Fuck! I think if a guy wants to do something, he just should do it. I don't want no priest tellin' me what to do!"

"So you don't go to church?"

"Sometimes I go to confession, but I don't tell 'em everything. As long as you give 'em some idea what you do, then you don't go to hell or nothin'."

"So what do you tell him?" I asked.

"You know, like a basic outline."

"Like what?"

"You know . . . like . . ." Brian made the absurd gesture of looking around him to make sure we were alone before whispering, "Theresa Caldone." He whacked the air with his palm. Then, having made his point, he smiled and leaned back in his chair to finish his cigarette.

Theresa Caldone? "Wow!" I thought to myself. Even I had heard of the legendary Theresa Caldone, who lived above Doogan's Bar with her mother, not so much on the wrong side of the railroad tracks as actually underneath them.

So Brian had been doing it. This only made me hornier. My mind raced. I wasn't even sure what I wanted. I just wanted more—a touch, a taste, another secret revealed—when all of a sudden Brian jerked forward, writhing as though trying to scratch his shoulder blades.

"What's the matter?" I asked.

"I got an itch. A fuckin' spider must've bit me!" Then, turning his back to me, Brian demanded, "Do me a favor. Scratch my back."

So I reached over, and with all my strength I ran my fingers across his shoulder blades. Brian arched his back and sighed with satisfaction. So close, I could smell that his shirt smelled like Clorox, and I was shocked that someone who talked so dirty would have such clean-smelling laundry. Brian continued to purr and I continued to rub, sniffing bleach shamelessly as my fingers ran down his spinal column. Meanwhile, I was starting to figure out a few more things about Brian. First of all, he trusted me, and second of all, he wasn't very bright. I had no way of knowing this then, but I had just discovered my type.

Unfortunately, another characteristic of my type is that they're impulsive and prone to sudden urges to flee the premises. Just as my fingers started moving down his spine, Brian jumped up.

"Come on, man. We gotta go."

Then he pulled the scotch out of his knapsack and slid it into an old cabinet covered with peeling contact paper with daisy designs.

"We'll save this for the weekend, man. Wanna come back here later and get plastered?"

"Yeah."

"And don't you tell no one about this place."

Then we exited, closed the place up, and started retracing our steps through the woods and back to the bicycle. As we drove through the streets, I again held on to Brian's belt buckle, and this time, as I stared at Brian's buttocks, I knew that, on some level, his ass was already mine. It was only a matter of time.

Then again, I was terrified. How did I know if I'd ever get the chance to be alone with Brian? And how did I know whether Brian would ever allow me to touch him again? This was my first clumsy seduction, and I didn't know yet that, merely by my wanting him so badly, the odds were in my favor. A few years ago I found a quote: "Old age and treachery will always triumph over youth and beauty." Looking back at my brief tryst with Brian, I'm amazed at how old and treacherous I was by the age of twelve. Having grown up Jewish and gay in a world that was Christian and straight, I'd already developed a wary detachment more suitable to a person four times my age. Even though Brian was sixteen months older, I was the ancient one; and even though my passion for him far outweighed his passion for me, there was never really a moment when I couldn't have called the shots.

But at the time I mostly felt like there was hurricane inside my chest making it hard to walk straight. I was hopeless and frightened, especially when Brian told me over the fence that he wanted to camp out in the woods that Friday night. The plan was simple: he'd tell his parents he'd be at Jerry's and I'd tell my mom we'd be at the McDermotts'. Everything was all set to go except I had to convince my mom to buy me a sleeping bag. I waited for a moment when I knew she'd be deliriously happy. Luckily, they were showing *Perry Mason* reruns on channel five and my mother had a huge crush on Raymond Burr. I stumbled upon her Wednesday afternoon with Rachel, watching television and knitting another ugly afghan to drape over the recliner.

"Look at him," my mother exclaimed as I sat down and pretended to take an interest. "For a large man he moves with such grace!"

I decided to get right to the point. "Mom, can I have twenty dollars to buy a sleeping bag?"

The King of Kings and I

Baby Rachel, now almost four, piped up, "What for?"

"It's none of your business," I told her.

My mother had the next word: "No."

"Why not?"

A commercial for Clorox came on and my mother pulled out another ball of yarn. "Why do you want a sleeping bag?" she finally asked.

"I want to sleep outside," I said.

"You've got a perfectly good bed inside. I don't want you sleeping outside by yourself."

"I won't be by myself," I implored. "I'll be with Brian McDermott."

I had completely miscalculated. At the sound of our neighbors' name, my mother sighed as though her crocheting had suddenly become excruciatingly difficult. "From next door? Those McDermotts?"

So I tried a different tactic. "Mom, you promised I could have anything I wanted for my birthday as long as it was under twenty dollars. A sleeping bag only costs eighteen ninety-five at Pergaments."

Luckily, Raymond Burr had come back on the screen and my mother no longer wanted to be bothered.

"Go get me my purse," she demanded. "Although God knows why you want to sleep outside on the ground with someone you hardly know."

My next clear memory is of Friday night: Brian was walking ahead of me, clearing a path for the two of us. I was lugging my sleeping bag, and Brian had met me at the entrance to the woods with a flashlight. We had little to say to each other, and the only sounds I heard were power cables, a few crickets, and the chafing of wide-wale corduroy as Brian's legs rubbed together. In the stillness of the night I felt certain that Brian could hear my thoughts of terrible longing. Why wasn't he running away from me in sheer terror? Then Brian pulled on the rope and we entered the underground chamber.

The night was warm, so we decided to leave the door open. We laid out our sleeping bags. Then my new pal opened the bottle of scotch, took a swig, and passed it to me. The alcohol tasted awful, like Listerine or something else I'd been warned not to swallow. Outside I could hear the droning of the electric cables as the power surged to millions of TV sets, lamps, and kitchen appliances. We weren't as far away from civilization as I might have hoped.

"Be careful!" Brian warned as I took a long swig and grimaced.

"I don't feel anything yet."

"You don't feel drunk right away, man." Brian started laughing and nearly fell off the chair. "For a smart kid, you're pretty fuckin' stupid."

I took another swig and passed it back to Brian, who put the bottle to his mouth without even wiping off my germs. When he handed it back to me, I did the same, feeling with my lips for traces of his saliva. Then I don't know what happened. The booze must have kicked in, because somehow I'd fallen on my back and was laughing. Brian had done the same. Then we both laughed again because we couldn't remember what we were laughing at.

Brian reached up and closed the door. "Shh!" he said. "People gonna hear us."

"Who?"

"Anybody, man."

Then it got quiet.

"There's nobody out there," I whispered.

"I know," Brian replied. "I wanna show you something."

Then Brian turned off the searchlight and we lay there side by side in the dark without talking. I just lay there, listening to the humming of the overhead cables and forcing my pupils to dilate, actually willing myself the ability to see in the dark. Above me I could make out some moonlight seeping through the branches of our makeshift roof, and strangely enough, it reminded me of the sukkah that Rabbi Mintz had built for us in the woods behind the temple. For a moment I felt sad; I wanted to leave. But just then I heard another intense rhythmic sound, no less mighty than the electric energy that powered all of eastern Long Island. It was the sound of Brian breathing. At first it was harsh and labored, as if someone had just punched him in the stomach.

"Whatcha doing over there?"

Brian was lying on top of his sleeping bag. His pants were down to his knees, and he was rubbing himself between his legs. Every few seconds he'd stop to spit on his hands and then he'd go back to stroking his penis, which had grown absolutely huge. At first I didn't want Brian to know that I was watching, but then he looked at me and smiled.

"Ever rub your dick like this?" he asked.

"Yeah."

"It's better when you do it with someone else."

"Yeah?"

"Watch me," he said.

I did as I was told. I watched him, thrilled by the size of his pelvic bone, two hills rimming the soft white terrain around his belly button. I was enthralled by how closely the reality of Brian's cock matched the way I'd pictured it hundreds of times before in my fantasies. But mostly, I was fascinated by the intense look of concentration on Brian's face. I'd never seen Brian concentrate on anything before. Then every few seconds Brian would glance at me to make sure I was still watching. And he continued to fiddle—sometimes fast, sometimes slow—creating music that could be heard only in his head.

I reached out and touched Brian's shoulder. Rather than pull away from me, he started groaning, making little yah-yah sounds of yearning—indecipherable sounds that, for a moment, reminded me of Hebrew. Now it seemed like Brian was praying. Like the two of us were in a holy place and what Brian held in his hands was no less sanctified than the lemon and palm branch that Rabbi Mintz had shaken when he celebrated the harvest festival. Then Brian's body spasmed and it was over. Only then did he become embarrassed, turning away from me just long enough to clean himself.

"Now you do it," he said. "Do what I did."

I slowly unbuckled my pants and felt for my penis. I was scared by the size of it; it was as big as my friend's. I started rubbing it the way I'd seen Brian do, who lay next to me resting his head on his elbow. I stroked myself for a minute or two but something was wrong. I didn't want him to watch me. I wanted to watch him. "Turn around," I said. "Press up against me."

Brian immediately obeyed me, shoving his naked butt up against my side as I stroked myself with one hand while running the other hand up and down his leg. I kept thinking that Brian would turn around and smack me in the face, or mock me. But that never happened. Brian just kept pressing himself up against my hand. At one point he even reached behind him and grabbed whatever he could— which happened to be my knee—but he never said a word. Then, much too quickly, I exploded, like I'd been turned inside out, and the better part of me splattered onto my stomach like a bucket of warm chicken soup.

"I told you it would feel good."

Then, without saying another word, Brian turned off the searchlight and the room was dark. My friend seemed to have already faded away, so I just held on to his back and listened to him breathe and waited for him to fall asleep. I looked around me at the walls of our sukkah. "This is our home now!" I smiled to myself. And then, because I was drunk—and only because I was drunk—I fell asleep and slept soundly, without a trace of anxiety.

How strange it is to look back at the night of my first homosexual experience. What's odd is that I don't remember feeling particularly guilty or ashamed. Like I said before, sex for Jews is less of a mortal sin and more of an opportunity to strike out. In my case, I had just hit a home run with this great-looking Gentile, and I was in heaven. My only problem was that, according to Brian's religion, gay men aren't supposed to go to heaven. Unlike me, Brian did not sleep contentedly. Nor was he feeling particularly romantic the next morning when he tried to sneak away without me. Nowadays, having experienced several one-night stands with former altar boys, I wouldn't be surprised by Brian's behavior; but at the time it caught me completely off guard.

The first thing I remember was regaining consciousness and not wanting to open my eyes. I sniffed at the air, and the smell of bleach mixed with moist earth let me know that I hadn't been dreaming. Ah, bliss! Then I reached over next to me, bravely hoping to caress the now familiar mound of Brian's back, but the bag was empty. I sat up with a start, to find out that I was alone in a dirty hole in the ground. Steely sunshine was pouring through the door we'd closed the night before, and I heard some rustling in the bushes outside. I quickly pulled on my pants and climbed toward the light. Outside I pushed through the scratchy underbrush and saw Brian retrieving his bicycle.

"Whatcha doing?"

Brian spun around like an animal cornered by a hunter.

"I forgot. I got somethin' I gotta do."

"Where ya going?" I asked.

Brian shook his head without answering.

"Can I come?"

Brian shook his head again. This time I knew he was annoyed at the question. But he hadn't actually said no, so I jumped on the back of his banana seat.

"Where ya think ya goin'?" Brian asked without turning around to face me.

"I thought we were hanging out together," I said.

"Jeez."

After a long moment Brian finally dropped his full weight down on the pedal. We were off, riding slowly out of the woods. The gravel path was bumpy, and I had a hard time balancing myself, so I grabbed Brian's hips. His back stiffened and he pulled away from me.

"Hey, whatcha doing back there?"

This time his angry tone frightened me.

"Nothing!" I replied.

So I grabbed the seat behind me and, with great difficulty, managed to stay upright as we passed through a hole in a chain-link fence and out onto the streets. It was a bright warm day, and I was starting to feel dirty and overheated. The bicycle swayed. I felt nauseous and remembered how much we'd drunk the night before.

"Where we going?" I asked.

There was no answer. And suddenly I became aware of the two of us, an odd couple on a suburban street in the middle of the afternoon. What were my neighbors thinking as we rode by, still covered in dirt from Brian's secret hiding place? Was it only my imagination, or were the adults peeking at us from behind their curtains, and were little children abandoning their tricycles and scurrying up their driveways?

"Hey, where we going?" I repeated. Perhaps he hadn't heard me the first time.

"Confession!" Brian yelled back. "I gotta go to confession."

We rode out of the development onto Central Avenue, past the firehouse, past the pizza place, and into the Sunoco gas station. Brian washed his hands in the men's room; then we rode away, pedaling over the wire, which made a loud dinging noise. We rode onto Stewart Avenue past a big white house inhabited by nuns and then past a small stone house where an old priest lived behind lace curtains. Then we pulled up to the front door of Saint Martin's Church, a perfect replica of Ghiberti's Gates of Paradise molded out of aluminum, and Brian, without saying a word, ran up the steps and slipped inside the church.

I sat down on the concrete and tried to get my bearings. At the gas station another car ran over the wire. *Ding!* It was the only other sound on earth except the very loud voices chattering inside my head: "Confession? What is confession?" It was something about telling a priest how awful you felt for your sins—kind of like Yom Kippur by appointment. Confession? Could it be that Brian was confessing about me? Had I suddenly become a person like Theresa Caldone, an irresistible sexpot ruining good Catholic boys with my animal magnetism? I laughed at the thought, and yet . . .

Confession? What time was it? Was my mother expecting me home? Had she already counted the bottles in the liquor cabinet and discovered that one of them was missing? All of a sudden it hit me that what had occurred the night before had not been accidental. I had planned the whole thing. I had planned and schemed for months. Then I had a sudden flash of insight so powerful that my knees buckled and I slid down a concrete step. There at the entrance to the church I realized something very important.

A major piece of the jigsaw puzzle had suddenly dropped into place. I gasped at the finished picture. All my scheming that year was leading me toward one thing, and one thing only: my future as a gay man. And this vision so terrified my twelve-year-old self that I had to lean my face against the iron banister, trying to breathe, trying to connect to something cold and familiar. I felt entirely alone. I looked across the street at a row of ugly houses. I hated Long Island. I had never fit in here. As a Jew, I'd long been accustomed to feeling lost in space. But this was even worse: I was now lost in time as well. By realizing my future I'd forfeited my past, and if I had died at that moment I would have drifted into some dark eternity where no one in my family had ever gone.

I closed my eyes and tried to humbly confess, but, like I said before, Jews aren't trained to feel guilty about sex, and besides, I was way too anxious to feel humble. "O G-d, why did you let me do this? I gave you several chances to stop me! You kept quiet when I stole the liquor. You kept quiet when I put my hand between Brian's thighs. Is this some kind of a joke? Because nothing is going to keep me from wanting Brian—"

Just then Brian ran from the church and flew onto his bicycle.

"Brian!" I called.

But Brian didn't answer me. He jumped on the pedal and was away in a flash.

"Brian!"

I ran down the steps and onto the sidewalk.

"Brian!"

But then I heard myself screaming and I stopped. Another piece of the jigsaw puzzle had just fallen into place. I looked around me to make sure nobody had heard me acting like a faggot. Then I sat down on the curb to be a little less noticeable. "How unfair!" I remember thinking. "How completely unfair!" Brian had been able to go into a church and confess his sins, while I would have to carry this sickening feeling around with me for the rest of my life.

I had such an awful ache in my stomach. At first, I thought I would die. I really did. But, somehow, I continued to breathe. I crossed my hands against my stomach and held myself as tight as I could. Very slowly, the pain subsided. More time passed and the curb started casting a shadow on the road. Then some minutes went by without any thoughts at all. A solitary car passed. Apparently, people were still going about their business, and I would have to go about mine. Just for the hell of it, I began pulling out weeds growing between the cracks in the sidewalk.

What should I do next? It was, after all, a beautiful Saturday afternoon, with no homework and plenty of sunshine. My first choice, hanging out with Brian, was now out of the question. "Oh, well . . ." I thought to myself. I could have gone to the movies. I could have gone bowling. The one place I couldn't go was home. How could I explain to my mother where I'd been without telling her what I had become?

The King of Kings and I

I absentmindedly yanked out another weed from between the cracks in the cement and shook every last trace of dirt from its roots.

Needless to say, Brian and I never had another conversation. His father, Mr. McDermott, returned from Texas the following week, and my friend began spending more time at Jerry's. Nor did I ever go back to our honeymoon hole in the woods. I did, however, get my sleeping bag back when it turned up a few days later on my patio; sorry to say, it didn't have a love note from Brian attached. But I wasn't that upset. It didn't take nearly as long to fall out of love with Brian as I would have thought. I don't remember why. Perhaps some long-forgotten crisis arose that spring to take his place.

The truth is, children's lives are crowded to the breaking point with all sorts of disruptions, and if adults changed their jobs as often as kids changed their classrooms, sales of Prozac would triple overnight. That fall I entered junior high school, where I was put in classes with smart kids from across town and started getting crushes on a higher grade of unavailable men. In all likelihood, Brian's thuggish charm simply started wearing thin.

As for Brian, he eventually dropped out of school and rented a room above Doogan's Bar, where he married and divorced Theresa Caldone. A few years later he married a plain girl named Mary from Mineola and they had four daughters: Janet, Jodie, Janie, and Jackie. The last time I caught a glimpse of him was three Thanksgivings ago, from my old bedroom window; he was playing catch in the street with his two elder daughters. Careful to remain in the shadows, I examined Brian, and, I must confess, he didn't look nearly as bad as I would have thought. To my surprise, he was fairly trim and sported a stylish haircut, which led me to believe that he might still have been seeing boys on the side.

But I'll never forget that day picking weeds in front of Saint Martin's Church, because just when I thought I'd have to go home and face the music, I saw two familiar figures coming down the street:

Debbi McDermott leading the ancient Mrs. Potts. They were walking so slowly that they had to have left home the previous November to have gotten so far on foot. Sensing a way out of my dilemma, I jumped up and pushed open the Gates of Paradise as Debbi helped Mrs. Potts up the stoop one slow step at a time. "Bless you," Mrs. Potts whispered as she walked past me into the dark, still air of the church. "Thank you so much!" Debbi said as she helped Mrs. Potts light a candle and place it on a shelf.

That afternoon I stayed for Mass, sitting in the back pew, and when I got home that night I explained to my mom that I had started doing volunteer work, helping homebound women with arthritis. To make good my claim, I soon started sweeping Mrs. Potts's driveway every Wednesday and accompanying her to Mass on Saturdays. That year, I must have sat through Mass more times than Cardinal Spellman, leaving the world behind and hanging out with old ladies in cloth coats who wanted nothing more than to be gathered up in the arms of their Savior. I enjoyed Mass. I had no idea what the priest was doing; I was just glad that his back was turned, leaving my mind to roam freely through the church.

I would count the buttresses, the pillars, and the sections in the stained-glass windows. I also had my favorite icons—such as Saint Sebastian, who managed to look dreamy even while bleeding to death. But he was no more beautiful than a large wooden statue of Jesus hanging on a cross. It was easy to see why he looked so sad in Debbi's painting, considering the gruesome way he ended up. Debbi explained to me that Jesus allowed himself to be killed because he so much loved his fellow man. "Ouch! Love hurts," I had to agree. But what fascinated me most about Jesus was his bare pelvic bone exposed ever so slightly. "Who needed Brian?" I remember thinking to myself. "I have the man man now." And when I caressed Jesus' body in my imagination, the constant aching emptiness would temporarily be replaced by some good honest yearning.

CHAPTER 2

Buddhism for Beginners

I graduated from high school just in time for the seventies. Looking back, I see that the only thing we did in those years was gradually lower our expectations, because if Ronald Reagan had been elected president any sooner after Woodstock, we all would have died from the shock. I also think of the seventies as the New Jersey decade, a time period with no real identity. Just as the Garden State is made up of one part suburban Philly and two parts suburban New York, the first half of the seventies was an extension of the sixties, and the last half was a prelude to the eighties. Each year rolled by like an exit not taken on the turnpike going from Hippie to Yuppie, from free love to free market.

Jaffe Cohen

Me personally? I wasn't old enough to be a hippie. I was part of the "little-brother generation": too young to fight in Vietnam, but just old enough to get really stoned at antiwar demonstrations. The end of the sixties had been a giddy time for all of us in high school. The pot-heads felt triumphant because by 1970 even the jocks were smoking dope, laying aside their penny loafers and wearing sandals to lacrosse practice. By the time I went to college in September, however, there were already signs that Woodstock was turning into Wood-stuck. Signs of tragic decay were everywhere. The Beatles had broken up. Jimi Hendrix had died. Elton John and Neil Diamond, on the other hand, were well on their way to fame and fortune, and Qiana shirts were coming into vogue. The gas crisis was only a few years away, and within five years all of us middle-class freaks would be scrambling back into corporate America, apologizing for the happiest times of our lives. The early seventies, therefore, had an undercurrent of desperation, like a pleasant Sunday afternoon before a long, boring week of work. Luckily marijuana was still pretty cheap in 1971, so most of us were too stoned to *really* understand what we were losing.

For me, 1971 was the year I left my parents' house. It was also the second full year of Gay Liberation. The Stonewall riots had occurred two summers before, and this news had filtered out to the suburbs on page four of *Newsday*. I remember how I'd found this newspaper on the front porch and stared in horror at the photograph of homosexual activists being shoved kicking and screaming into a police van. Without a second thought, I threw the paper in the trash and, that evening, told my father that the paper had never been delivered, that the newsboy had been hit by a truck.

You see, by the time I graduated from high school, I was in a state of denial—no less toxic than the state of New Jersey. I'd *forgotten* that I was gay, which, considering how horny I still was for guys, was like Rush Limbaugh forgetting he liked to eat. This forgetfulness wasn't my fault: I saw no future in being queer; I had no teachers or guidance counselors suggesting "big queen" as a career option. Consequently I ignored my sexuality so completely that my erections felt like they were happening to somebody else, somebody fictional. The real me was the person waiting for the swelling to go down. I even went so far as training myself to be aroused by females by masturbating to pictures of half-naked women. Unfortunately, the only pictures I could find in our house of half-naked women were the lingerie ads in the *New York Times* Sunday magazine section. Needless to say, I never really got turned on by female models in overpriced panties, although to this day I get strangely excited whenever I see a guy reading William Safire.

Not knowing who I was meant I didn't know where I belonged. Certainly not in the suburbs, where every screen door was embossed with the name of a heterosexual nuclear family. And yet I had no desire to leave the development; in fact, if my grades had been lower I would have stayed at my parents' house another twenty years, planned their meals, and taken pottery courses at a local community college. Unfortunately, this would have been unthinkable for a Jewish child with a 3.8 grade point average, and so on September 1, 1971, my unhappy mother abandoned me in the parking lot of Walt Whitman Dormitory on the campus of the State University of New York at Stony Brook.

I had chosen this college only because of its proximity to my mother's washer and dryer. Now, my mother was even less anxious for me to leave home than I was. I know this because she drove me to school, something she had never done when I was in grades K through 12. My mother, Roz, hated to drive. To this day she drives only with the greatest reluctance, and always scurries home before dark. I don't think she even knows that the car has headlights. And she always pulls herself close to the steering wheel, rides the brake, and lurches to a complete stop fifty yards before each intersection. Watching her drive anywhere is like watching a circus elephant try to stand on a ball: eventually she gets there, but at such a lumbering pace, you wonder, "What's the point?" We made the forty-mile trip to Stony Brook in a record two and a half hours.

What my mother lacked in driving skills, however, she more than made up for in housecleaning genius. Some women carry makeup in their purses; my mom packs Brillo pads and Bon Ami cleanser. Within seconds of entering my cinder-block cubicle, painted bright yellow to cut down on the teen suicide rate, she pushed up her sleeves and went to work on the bathroom floor, scrubbing for two hours a surface that, to my eyes, had been perfectly clean when we'd walked in the door. Me? I very slowly unpacked my suitcase into a plywood dresser whose mahogany facing was already starting to fall off. I almost started crying several times, but I didn't want to upset my mom, who was working so hard to create a toilet as antiseptic as the ICU at Mount Sinai Hospital.

When she was done scouring, she made my bed, cleaned the windows, and measured them for drapes. On her way out the door she announced, "I'll give you Grandma's old curtains."

"No thanks," I said glumly.

"Why not? They're good material."

"You've already given me Grandma's lamp, Grandma's bedspread, and Grandma's doilies."

"So?"

"I'm just afraid that Grandma's gonna come back to life and she'll think that she lives here."

My mother sighed and put her purse over her shoulder. "If you don't want them, I'll find other uses for them."

As what, I couldn't imagine.

"No, I'll take them."

Then I offered to walk her back to her car. The western sky was a ridiculously happy shade of orange. Neither one of us knew what to say as my mother checked in her purse for her car keys.

"Where do you have to be now?" she finally asked.

"There's an orientation meeting at seven."

"It's 7:30. Don't you think you should go?"

"Yeah," I said.

"You know how to get there? Did they give you a map?"

"Yeah."

My mother looked over my shoulder, squinting at the orange sky.

"Well . . . good-bye."

The she hugged me with a ferocity that squeezed the air from my lungs.

"Don't forget to call," she said.

"I'll call soon," I replied.

"If there are any problems . . . call."

"As soon as they give me a phone."

"There *are* pay phones."

"I'll call."

"Do you have quarters?"

"I'll get some."

My mother pulled her change purse out of her pocketbook and snapped it open.

"I've got a couple."

I held out my hand and my mother gave me three quarters. "If you have to, call collect, but it's more expensive."

I couldn't bear it any longer.

"Go on. You don't want to drive after dark."

My mother opened the door and hesitated.

"If there are any problems . . ."

And suddenly it occurred to me that I didn't *have* to go away to college. Nobody was making me go. Certainly not the woman standing in front of me. If I decided to go back upstairs and unpack the dresser, nobody's life would be affected but my own. Not that much money had been spent. Not that much time had been wasted.

My dearest desire at that moment was to jump inside my mother's pocketbook and be held close to her heart. And yet . . .

"I'd better get going," I said.

Then she disappeared inside the car and started the engine. In no time at all she was spitting up gravel as she scurried from the lot. There was nothing left of my mother now but an oil stain on the asphalt. I burst into tears. Thank god she wasn't seeing me like this. Thank god.

Now what to do? I pulled the acceptance letter out of my back pocket along with a pamphlet containing a map of the campus. I needed to find the Walter Shapiro Lecture Hall. I started walking.

I walked out of the parking lot into a different parking lot, which led into another parking lot which ended in a tar path which weaved through a construction site. I made my way around a bulldozer and a metal drum hissing steam from some unseen hell. I scanned the horizon. In those years Stony Brook was rapidly expanding from three ugly buildings to three dozen ugly buildings, and even through my veil of tears I could see that I'd been abandoned in one of the most unappealing spots on the face of the earth.

I made my way across plank-covered mud-splattered pits, around abandoned cranes. The early seventies were awful years for architecture. We were somewhere between modern, postmodern, and just plain hideous, so every new building resembled either an oversize lunar module or a concrete bridge abutment. The style of architecture back then was so raw that it was almost impossible to tell which structures were being built and which were already complete. The older buildings were red brick, like actual school buildings, but the newer ones were often nothing more than monstrous concrete slabs—mausoleums that might have been labeled "Here Lies English," "Here Lies Chemistry."

Even worse were the whimsical structures. The Theater Department, for instance, was a twisted hunk of stainless steel that looked like a 747 crashing into a duck pond, and the Walter Shapiro Lecture Hall was an asymmetrical mound of cement that resembled an Egyptian pyramid whose slave workers had suddenly walked off their jobs and taken a five-thousand-year lunch break. This playful monolith had four trapezoidal entrances, leading into four distorted hallways—a labyrinth that would have foiled even the most intrepid of grave robbers.

Finally, I gave up trying to find my room. I pushed my way into the first open door I could find, into a chamber none of whose walls stood straight, a fluorescent *Cabinet of Dr. Caligari*. Seated cross-legged on some gray industrial carpeting were a dozen of my contemporaries, already cranky from lack of back support. The leader of this sullen group, a wild-haired graduate student wearing a peasant blouse, was breast-feeding her baby. She frowned at me as though I might have come to kidnap her child.

"Excuse me. Is this Lecture Hall Four?"

"No, this is Three."

"Oh . . . umm . . ."

I scanned the room. Most of the other kids had already been to the bookstore that day, so the floor was littered with Norton readers and overpriced psychology texts featuring B. F. Skinner on the cover.

"If you don't mind, I was just explaining core courses."

"I'm sorry."

I didn't move. After a moment the group leader finally decided she'd look better to the group if she showed me some compassion. Burping her baby, she explained, "Room Four is right next door, but in order to get there you have to turn right, walk around the corner, take the second staircase down, turn left past the elevators, which aren't working, and—"

"Oh," I replied. "Can I just stay here?"

"Let me see your schedule."

Without disturbing her child the group leader managed to take the paper out of my hand, but the greedy little baby, thinking it was more food, grabbed for my schedule and tried to eat it.

"No, Seabreeze. This doesn't belong to you."

Meanwhile all the other kids stared at the ground or checked their notes, except for one guy who caught my eye just as I was catching his. We locked eyes for only a moment, just long enough for us both to realize that we looked almost exactly alike. He had the same mouth of a sad clown; his cheeks were rosy and his eyes were bright blue. I suppose you might say that it was love at first sight, but it wasn't sexual or particularly romantic. This is not to say that it wasn't highly dramatic. Upon finding my long-lost twin, I probably felt what some Cheyenne Indian felt the first time somebody took his photograph: "What is my soul doing sitting in front of me?"

"You can stay here," Seabreeze's mother finally announced without much enthusiasm. "My name is Ocean Rosenthal."

So I joined the group, sitting next to my new friend.

"Are you two related?" the group leader asked. We looked at each other and shook our heads. Then, after I introduced myself, giving my name, my favorite primary color, and a pet psychosis, Ocean continued her presentation by explaining that, in the interest of turning out well-rounded students, Stony Brook was requiring all freshmen to take classes completely outside their majors. This, I quickly deduced, would not only make our lives miserable in the short run, but also have no effect in the long term unless we wound up contestants on *Jeopardy*. My new friend, who had been studying the academic catalog, raised his hand vigorously.

"Yes, Ira?"

"So as a theater major I would still have to take calculus, even though, on page seventy-four, it says I can petition to substitute to take two sciences instead of a math?"

"Really?"

The King of Kings and I

Ocean shifted Seabreeze to her other breast and thumbed through her catalog. I did the same, flipping to the science section. Which two sciences should I take? I snuck a peak at Ira's handout. He'd circled earth science, so, without hesitation, I did the same. I also noticed that Ira had done nothing to hide his schedule. In fact, he seemed to nudge his paper toward me to make it easier for me to read. After the orientation meeting was over Ira approached me and said, "A couple of us are going over to the student union. You want to come?"

I had nothing to do but head back to my room. "Yeah, sure," I said. So I exited the lecture hall with Ira and a few assorted geeks who looked like they had little in common other than incipient drug addiction and having been sentenced to the same dreary residence hall. In retrospect, this ten-minute walk through darkened mud pits to the student union, a building so stark even Saddam Hussein wouldn't have used it as a hideout, was a defining moment in my life. It was my first glimpse of the cast of characters who would feature so prominently in the next few years of my life.

Leading the way was Andy Ives, a tristate Frisbee champion and the first of us to become a major pothead. He was the only one among us who would thrive on the college food plan, becoming addicted to meat loaf and gaining thirty pounds by Christmas. Then came Barry Liebowitz, a knock-kneed whiz kid from Ozone Park, Queens, who would later give up his dream of teaching algebra to move to Colorado and raise free-range turkeys. Behind him skulked his prodigiously talented thespian roommate, Aaron Grossman, seventeen going on seventy, who had already won raves for his King Lear at Oceanside Junior High School and would soon direct and star in his own one-man adaptation of Ibsen's *Peer Gynt*. Next to Aaron strolled Vinnie Passalacqua, so relaxed that he wouldn't register for classes until Thanksgiving. Then came David Albright, an outrageously effeminate French major who would worship Dionne Warwick and play her records endlessly. And finally, ambling at his own pace, was

David's roommate, weirdo Scotty McWilliams, a six-foot-three Jesus look-alike who in December would drop acid during 2001: A Space Odyssey, wallpaper his dorm room with aluminum foil, and float weightlessly for the entire semester.

But for me, the most fascinating of all of us was still Ira, who maturely suggested that we move two tables together to keep the group together. Unlike me, Ira had come to Stony Brook for a very specific reason: to study theater seriously with a man named Alfred Bennet-Hughes, an imported English homosexual who would later gleefully feel our stomach muscles under the guise of teaching Shakespearean voice production. Like Aaron Grossman, Ira had been a devout theater major in high school and had worked extra-hard to get the "lawnguy-land" out of his voice. Even at seventeen his consonants were so clipped that, when cast as Nicely Nicely in Guys and Dolls, he had to pretend to be from New Yawk. To tell the truth, I was a little put off by his preten-tiousness, yet there was something intriguing about him. In spite of his artificial speaking voice and slightly affected manner, I desperately wanted to become his friend. It was like he had already taken a few baby steps down a path I had yet to enter.

After a few minutes Ira made a quick run back to his dorm to see if his roommate had arrived yet. Without his moderating influence, the dinner conversation quickly devolved into a scathing critique of the cuisine once Andy grunted, "These potatoes taste like shit."

Barry agreed. "Chemically speaking, they're only one molecule away from Spackle."

Aaron just glared at the rest of us, looking like Richard III with acne. Scotty, who was quietly enjoying his meat loaf, turned to Vinnie and asked, "Did you bring your TV set to the room?"

"Yeah," Vinnie answered, "but there's nothing on tonight."

"No, man!" Scotty protested. "My favorite show is on!"

"What's that?" Aaron leaned forward, looking at Scotty as if he were studying a painting, not sure it was real.

"*Flipper*, man. They're running the original episodes!"

This surprised me. I wondered if Scotty's interest in the show, like mine, was with Luke Halprin, the gorgeous blond boy who every week took off his shirt and dove into the water. Meanwhile, Andy threw down his fork of potatoes. "That show is so fuckin' stupid! It's the same plot every week. Every week the fuckin' fish is saying to the boy, 'Eee-ee-eee'!"

"Flipper's a mammal," Barry corrected him.

"Flipper's a fuckin' retard and that kid's even stupider. Every week he's gotta ask the fish, 'What are you saying, Flipper? What are you saying?' For Chrissakes, Flipper's saying, 'Get in the water and follow me, you stupid jerk. Read your fuckin' script!' Jeez!"

Scotty, probably already stoned, shook his head thoughtfully. "Wow. That's right, man. Wonder what it would be like to live underwater." Then, crestfallen, he went back to his meat loaf. "I like that show."

The conversation might have ended there if Barry hadn't regaled us with the following fact: "Dolphins have ten-inch penises."

Andy jumped on this. "You are really disgusting. Jeez."

But Barry continued, "And sometimes when you swim with the dolphins they like to rub it up against you."

"Really?" Scotty said. "That would be cool!"

At this David Albright, who had been quiet until now, pursed his lips and looked aside. Aaron remained silent, but his gaze grew more clinical. Andy, however, jumped on Scotty like a trial lawyer interviewing a hostile witness.

"You'd like that, wouldn't you? Getting a big fucking fish dick shoved up your ass. I knew you were weird!"

Scotty, fortunately, didn't answer Andy's accusation. His mind was somewhere else—swimming with the dolphins, I imagined.

"You guys are disgusting! Barry, give me the rest of your potatoes." Andy grabbed Barry's side dish and shoved a forkful in his mouth, beginning the life of self-indulgence that would soon ruin his boyish figure.

Just then Ira returned with the news that he'd found a note on his door indicating that his roommate wouldn't be coming after all and that he'd be reassigned a new one.

"Wonder who you'll get," Barry said.

I looked down and almost blushed, wondering if my life had just changed for the better. Just then Andy swallowed his bread and tried to pull the conversation back to the previous topic. He turned on Ira. "Hey," Andy asked, "you know that TV show *Flipper*? If I gave you fifty bucks," Andy continued, "would you jump in the water with a horny dolphin?"

"No way," Ira replied honestly.

Andy then turned his attention to me for the first time. "How about you?" he asked. "What's your name again?"

"Jaffe," I replied.

"If I gave you a hundred bucks would you have sex with Flipper?"

I thought for a second. This would be the first time I spoke in front of this group, and whatever I said would establish my identity and possibly haunt me for years. I chose my words carefully.

"No," I replied, "but Mr. Ed is kind of cute."

Everyone laughed except for Andy, who pushed away his plate. "Man, I can't eat with you guys anymore."

And across the table, Ira nodded his approval and I somehow knew that he had already chosen me to be his new roommate. Twenty years later, in Greenwich Village, I asked Ira what he'd been thinking that first night in the student union, and Ira remembered that we'd both had the exact same thought. Neither one of us particularly wanted to be poked by a porpoise. On the other hand, if *being* Flipper meant that every week Luke Halprin would jump in the ocean and climb on our backs, both of us would gladly have learned to breathe underwater.

The King of Kings and I

*   *   *

Ira and I actually turned out to be more different than we at first thought. In fact, the longer we lived together, the more we seemed like Goofus and Gallant, those two cartoon brothers from *Highlights for Children* magazine, one of whom had perfect oral hygiene while the other used his toothbrush to clean his sneakers. Bottom line, there seem to be two types of people in the world: managerial types like Ira; and people like me who have very few opinions about what to eat, where to put furniture, and which shirt looks best on us. These types often marry each other, and from the moment I moved into Ira's dorm room, I gained not only my first real friend since leaving Brooklyn, but also my first real glimpse of what I'd be like as a spouse. It was frightening. I must say, however, we weren't the only odd couple in the dorm. Up and down the hall our schoolmates were working out their own relationships with varying degrees of success.

Next door to us, Barry Liebowitz and Aaron Grossman managed to coexist in a loveless union. They lined their beds up against opposing walls adorned respectively with a framed periodic table and an autographed picture of Lee Strasberg. Across the hall from them, Vinnie and a friend from Manhattan named Taylor Redfield quickly got rid of their bedsprings, lay their mattresses on the floor, and smoked dope constantly. Next door to them, mincing David and odd-ball Scott were the strangest couple of all. David spent all his time tending to his complexion and writing long passionate letters home to his great-aunt Marbelle in Utica, New York, and Scott, to his credit, never seemed to think this strange.

Andy Ives, on the other hand, took whatever opportunity he could to torture David, hiding his overpriced shampoo and calling him Suzy Q behind his back. To mankind's benefit, Andy was never assigned a roommate, which allowed him to close his door, eat by himself, and masturbate whenever he wanted. Oddly enough, it soon appeared that Andy the frustrated jock was more out of place than

61

David at that particular school in those liberal times. Of all of us living on the hall, Andy would have been happiest going to a college featuring more traditional fraternities like the Ku Klux Klan or the Gestapo.

Despite our differences, my friendship with Ira thrived that first semester. Maybe because we looked so much alike we were instantly familial. We had an unspoken agreement that we would always go a little out of our way for each other. We always sat together in the cafeteria and took each other to movies on Friday nights. My third week in the room, we were lying in bed reminiscing about old times, bemoaning the loss of childhood as only seventeen-year-olds can do, and Ira asked me if it would be all right if he fell asleep while I continued to talk. He didn't want me to feel lonely. "Sure," I said. "Just because one of us is talking doesn't mean the other one has to listen." Then, after he might have been asleep, I added, "Just so long as I know that you're there."

And for a very short while I was happy at Stony Brook. Ira and I had been blessed with the largest room at the end of the hall. So Ira decided we would always leave our door open. Then we moved our beds into a charming L shape and bought some throw pillows at a yard sale so that our hallmates would automatically enter our room and plop themselves down. Ira, slightly less solipsistic and depressed than the rest of us, became our unofficial Pearl Mesta, and I was his quiet little helper. This suited me just fine. My only other interests at the time were Joni Mitchell records and doodling in an artist's pad. I would sit for hours, scratching away with my Rapidograph, imagining myself a lovely canyon lady wearing wampum beads, and filling my drawing book with lines. On my own, I might have turned into a recluse; but as Ira's roommate I found myself at the center of what little social life occurred in our dorm. I became the quiet guy in the corner you passed the joint to simply because he was there.

The King of Kings and I

At first we were one big asexual family, but then the heterosexuals among us began to weed themselves out. First Andy met a girl in his physics class. Then Barry started spending most nights in Margaret Sanger Dormitory with Rhonda, his chemistry lab partner. Even Scotty learned the guitar and started serenading an exchange student from Portugal. By Thanksgiving our only regular guests were Aaron, who gossiped cruelly with Ira about the Theater Department; and David, who brought over his Edith Piaf records and lip-synched to "La Vie en Rose."

The question you might be asking yourself is whether or not we knew we were gay. Not quite. I was still remarkably naive. Looking over a few letters I'd written home to my mother that year, I recently found one that boasted: "I recently met some really great guys here on the hall. They're so funny and vivacious. You'd really like them because they really like to watch Esther Williams musicals from the fifties just like you." First of all, *vivacious* is a lovely adjective—if you happen to be Liza Minnelli. But for a seventeen-year-old boy *vivacious* usually means queer. Second, with the possible exception of her stepson Lorenzo Lamas, there are no straight boys on the planet born after 1940 who would have any interest whatsoever in the movie career of Esther Williams.

Now, one of the reasons it wasn't glaringly obvious we were gay is that some of us still had, or pretended to have, girlfriends. Even David kept a picture of his sweetheart, a plain-looking girl not unlike the young woman who recently carried Michael Jackson's baby, which he pinned on the wall right next to his poster for the New York City Ballet. Aaron occasionally kept company with a Korean girl at the international dorm, and Ira still kept in contact with his high school honey, the star of Wantagh High School's drama club, the irrepressible Janet Eisenberg, who was destined to play a major part in my life as well.

The previous summer Janet and Ira had toured the Catskills together in a hideous cabaret revue called *Tony's Tonight!!!*, a five-hour ordeal featuring the first few notes of several thousand forgettable songs from Broadway musicals. Janet was what is known in show business as a "triple threat." In other words, she was only modestly talented, had low self-esteem, and talked endlessly about herself. As Ira gallantly explained, she couldn't dance but she "moved well." She also had a nasal high-pitched singing voice that could either shatter a jar of gefilte fish or convert a dog to Judaism. It wasn't that she couldn't hold a tune. It's just that she held them so enthusiastically she tended to strangle them to death.

Janet and Ira had parted company when Janet left for Boston to study voice at Emerson College. She didn't show up at Stony Brook until Thanksgiving, and I must admit I took an immediate dislike to her. She brought out everything in Ira that was superficial and arch, gossiping about the theater and mocking whomever they believed to be chronically untalented. Despite being Janet's so-called boyfriend, Ira acted even more effeminate when Janet was around, spending all day Friday frosting her hair and comparing facial scrubs. On the plus side, Janet did have a vivid imagination—as well as some great acid she'd scored in Boston Common the week before. Saturday afternoon she and Ira planned to trip together—they'd done this before—and Janet was just about to slice the pill into two pieces when Ira suggested that it would be more fun to take me along. Janet, basically generous and good-hearted, agreed, and we split the acid three ways.

It was my first trip on acid. At first nothing happened. I kept staring at the walls waiting for some nifty hallucinations, but the walls remained upright. Then we got into Janet's Buick because Ira wanted to show Janet some of the beautiful countryside not too far off campus. As the drug took effect we drove slower and slower, cruising along at seven miles per hour on a one-lane highway, until we finally stopped by the side of the road. Janet wanted to "experience" the grass. Left to my own devices I might have been perfectly content to contemplate the sunlight glinting off the door handle, but Janet and Ira pulled me through a fence into what turned out to be the most gorgeous meadow I'd ever seen. Then the two of them started singing show tunes and I must have been really tripped out, because two nasal adolescents singing *Brigadoon* suddenly sounded like the Mormon Tabernacle Choir.

"Look at the sun!" Janet exclaimed, pointing west. "Wow!" It was one of those late-autumn days when the sun seems to do nothing all day but set. Then Janet stood still and grabbed Ira's hand. "Can you feel the earth moving?" Ira grabbed my hand and the three of us felt the movement of the planet and we gave thanks for having each other. "Old loves," Ira said, looking at Janet, "and new loves," he said, looking at me. I was so moved. Ira and Janet—they were my soul mates. How could I ever have thought ill of either one of them? We started harmonizing on "Where Is Love?" from *Oliver!* and Janet burst into tears. Then a cow munching grass, probably no stranger to tripping undergraduates trespassing on his lunch, ambled into view, and the three of us screamed and climbed up a tree and made it our home.

We all found branches that suited our personalities. I hugged the tree trunk. Its bark flowed through my arms like a river of warm water. The world was a miracle, and I was determined to make the most of the view. "I'm gonna climb higher," I said. Ira and Janet beamed at me. "Do you want to come?" I asked.

"Come back and tell us what you see up there," Ira said.

"Good-bye," I said like a soldier going off to war. Ira and Janet bade me good-bye and waved like two parents in a Norman Rockwell painting. "Come back soon," Ira added.

Leaving Janet and Ira behind, I slithered upward through the branches, pulling myself to a place where there was more sky than green. I breathed deeply and the moon appeared. I had a revelation. "Isn't it amazing," I thought to myself, *"that any of this exists at all?!"* Poised between heaven and earth, I felt that, as gorgeous as the world seemed at that moment, nothing was more miraculous than the fact that *it was there!* "None of this *has* to be," I remember thinking to myself. "All this could just as easily *not be here*. The air, the stars, the Stony Brook campus in the distance. How incredible that *the void filled itself up with stuff!* Look at all this stuff!" The sheer *generosity* of creation in the way it came into being—what a *miracle!* Suddenly I became aware of a second miracle. Beyond the miracle of creation was the miracle that *I was there to perceive it*. "Aaah!" The joy was too much to contain. I started to sob with happiness.

Then I listened to sounds. A car went by. The wind rustled some leaves. Some garbled words banged around in my head. Everything was just stuff. Even *the thought of "stuff" was nothing but stuff*. My thoughts were merely sounds going on inside my head, no more capable of hurting me than the sound of the wind. *"I'm free!"* I realized. "But who am I?" I asked myself. I waited for an answer. "I am *a heart with a memory!*" I said the phrase out loud to myself. "A heart with a memory. Wow!" How could I have ever believed that life was anything less than pure bliss?

So I sat. And I sat some more. But the spell had already been broken. Very slowly, like a car engine coming back to life on a cold winter morning, my thoughts started to sputter in more familiar territory. First came the thought that I had taken a drug that would soon wear off. Then came the thought that the drug was wearing off. Then came the thought that I was lonely, unbearably lonely. I wanted to be back with my friends. I reluctantly climbed back down to find Ira, who, along with Janet, was still singing "Where Is Love?" from *Oliver!* Apparently I'd been gone only about forty-five seconds.

"I'm back," I announced.

"Oy! Our dah-link baby has returned to us!" Ira said, pretending to be his grandmother. "I'm kvelling!"

"Come, dah-link!" Janet reached out to me and squeezed my head into her bosom. Then we just huddled together and listened to the silence. Janet swore that she could hear the tree growing.

"Come listen to the bark of the tree."

"The tree's barking?" Ira asked.

Janet again put her ear to the branch.

"Wow! It is! It's going, 'Woof, woof, woof.'"

"It must be a dogwood," I concluded, and we all laughed.

"I'm so glad we found each other," Ira whispered to me.

"Me too."

Ira put his arm around me, and the two of us beamed at each other.

"What are you guys whispering about?" Janet asked.

"Oh . . . nothing," Ira replied, looking somewhat guilty.

On the way home Janet started complaining that she had a headache, but I suspected she was beginning to get jealous of me. As generous as she was, I don't think she relished sharing her boyfriend. For myself, I wasn't attracted to Ira sexually, but I was beginning to realize that Ira's friendship with me had a much stronger chance of lasting than his romance with Janet. They seemed way too comfortable with each other to be a "normal" couple.

That night, Ira and Janet went to the student union to see a screening of *The Strawberry Statement*. When they returned a few hours later, I pretended to be asleep in order to test my hypothesis. Would Janet and Ira actually have sex? The bedsprings croaked and squealed as two people crawled onto a cheap dormitory mattress hardly big enough for one.

"Good night, honey," Ira said.

"Good night, sweetie," Janet replied. Then, after a moment, Janet added, "Is this OK if I stay here?"

"Sure. Are you comfortable?"

"Yeah."

"I'm so tired."

"Me too."

"I had the best time today," Ira said.

"Me too," Janet replied.

Then they were both quiet for a minute.

"Isn't this cozy?" Janet asked.

"Oh, yeah," Ira replied.

Then they were quiet again.

"Do you think Jaffe is sleeping?" Janet asked.

"Good-night, Jaffe," Ira called across the room.

I didn't answer. Then an eternity passed in which I couldn't make out any words. Finally I heard Ira grunt, "My arm's asleep," and Janet mumbled, "Sorry." The next morning when I got up to go to the bathroom, I nearly stepped on Ira, who'd crawled out of bed and made a little nest on the floor with an old comforter and a few army blankets.

The next morning I felt a little sorry for Janet. She complained about her headache being worse as she boiled water on our hot plate. Hoping to make Ira laugh, she again pretended to be an old yiddishe mama: "You vant mebbe a glass of tea, dah-link?" But Ira didn't improvise anything in return. He just replied in his regular voice, "No thanks," and Janet made the tea for herself. Then on the way back to her car she and Ira reminisced about *Tony's Tonight!!!* and even warbled "Wunderbar" from *Kiss Me Kate*, but neither one of them could remember the words to the second verse. We all exchanged hugs, and then Janet slid behind the wheel of her father's Buick and floated away gently. Watching her go, I knew somehow that I wouldn't see her again for a long, long time. I wasn't sure what Ira felt, though. On the way back to our room he asked me what I thought of Janet.

"She's fun," I said unconvincingly. "I had a great time yesterday."

"Me too," Ira sighed. "That was great."

We got back to our room.

"Were you jealous?" Ira asked.

"No. Why should I be jealous?"

"I don't know," Ira said.

We flopped down on our respective beds.

"She makes me feel like such a kid," Ira finally announced dramatically. "When I'm with her I feel so theatrical."

"Oh," I said.

"What do you want to do the rest of the day?" Ira asked.

"I don't know," I replied. Then I added, "Maybe I was a little jealous. At first."

"Don't worry about it," Ira reassured me. "I realized something yesterday. You're my best friend."

Later that night, neither one of us went anywhere. Most of our friends hadn't returned from Thanksgiving with their families, so I took out my art pad to draw while Ira memorized a speech for his Shakespeare vocal-production class. I wanted to draw a picture that would be a souvenir of my first LSD trip. Trying to picture what the setting sun had looked like drenched in acid, I took an orange crayon and started making orange swirls. Round and round I drew circles of gold, until I was hypnotized by the motion of my hand. How wondrous life had felt. I wanted to continue to be able to feel that all the time, so I resolved to be more honest with my emotions.

"So, how do I make you feel?" I finally asked Ira.

"What do you mean?" Ira asked, hardly looking up from his book.

"If Janet makes you feel theatrical . . . how do I make you feel?"

Ira thought for a long moment. "Real," he said.

"What do you mean?" I asked.

"I'm not sure," Ira said.

"I know what you mean," I said.

Then I went back to my drawing, making swirls of orange color. Round and round I went until the color was so thick I could use my fingernails to scratch letters in the sun. Very carefully I etched the word LOVE into my creation, hoping I would one day know its meaning. In the meantime, Ira would do just fine.

Since the dawn of man's arrival—if man did arrive at dawn, my ancestors probably arrived sometime after lunch—there's been this idea kicking around that happiness lies within and people don't

need too much "stuff" to be joyful. The Hindus have their holy beggars, and even Jesus, whose life story is currently being marketed by
some pretty hideous money-grubbing organizations, is quoted as
having said that it's harder for a rich man to get into heaven than for
a camel to go through the eye of a needle. Unfortunately, the last few
centuries of Western capitalism have not been very kind to this concept, and the past twenty years of postmodern consumerism have
buried this idea completely under a pile of new gadgets, designer
labels, and easy credit.

Nowadays it's odd to think that bodhisattva can't be charged at
Bloomingdale's. But such was the craziness of my youth that, for one
brief moment, several million middle-class college kids really
believed that Love was the answer and materialism was absurd. Even
though many of my generation have grown to believe that *real* life
didn't begin until we started making a *real* living, I'd still like to defend
the sixties. We were right! Flower power was more than just an excuse
for goofy posters and ugly pink bathroom mats. Our only fallacy was
that we miscalculated, by several thousand years, how long it would
take the world to catch up to us.

In any event, the following semester my soul searching intensi-
fied. I went through more majors than the Who went through guitars.
I soon narrowed my scope to something in the arts. I took figure
drawing, but my subjects always looked in dire need of skeletons. I
tried ceramics, but whenever I threw a pot, the teacher would throw
it right back. Thinking I might express myself physically, I took an
introduction to mime, but I did poorly: I couldn't keep my mouth
shut. The second day I was almost tossed out by the teacher. Walking
up imaginary steps, by sheer force of habit I broke out complaining,
"Oy, these steps! I can't take these steps!"

For the most part, though, I tried to avoid theater majors, who
were all way too vivacious. That spring, the Drama Department produced *Damn Yankees*, so Ira and I and eight other limp-wristed per-

formers who had never gotten to first base in high school were absurdly miscast as World Series contenders. Our room now overflowed with guys chattering about Gwen Verdon and Ben Vereen. The biggest "Mary" of this bunch was an overweight multitalented viper named Billy Quintana, who'd been typecast as the Devil. Now, Billy Quintana was a major queen! I saw his driver's license photo: it was taken over his shoulder, and he had a rose in his teeth. This dormitory diva would run into our room at all hours, with a pink towel wrapped around his head, singing "Boogie Woogie Bugle Boy" because he loved anything associated with that decade of World War II and the great MGM musicals.

Apparently, Billy was one of those gay men who identifies so strongly with his mother that he tends to feel nostalgic for her childhood instead of his own. Unfortunately, despite living in the past, Billy had a skewed knowledge of history: the only literature he ever read was back issues of *Variety*. He actually believed that Mary Martin defeated the Japanese in World War II and that the Wild West was tamed by Ethel Merman. Ira, to my dismay, began taking on Billy's obsessions. One day after Billy left, Ira sighed, "Oh, Jaffe, I miss the forties!" "Ira," I reminded him, "you weren't born until the fifties."

There was no doubt about it. My roommate was now flaming brighter than Dresden after the firebombing. Always fastidious, Ira now became obsessed with his appearance. Once content to wash his hair with Johnson's baby shampoo, Ira now spent more money on hair products than most people spend on their mortgages. He also spent more time examining his face than Rembrandt, shamelessly plucking, tweezing, and lip glossing until he resembled a Jewish Farrah Fawcett with a slight five o'clock shadow.

Needless to say, Ira's days as a leader of men were long past. Gone was the time when Andy or Taylor would casually drop by. Now they scurried past our open door as fast as they could, leaving Aaron Grossman and David Albright as our only remaining friends. David bonded with Billy immediately because they both swooned ecstatically over every note that Miss Judy Garland ever sang. They worshiped her Carnegie Hall album and argued endlessly over whether or not Judy would have been fabulous in *Annie Get Your Gun* if MGM hadn't fired her. "Judy wasn't well in those days," Billy would sniff. "She *never* could have done it!" "That's not true," David would counter. "All she needed was a little rest!" And then one of them would complain about how unfairly Louis B. Mayer had treated her and the other would, invariably, burst into tears.

Meanwhile Aaron Grossman, who preferred Dame Judith Anderson to Judy Garland, despised Billy Quintana. Billy, likewise, despised Aaron as an old party pooper, and if Billy happened to flounce into our room when Aaron was already there, Aaron would loudly excuse himself and exit. This would then give Billy free rein to say the nastiest things about Aaron. Quoting Harold from *The Boys in the Band*, he'd take a hit of a joint and announce, "Aaron Grossman! King of the Pig People!" Ira, the gracious host, always fretted about their feud. I, on the other hand, thought their oversized feelings would have been more appropriate for a theater the magnitude of Shea Stadium. Somehow I'd already guessed that, as differently as Billy and Aaron behaved, they were quite similar beneath their Danskins. In any event, when the school term ended in June, I was almost relieved to go back to my parents' house.

Unfortunately, I'd forgotten how little there was to do in Bethpage. Everyone my age was either working nine to five or too ashamed to show their faces on the street. I was lonely, but determined to put my solitude to good use. I made up a reading list including the works of Hermann Hesse, Thomas Merton, and Lao-tzu, but before the week was out I started reading anything that happened to be lying on the bathroom floor. By mid-July I had finished two chapters of Jacqueline Susann's *Once Is Not Enough*, at which point my mother suggested I get a job.

The King of Kings and I

What a nightmare! After only one year of a liberal-arts education I was *completely* unemployable. Art classes had made me pretentious, poli-sci classes had made me angry at the system, and psych 101 had made me painfully self-analytical; in short, there wasn't a job on the planet that would have tolerated me for two seconds. Finally in late July I found a part-time job working for a Tupperware distributor. I was incarcerated in a dusty warehouse—picture Alcatraz in pastel-colored plastics—until one day a box of salad spinners fell on my head and broke my glasses. This convinced my mother that my life was in danger, and she reluctantly allowed me to quit my job and return home, where I finished Jacqueline Susann and rested up until September, when I returned to school.

Unlike me, Ira had used his vacation bettering mankind by teaching drama in a nursing home. My first afternoon back, he proudly displayed photographs of the musical *Mame*, which he'd directed, starring wheelchair-bound seniors. I wanted to tell him how proud I was to be his friend, but just then Billy Quintana burst into the room to brag about his summer. First he flipped through Ira's photographs and exclaimed, "Honey, this isn't *Mame!* This is *maimed.*" Then he regaled us with stories about how he'd been working as a busboy in a very chichi Manhattan restaurant and how all his new city friends wanted him to crash at their apartments. "And," he said, winking at Ira, "I could probably bring a friend." Needless to say, I didn't see too much of Ira that semester. He was always rehearsing one thing or another, and weekends he and Billy often took the train into Manhattan.

The only other change on the hall was that Vinnie Passalacqua's roommate, Taylor Redfield, had gone to Europe that summer to follow the Dead and had disappeared somewhere south of Munich. I discovered this one afternoon in the philosophy building. I'd been closed out of "Ancient Wisdom," and I was checking the bulletin board to see if there was anything else I could take. I was so anxious to find a new class that I almost didn't notice Vinnie ambling up beside me and saying hello. He'd gotten a haircut over the summer, and his eyebrows were black and beautifully shaped against his pale skin. I offered some advice.

"A couple of these, you don't need a prerequisite," I suggested.

"Yeah . . . maybe . . . umm . . . yeah."

"'Death and Dying' might be easy."

"Yeah, it might be. I mean . . . you know . . ."

Vinnie and I had never really spoken, and this may have been the first time I'd heard his voice. Freshman year I'd found his introversion boring, but this year his mere familiarity was reassuring. I pressed forward, but I had to lean in close to decipher his stammer.

"So what are you going to take?" I asked.

"I don't know. I was looking for something more . . . umm . . . yeah."

"Me too," I lied.

"More . . . yeah."

"Traditional?"

"Yeah . . . traditional."

"Maybe something Eastern?" I asked.

"Yeah . . . Eastern," Vinnie replied.

We continued to scan the course listings. Vinnie, unlike the rest of us, had never lived in the suburbs, and we all thought he was cool because he'd attended Manhattan's prestigious High School of Music and Art. Not only that, he'd actually smoked dope with his parents, which made him about ten years ahead of his time. Until that day I would have described Vinnie as morosely self-sufficient. I'd also thought he was too bony to be attractive. But that day, with his new haircut, Vinnie warranted a second look. He wasn't so much painfully thin as poorly dressed. In fact, beneath his torn jeans and Indian shirts may have beat the heart of a mesomorph. A dollop of maternal instinct and a pinch of sex drive suddenly erupted from the pit of my stomach, and I coughed out another suggestion.

The King of Kings and I

"Professor Finkelstein's 'Buddhism for Beginners' is still open."

Vinnie saw where I was pointing on the bulletin board. "Buddhism. Yeah."

"Tuesday and Thursday, 1:10 to 2:45?"

"Umm . . . yeah. I'm free."

"There's no prerequisite."

"Let's take that," Vinnie said.

"Cool," I said, feeling like I might have just made a new friend.

In the weeks that followed, Vinnie became my obsession. Because he said so little, I imagined that his unexpressed thoughts were much deeper than they actually were. Most days at sunset Vinnie would smoke a joint, sit on a ridge behind the lecture hall, and just stare off into space. The third week of classes I managed to rearrange my schedule to walk the path right below his perch.

"Hey, Vinnie! How's it going up there?"

"Great," he said.

I clambered up beside Vinnie and he passed me the joint. Guessing that he loved nature, I tried my best to blend into the environment. I let him speak first.

"It's beautiful," he finally said.

In front of and below us was a huge muddy hole housing the foundation of the proposed humanities pavilion. But beyond this pit the sun was a breathtaking shade of orange, which reminded me of my acid trip.

"Hmm," I said.

"Yeah," Vinnie replied. I was *so* impressed.

"The miracle of creation is that none of this has to be here."

Vinnie's eyes widened. "Wow. Yeah, right."

I had never tried to explain this revelation to anyone before, but, made bold by Vinnie's apparent interest, I continued, "You start out with something . . . not really something . . . Actually, you start out with nothing. OK . . . picture nothing."

"Hmm." Vinnie took another hit of his joint.

"And nothing turns into something."

"Wow!" Vinnie said.

"Isn't that amazing?"

Vinnie passed me the joint and asked, "You think we'll have meat loaf for dinner?"

I took Vinnie's non sequitur in stride. The absurdity of it seemed to reinforce rather than contradict my point.

"What's today?" I asked.

"Thursday," Vinnie said.

"Probably," I replied.

We took several more hits from Vinnie's joint and then I sat quietly, hoping that Vinnie had noticed how brilliant I'd been.

"You know . . ." Vinnie finally uttered, "according to quantum physics everything—matter and energy—it all pops out of nothing. So everything could disappear again just like that." Vinnie snapped his fingers. Then we both sat silently watching the sun set over the unfinished campus. A huge phallic building crane jutted three stories into the sky without spoiling the view. As long as Vinnie made no effort to leave, I figured that he was enjoying our time together as much as I was.

From then on, Vinnie called for me every day and we went to Buddhism class together. After that we spent our evenings together lying on the floor of his room and imagining ourselves superior to everyone else on the hall. To our left, Andy Ives and some of his new friends had bought a TV and were watching Howard Cosell on *Monday Night Football*. To our right Ira, Billy, and David were singing the score of *Pippin*. Only Vinnie and I seemed to realize how ridiculous it was to be holed up in a dormitory on Long Island when there were infinite numbers of worlds yet to be explored, none of which were listed in our academic brochures.

The King of Kings and I

"Buddhism for Beginners" had turned into a huge disappointment. Professor Finkelstein was teaching enlightenment as a historical concept rather than as a goal worth pursuing, so Vinnie and I began pondering other journeys. My brother Bernie, a "head" since high school, was then living in Tucson, engaged in the "import-export business." He imported marijuana from Mexico and exported it to students at the University of Arizona. One night Vinnie and I decided that the following semester we might drop out of school and hitchhike cross-country. Normally this idea would have terrified me, but with Vinnie by my side I could have done anything. Besides, it was 1972. The sixties were almost over. We only had one last chance to be free!

Looking back, I see that of course I was in love with Vinnie. Nowadays I would suggest investing in a condo together, but in 1972 I had no concept that two men could be lovers, so I took it day by day and I was reasonably content. As long as he kept calling on me for class, as long as we studied together, as long as he treated me like his best friend—I was happy, and, paradoxically, his kindness to me cut down on my need to get down his pants. When the itch of sexual desire reared its useless head, I scratched it by myself and forgot about it.

Furthermore, Vinnie, under the influence of Eastern philosophy, began toying with the idea of celibacy. Professor Finkelstein had taught us that desire was the root of all suffering. Though this idea was more familiar to Vinnie, a lapsed Catholic, it also made a certain amount of sense to me, a frustrated Jew. Certainly my life would have been a lot happier without desire, but I had less faith than Vinnie that people could change. Was it actually possible to cut down on one's inner cravings? Was there some kind of dietetic candy for the soul? In reality I never *really* believed that celibacy was such a great idea, but Vinnie always wanted to talk about it. And the more he talked about celibacy, the hornier I got.

Celibacy also kept me awake most nights, because Vinnie turned out to be the type of shy person who suddenly turns voluble long after sunset when the rest of the world is dying to go to sleep. One Friday night after Ira had gone to Manhattan with Billy Quintana, Vinnie came over to our room to plan our trip to Arizona, and he wound up sleeping in Ira's bed. So there we lay—perpendicular, with our feet almost touching—as we both tried desperately to figure out questions that had been plaguing theologians for generations.

"If you didn't *want* anything, there'd be no reason to be reborn," Vinnie explained. "You'd be a completely realized being."

"I can't even imagine what that would be like, not to want things."

"I can . . . sometimes. Sometimes I feel completely satisfied. There's nothing I want. But as soon as I get that feeling—bam!—then I get the thought I want to stay like that forever and it's over."

"Oops," I said.

"Yeah. But I'm not gonna worry about it. Remember what I told you. This could all disappear just like that." Vinnie held up his hand and snapped his fingers.

Meanwhile, I was starting to feel uncomfortable. This was the first time we were sleeping in the same room, and the yearning was starting to hurt. Was going out west together such a good idea? On some level Vinnie must have been feeling the same thing, because he began talking about sex.

"Sex is the most powerful desire, man. Sex is so weird. Don't you think sex is weird?"

"Umm . . . yeah."

"Like, our society makes it seem like wanting sex is the same thing as loving someone. I mean, how can you love someone if you desire sex from them? Like, let's say you desire to have sex with a girl—or even a guy—whatever. You following this?"

"Yeah. Sure."

Had Vinnie said what I thought he did? I held my breath and tried not to show how excited I was that Vinnie had mentioned the possibility of gay sex without cursing or vomiting. Vinnie continued to talk.

The King of Kings and I

"So if you want something from this person, you're not really perceiving that person's soul. It's like two opposites—love and desire. The Hindus were right, man. Just tie a wet diaper around your crotch and let the kundalini rise up your spine. You know what I mean?"

"I'm thinking."

"Do you agree?"

"I'm not sure."

I really did have to think about what Vinnie was saying. My future happiness hung on my every word.

"Why are you being so quiet?" Vinnie asked.

"I'm just thinking."

"What are you thinking?"

I took a deep breath to quell the fear.

"You know, Vinnie," I said haltingly, "sex might also be a way of expressing your love to someone."

Vinnie was quiet for a moment.

"What do you think?" I asked.

"Nah. That's like some fucked-up medieval notion."

"You're probably right," I sighed.

Again, Vinnie didn't respond. For a moment I thought he'd fallen asleep. I was just about to blow out the candle when my friend murmured, "Hey, I like the way you and Ira have rearranged your beds."

"Yeah. It's easier to talk this way."

"Do you ever talk about these things with Ira? You two guys seem really close. Like you were married or something. What does he think about you and me hanging out so much?"

"He's busy with his friends."

"Yeah, *those* guys."

What did Vinnie mean by "those" guys? I kept quiet, as though deaf to his innuendo.

"Who'd he go to the city with?" Vinnie asked.

I considered pleading ignorance, but then it occurred to me that telling the truth might flush out Vinnie's motives.

"Billy Quintana and David Albright," I said nonchalantly.

I let another moment pass.

"You think those guys are gay?" Vinnie finally asked.

"I don't know. Maybe." Then, trying to sound casual, I added, "I mean, I don't think it would bother me if they were."

"Me neither," Vinnie said, equally nonchalant. "If two guys love each other, theoretically two guys having sex might be OK as long as they weren't coming from a place of desire."

"Yeah," I said. "Like if they just sort of bumped into each other by accident? That would be OK?"

"Yeah," Vinnie said.

"Well, good night," I said.

"You see how much time we waste talking about sex?" Vinnie concluded. "If we used that same time meditating we'd be Buddha by now. We wouldn't have to go through any more lifetimes. We'd be free!"

"Yeah," I said.

"When we go out west, man, we're just gonna experience. No thinking. Won't that be great? Sleeping out in the desert. Sleeping under the stars. Good night."

"Good night," I repeated.

Then I lay there for a few moments waiting for Vinnie to fall asleep. I tried to picture the joy of sleeping under the stars, but the only stars I could picture sleeping under were Paul Newman and Robert Redford. After a few minutes I heard my friend snoring. "What a lovely sound," I thought to myself as I reviewed bits and pieces of our conversation. Suddenly it hit me. "Of course!" I yelled to myself with such a force that it pushed my head off the pillow. "Vinnie's gay!" I reviewed the evidence. He'd never talked about a girlfriend. He and Taylor had seemed awfully close. Of course Vinnie was gay! All of a sudden our trip out west held the possibility of being a honeymoon—except . . .

The King of Kings and I

Maybe Vinnie didn't love me. I buried my face in my hands. How awful. I knew then that I wanted Vinnie even more than I'd wanted Brian McDermott. Something had to give. I very quietly got out of bed and knelt beside Vinnie where I could see him more clearly in the dark. I didn't touch him, but I whispered to him, letting my words tickle his neck and slide down his back. "If I could have you, I would never again desire anything else in this world ever again. And if you felt that way about me we could be desire free! We'd be enlightened!" After a few minutes I realized that Vinnie wasn't about to wake up, so I crawled back into my bed, and eventually I must have dozed off.

In the ancient language of gay men, *queen* is a synonym for *human being*. I've always found this term compelling and oddly to the point, because it implies that we're all more feminine and more regal than one might suppose. It's especially amusing when *queen* is applied to men whose feminine sides are not so obvious. For instance, Ronald Reagan is an old queen. Colin Powell is a black queen. Dan Quayle is a dumb queen. And Aaron Grossman, my fellow college student, was—I imagined—an evil queen.

Evil queens are fascinating. If there's a force of good in the universe that keeps the planets spinning, evil queens never seem to notice. They live in dismal worlds of their own creation, nursing slights more energetically than Florence Nightingale nursed the whole British Army. They prefer indoors to outdoors because natural light tends to distract them from their revenge fantasies. Historians owe their livelihoods to these men. Without evil queens Genghis Khan, Napoleon, and Mussolini, nothing much would have happened and the story of mankind could have been transcribed on an envelope.

The truth is, evil queens are the engines who get the plot moving. They lurk in the shadows until their time is right and then pounce when the possibility for success is within their reach. It was early December and I was just returning from the student union when Aaron accosted me on the way into the dorm. Looking back, I'm sure he must have been staking out my room, because no sooner had I jingled my key chain than he was on top of me like an oil spill.

"Jaffe, you're precisely the gentleman I've been looking for."

"Oh hi, Aaron," I said, already trying to figure out a plan of escape.

"How *are* you?" he said.

"Great."

"It's marvelous to see you. You're looking rather hale! Thriving on the institutional food, I see."

My eyes glazed over as I pondered Aaron's sudden friendliness. We'd never had anything in common. For over a year we'd been like distant cousins forced to sit side by side at a bar mitzvah with nothing to talk about. There was something repelling about Aaron—not that he was ugly. He had a strong jaw and a noble brow; almost a parody of good looks. There was, however, something askew about Aaron: his handsome head was a little too large for his body, and although he was only eighteen, his hairline was already starting to recede. Mainly, though, it was his huge ego, the belief that he already knew everything—a case of advanced pedantry—that made him appear so freakish, and I'd always shied away from Aaron as one might shy away from a nine-year-old with a hairy back. I braced myself.

"Listen, Jaffe," Aaron hissed warmly, "I happen to have a project you might find amusing."

"Really?" I was shocked.

"By the way, I heard you were quite excellent in your mime class."

"You did?"

"However, you're busy. I'm busy. I'll cut to the proverbial chase. Ira may have informed you that I'm taking a directing class."

Actually, Ira had told me about Aaron's acceptance into Professor

The King of Kings and I

Bennet-Hughes's very exclusive directing seminar, supposedly the first time since Sophocles that a sophomore had been given such an honor.

"And," Aaron continued, "I'd like you to play a part."

"Really?"

I had to admit, I was hooked. The instinct that every young homosexual has to be onstage wasn't completely dormant in my soul.

"Let me explain. I'm adapting *Alice in Wonderland* using the ideas of Antonin Artaud. The project will evolve out of group interaction—nothing too demanding."

"And this will be for a performance?"

Noting my interest, Aaron continued, almost crawling onto my shoulder to better whisper in my ear.

"Oh, yes—early next semester, for some of the visiting faculty. I thought we'd start rehearsing before Christmas break. I've asked a couple of guys on the hall to work with me on this. Are you interested?"

"Umm . . . maybe . . ."

"Because I've already solicited Ira to play Tweedledee, and I'd like you to come on board as Tweedledum."

"I don't really think of myself as an actor," I replied modestly.

"Don't worry!" Aaron gripped my shoulder with his oversize knuckles, and my skin not only crawled away, it slid under my door and hid under the covers. "To tell you the truth, Ira may have more technical training, but you—*you're* the natural performer."

"I am?"

"You have a wonderful . . . spiritual . . . quality."

"I do? Who else did you cast?"

"Our friends! David and Billy—"

Well, I certainly didn't want to spend any more time with this vivacious crowd. "You know, Aaron, I'm really pretty busy right now—"

Aaron's grip suddenly again tightened on my shoulder as he hissed out one last enticement. "I almost forgot to tell you. I've asked Vinnie to help me."

My heart skipped a beat.

"Y-you did? Is he . . . is he going to do it?"

Aaron nodded his head and looked me square in the eyes. I tried to avert my gaze, but I'm sure Aaron must have caught a glimpse of my terror, which cheered him up considerably. "Come on," he said brightly. "If you don't do this, you'll be missing out on all the fun. Basement lounge at nine?"

I nodded my head yes.

Sad to say, nothing could have kept me away from what was about to transpire. Human beings are the only animals on earth who, despite the sounding of every possible anatomical alarm, can approach danger thinking nothing is wrong. I actually entered the basement lounge believing that Aaron's only concern was putting on a show and my only concern was giving him the best darn Tweedledum he'd ever seen. Unaware of the theatrical tradition of always being punctual for rehearsals, I arrived fashionably late to what looked like a hall meeting already in progress.

The walls of this lounge, like every other public area at Stony Brook, were cinder blocks painted a garish primary color—in this case, royal blue—and there were seven of us seated on cold linoleum tiles. I'd expected Ira, David, and Billy to be there, but I was a little surprised to see nonthespians Scotty and Barry seated side by side and, of course, Vinnie, who smiled at me as I entered the room. Apparently, the group had been listening to Aaron as he explained the madness behind his method. His squinty eyes scanned the room like Captain Bligh on the HMS *Bounty*, searching for possible dissension.

"Welcome, Jaffe," Aaron said slyly. "As I was saying, the essence of theater is having the chance to closely observe real people under real circumstances. So for *Alice in Wonderland* there will be no prepared script."

"Are you saying we're going to improvise?" Ira asked.

"Exactly," Aaron replied. "As the director I'll provide the setting and the initial motivations, but the actual text will come from you, the actors. We'll be stripping theater down to the bare essentials. There'll be no scenery, no props—"

"And no audience," Billy quipped.

"And no talking out of turn," Aaron warned him.

Improv theater? I was horrified. As far as I was concerned, improv theater, or drama based on the notion that *Hamlet* might possibly be written by nervous actors in black leotards, was the absolute pits. By 1971 the vogue for improv was already passing, and it would soon find its rightful place among bad comedians and nursing-home residents, where it would enjoy a status somewhere between "spin art" and bingo. I questioned why Aaron, a notorious control freak, would have chosen to work this way. His next statement answered my question.

". . . and the reason I want to work this way," Aaron continued, "is because what I'm most interested in exploring is the actor and . . . his body." At this moment Aaron seemed to look directly at Vinnie, undressing him with his eyes. I could see Vinnie trying to hold on to his clothes, but Aaron's eyes were just too fast for him. Vinnie's face turned scarlet and Aaron glanced at me as though to say triumphantly, "See what I can do." Hey! Vinnie was my fantasy, not Aaron's! I hurriedly tried to use my imagination to button Vinnie's shirt and zip up his zipper.

But even more queer surprises were in store. While Aaron turned back to his notes to see which parts we'd be playing, I witnessed a truly remarkable sight. Billy Quintana and David Albright had begun to hold hands! I was surprised by this open display of affection. I can't say I was shocked. If I'd seen either one of them kissing a girl's hand, *that* would have been stunning. I was merely unnerved, the way one might feel about seeing an actual duck-billed platypus after years of only hearing them described.

"Ah, here we are," Aaron suddenly exclaimed, "the parts you'll be playing! Now, you may have noticed that there are no women present. As in Shakespeare's time, all the parts, both male and female, will be played by men. Ira and Jaffe, of course, will mirror each other as Tweedledee and Tweedledum. Scotty, nobody can figure you out, so you will be the Cheshire Cat. Barry—I'm sorry but your rationality always strikes me as insane—you will be the Mad Hatter." The group chuckled appreciatively. "David's natural exuberance will be perfectly utilized as the March Hare. And Billy, please forgive me, but you will be the Red Queen." Billy pursed his lips and bowed to a smattering of applause.

"Have I left anyone out? Oh, yes, Vinnie. The only true innocent among us shall play the title role. You will be Alice." Vinnie bowed his head and chuckled demurely, and for the first time, it occurred to me that not only was Aaron trying to seduce Vinnie, but he might very well succeed.

Just then Aaron got up and shook out his arms. "Can we all get up?" One by one we all stood and formed a circle in the middle of the room. Aaron then led us in a series of "trust exercises," but the more we ran our fingertips across each other's faces and fell backward into each other's arms, the more suspicious I was that Aaron had called us together in order to get his rocks off. Every chance he could find, he left his paw prints on the group, and, much to my chagrin, his foremost target was Vinnie's back and shoulders, which he patted at every opportunity. And Vinnie—to my greater chagrin—didn't scream out in rage every time Aaron came near him, but rather seemed to enjoy the little back rubs and hair mussings. I couldn't wait for the whole thing to be over.

Finally, at eleven Aaron dismissed us and assured us that the next time we'd actually work on some scenes. I tried to leave with Vinnie, but Aaron interrupted us by asking Vinnie to stay behind for

notes. Out in the hall Scotty and Barry were just heading back to their
dorm rooms while Billy, David, and Ira were talking about going off
campus to a diner. They asked me if I wanted to come along with
them, but I was far too preoccupied.

"No thanks," I said as I paced the hall. "I'm gonna wait."

"Oh come, darling," Billy urged me. "If you're waiting for Vinnie,
he and Aaron will be in there forever. Wink, wink. Nudge, nudge."

"*Jalouse?*" David challenged Billy in ungrammatical French.

"Of that bossy Miss Thing? Are you cuh-razy? Come on, honey," he
said to Ira, pulling on his sleeve, "the limousine's leaving in five minutes."

"In a second," Ira said.

Billy and David danced down the hall, leaving me alone with Ira.

"Are you sure you don't want to come?" he said.

"No thanks, but . . . How long have they . . . you know?" I said,
pointing after David and Billy.

"A couple of days. You didn't know about it?"

"Not till tonight."

"So what do you think of it?" Ira asked.

"I mean . . . it's OK for them."

I could tell this wasn't quite the answer Ira wanted to hear, but I
just wasn't ready to lay my cards on the table. Neither was Ira,
although I was pretty certain both of us had been dealt the same hand.

"You sure you don't want to come out with us?" he asked.

"No. I think I'll just get to bed early."

"Oh, come on. We never *play* together anymore."

Ira's voice was a little too high pitched. His plea was a little too
melodramatic for me to want to take him seriously. Suddenly I realized that I hadn't even told him yet of my plans to leave school the
following semester with Vinnie. Was it possible that we'd drifted that
far apart?

"I promised Vinnie I'd wait for him."

"Jaffe, is there anything you want to tell me?"

"No. Do you have anything you want to tell me?" I inquired.

"No . . . well, reservoir!" Ira concluded cheerfully. Then he walked away, waving over his shoulder in a gesture he'd taken from Sally Bowles in the movie *Cabaret*. I had the distinct feeling that I should have gone with him, but a greater force kept me waiting there for Vinnie to escape from Aaron's clutches.

When Vinnie finally did emerge I did my best to appear calm as I walked him upstairs. I prayed I wouldn't have to beg him for details, but after three endless seconds in which he didn't offer any, I just had to ask, "What did Aaron say to you just now?"

"Not much. Just not to worry about being embarrassed. He picked up that I was a little uptight in the group."

"You didn't seem uptight to me."

"I was! I never expected to be playing Alice. I never really thought of myself as innocent."

We arrived at Vinnie's door, but rather than opening it and inviting me inside, Vinnie opted to talk in the hall.

"You know, if I had known acting was so much fun I would have taken a few more theater courses."

"Really? You don't find it spiritually superficial and distracting?"

"Maybe." Vinnie stretched to indicate he was tired. "Hey," he said, "you don't mind if we don't stay up late tonight talking? I'm gonna try to get some sleep."

"Nah . . . that's OK. I'll just—"

"I thought you went out with Ira and those guys."

"Nah . . . I was too tired."

For the first time, we faced each other with nothing to say. "Hey," I finally managed to squeak out, "only a month and we'll be heading out west."

"Yeah," Vinnie responded, not very enthusiastically.

That night I couldn't fall asleep. It was clear to me now that I wanted to make love to Vinnie, but I also wanted to wait until we left

The King of Kings and I

Stony Brook. Two guys having sex in the desert would be spiritual, whereas two guys having sex in a college dorm would have made us homos like David and Billy. After two hours of tossing and turning, I finally fell asleep and had a very un-Jewish dream. It was a Ken Russell extravaganza in which Vinnie and I were medieval monks and we were rehearsing a passion play–musical that Billy Quintana had named *The King of Kings and I*. Vinnie, of course, played Jesus; I played "I," and the two of us were very much in love. Every day we made out backstage until one day Aaron Grossman showed up as an evil rabbi and threw me into that special rung of hell reserved for bad actors in awful plays. There was no food; I had to mime eating. And there were no bars on the window, but I had to mime the walls closing in on me. I escaped into the sunshine but it was too late. I saw Aaron and Vinnie running away from me hand in hand, and I screamed at them, "Faggots! Faggots!"

That day went by excruciatingly slowly until that evening when I waited by Vinnie's door for him to return from classes. I had to tell him that I loved him. I practiced what I would say. In my fantasy, Vinnie would arrive home morose and confused, and he'd grab me in his arms and tell me how he'd been yearning to tell me the very same thing. My heart sank when I heard him whistling cheerfully as he entered the hall.

"Hey, Jaffe!" he said brightly.

Somehow I knew my cause was lost.

"Have you been waiting here long?" he asked.

"No . . . I . . . just got here."

Vinnie started opening the door to his room. "I had to stop by the Union store on the way back from classes." We entered his room and Vinnie chirped as he unpacked his bag. "You know, Aaron's a lot more interesting than I thought. He's into meditation, you know. He had really good ideas about theater as a mode of self-development."

I flopped myself down on the floor without saying a word.

"You OK?" Vinnie asked as he pulled some bottles out of a shopping bag.

"Sure. Whatcha got there?"

"Shampoo and stuff. Some conditioner." Vinnie went to the bathroom and turned on the shower. He left the door open a crack so I could call in after him.

"You don't usually use conditioner," I yelled.

"My hair gets knotted sometimes. Here, smell this." Vinnie held the bottle up to my nose. "Herbal essence."

"More like horrible essence," I quipped. "You gonna condition your hair when we're sleeping under the stars?"

"I don't know," Vinnie said.

While Vinnie was in the shower it again occurred to me that my friend didn't love me, but I pushed that thought aside. God may have created smallpox and the Long Island Expressway, but no way would he have created a universe in which one person could love another so deeply to no avail. It would have been physically impossible for Vinnie not to feel some of what I did. All he had to do was breathe the air around me. As I sat there waiting for Vinnie to finish showering, I felt like a car engine running in a closed garage, toxic and possibly fatal. I wasn't sure whether I wanted to make love to Vinnie or merely immobilize him with my deadly fumes. Finally I heard Vinnie finish his shower. He opened the door to the bathroom a tiny crack to let out the steam. Then he started putting on deodorant. "In case we sweat tonight at rehearsal," he said to me through the slit.

"Vinnie . . . I . . ."

"You sure you're OK?" he said as he came out of the bathroom pulling on a navy blue polo shirt.

"Vinnie, there's something I have to tell you."

"Tell me on the way to the rehearsal. How do I look, by the way?"

Vinnie did a little turn that looked almost dainty. The thought that he was dressing for Aaron drove me insane.

"It's OK."

"You don't like it?" Vinnie said as he removed the price tag.

"No, it's OK."

"But you don't *really* think it looks good on me?"

"What do you care what I think?"

Vinnie combed his hair in the mirror.

"You think caring what you look like is shallow?"

"No . . . but . . . I'm just surprised that all of a sudden—"

"I always cared about what I looked like."

"It's something we never talked about."

Vinnie unbuckled his pants to tuck in the shirt.

"There are a lot of things we never talked about," he said as we exited into the hall.

We were just about to enter the lounge. I could see that the other guys had already arrived. It was now or never.

"Listen, Vinnie . . . about us—"

"Oh, by the way," Vinnie interrupted, "thanks a lot for recommending me for this."

"What do you mean?"

Vinnie leaned over and whispered in my ear, "Aaron told me that you said I should be in this. That's why he asked me."

"He did?" I stopped dead in my tracks. "I never said that."

Just then David and Billy squeezed past us holding hands. Billy minced, "Come on, girls. It's show time!"

Then David gave Vinnie the once-over. "Lovely chemise," he said flirtatiously.

"I thought Aaron talked to you first," I said.

"We better get inside," Vinnie said. "Aaron wants to get started."

"Vinnie," I said, "I don't know if we should be going out west together. I . . . I haven't been completely honest with you."

Vinnie looked confused and eager to hear what I had to say, but just then Aaron rushed down the stairs carrying a clipboard. He grabbed Vinnie by his new navy blue sleeve, taking a moment to appreciate the material.

"New shirt?" he asked as he pulled Vinnie into the room. "Very nice!"

"Thanks," Vinnie said. Then he turned to me and added, "Hold that thought. I do want to talk—but later."

Then we both entered the room and took our places in the circle.

There are only three types of young men who become actors. First, there are the obvious homosexuals who join the high school drama club in order to be applauded for the same outlandish behavior that normally gets the crap kicked out of them in the school cafeteria. Second, there are the obvious heterosexual boys who smell a testosterone vacuum and join the drama club in order to hit on the girls who've been desperately trying to date the gay men. And finally, there are the majority of young actors who have no idea who they are or what they want.

Unfortunately, not many of us were purebreds like Billy Quintana, who never had any doubt he was traveling the gay lane on the highway of life. Most of us tended to swerve from one lane to the other. If we were homosexual, we often prayed that the solid line would open up and we'd get a chance to drive straight for a while. If we were heterosexual we often prayed that our awkwardness with women didn't mean we'd been driving in the gay lane all along without knowing it. Many of us even believed we were bisexual, but, like a dime standing on its edge, we all flopped to one side sooner or later.

Looking back at those first few years of college, I still find it hard to fathom the depth of our confusion. Why didn't Ira and I know for sure that we were gay? What about Barry and Scotty? Why were these two heterosexuals hanging around with all of us "queens"? If we didn't know we were gay, perhaps they didn't know they were straight? Adding to the confusion, the word *straight* had a very different meaning in 1971. *Straight* meant that you didn't smoke pot. It was an insult to be called straight. In 1971, being cool meant getting high, going to Jethro Tull concerts, and jumping up and down with your arms around both sexes. It was still a time of glorified jug bands like the Grateful Dead and the Allman Brothers, but the sexually ambiguous era of David Bowie was only a rhinestone's throw away.

In some ways, then, 1971 was the perfect time to come out. In fact, I never really *came* out. It was more like I *stayed* out when everybody else went back in. It was like a scene from *Buck Privates* in which the drill sergeant calls for a volunteer and the whole line, except Costello, takes one step back, leaving the poor schlepp standing out on his own. In the same way, as the decade became more conservative and most retired back into rigid heterosexuality, I—and a few million other queers—soon discovered that we had inadvertently volunteered to do special duty against the patriarchy.

But this perspective came with time—lots of time. A quarter century ago I had no politics, very little sense of history, and even less real empathy. I was never a camera like Christopher Isherwood. I was more like a fun-house mirror reflecting distorted images of myself everywhere I turned. Therefore, as I entered the basement room for my next and last rehearsal of *Alice in Wonderland*, I truly believed that Aaron was going to steal Vinnie away from me. And, in retrospect, I should have been so lucky.

After a half hour of stretching, Aaron called us back into a circle. We all linked arms as our director announced that the first scene we'd create would be Alice meeting the Caterpillar. Very meticulously, he explained his concept of the scene. "I see this hookah-smoking insect as similar to the Snake in the Garden of Eden. The Caterpillar is an animal of pure instinct, a phallic symbol perhaps. When he asks Alice repeatedly, 'Who are you?' he becomes that small nagging voice who spurs us to live our lives passionately. What the caterpillar is really saying to Alice is, 'What do you crave?'"

Aaron's eyes scanned the room like a searchlight, illuminating each face they passed. Barry, Scotty, and Ira nodded their heads thoughtfully. David and Billy, who already knew what they craved, looked vaguely bored. Vinnie, on the other hand, hung on to Aaron's words as though Aaron were the Buddha himself.

"Are there any questions?" Aaron asked.

Ira raised his hand.

"Which one of us will be playing the Caterpillar?"

"I will," Aaron announced, looking directly at Vinnie. "Are you ready to be brought out, so to speak?" Vinnie nodded his head. Meanwhile the hole in my stomach had just opened up to include the La Brea Tar Pits. Then Aaron let his eyes linger on me a moment, as if to say, "Get a load of what I'm going to do next!" I hated him. "But enough of my lecturing," Aaron concluded. "Everybody up!"

Then Aaron put on some cha-cha music and encouraged us all to "explore space," which in aeronautical terms means escaping the earth's gravity but in dance parlance means flinging yourself about the room like an idiot. For five minutes we crawled on our bellies and sliced the air with our elbows in arduous attempts to be spontaneous. I believe I must have been rubbing my nose against the venetian blinds when Aaron issued his next directive. "C'mon, everybody. Grab each other's hips. We're making a conga line!"

Aaron naturally assumed the position at the head of the line, grabbing Vinnie's hands and placing them on his hips. Barry, Scotty, David, Billy, I, and Ira followed suit, turning ourselves into a seven-headed Carmen Miranda. When the music finished, Aaron slowed his movements, spread his legs wide, and wobbled comically across the room. We instinctively held tight to each other and mimicked his movements. Then our leader started rhythmically pulsating like Martha Graham trying to give birth. We did this as well, contracting and expanding as one organism. Then Aaron mimed taking a bong hit and we all inhaled together. "Whish!" Then we all exhaled together. "Whoosh!"

The King of Kings and I

We did it again. "Whish! Whoosh!" Suddenly, Aaron gave the creature a voice. Speaking in a trippy basso profundo, like James Earl Jones on Quaaludes, Aaron intoned regally, "Enter the birth canal!"

Ira, who was on the end of the line, knew a cue to take center stage when he heard one. Crouching into a ball, he rolled between our legs and we all made primitive birthing screams as we pushed him through. "Aaah!" "Eeeh!" Finally making it through the tunnel, Ira turned and faced Aaron, who took another imaginary toke. "Whish! Whoosh!" Then we wiggled our arms toward Ira as the Caterpillar asked, "Who-o a-a-re y-o-u-u?—stretching each vowel sound into a symphony.

Ira, rather than speaking, did a little happy dance and sat down on the edge of the playing area. Aaron called "Next" and I, being the tail end of the Caterpillar, rolled through the birth canal. In response to Aaron's "Who are you?" I did a little confused movement and sat down next to Ira. One by one, Aaron called us and we all rolled through. One by one we faced Aaron until only Vinnie was left holding on to the Caterpillar's hips. "Alice!" Aaron rumbled. "Come through."

Vinnie then dutifully rolled into the center of the room and Aaron smiled triumphantly. As far as I could tell, this was the moment he'd been waiting for; he paused dramatically before announcing, "Aaah! Now our scene is about to begin!" Vinnie looked around nervously at the rest of us, who linked arms and closed the circle. Doing his best to mime panic, Vinnie searched for an escape route but there wasn't any. Exhausting all possibilities, he finally faced Aaron, who now spoke even louder. "A-and who-o-o a-a-re yo-u-u!"

"I'm . . . I'm Alice," Vinnie replied meekly.

"Yes, my dear, but—who are you?"

Vinnie took a moment to decide whether or not to take the question seriously. "I'm . . . I'm a seeker of truth," Vinnie replied.

"A se-e-e-ker?" Aaron asked, drawing out the first syllable to the width of the Pacific Ocean.

Then—I'm not sure who started it—Billy, perhaps—we all began chanting in unison, "Seeker, seeker, seeker . . ." letting our voices trail off like an echo returning from a faraway place.

"And what are you seeking here, with us?"

"Us, us, us."

Vinnie looked around him at the guys on his hall. Nobody was absolutely sure what game we were playing. Billy and David might have caught Aaron's drift. Ira, I believed, was thriving on the theatricality of it all. Barry and Scotty were simply trying not to look like complete idiots. And me? I was both titillated and horrified that Vinnie was about to be exposed. As for Vinnie, I wasn't sure why he'd come this far. Certainly he must have suspected that Aaron was trying to get him to admit he was gay, because his voice sounded so uncertain when he asked, "You mean why did I come to Wonderland? I don't know. I fell through a hole."

"You climbed through a hole," Aaron corrected him.

"Hole, hole, hole," we all repeated.

"Yes. Yes. I climbed though a hole because I was . . . I was bored with where I was."

"Bored?"

"Bored, bored, bored."

"And I don't think I was being myself."

"Aaah!" Aaron as the Caterpillar announced triumphantly. "And who are you?"

"You—you—you—"

"I don't know," Vinnie replied. "That's what I'm trying to figure out."

"And what did you think you'd find here?"

"You mean here? In Wonderland?" Vinnie glanced at me for help, and I wanted to call out, "No, you don't have to answer these questions." But, like everyone else in the room, I needed to see where the scene would wind up.

"What did I think I'd find here?" Vinnie repeated, still not sure whether he was answering as Alice or himself. "I thought I'd find a place . . . where . . . where the rules would be different."

"Why?"

"Why—why—why—"

"Because . . . because I'm different."

"How are you different?" Aaron asked.

"How I feel inside. What I want." Vinnie paused. "Do you want me to answer as Alice or Vinnie?"

Aaron was silent.

"Because if you wanted to confuse me, you certainly have."

Aaron smiled broadly but offered no more clues.

"How am I different?" Vinnie looked around the room sheepishly. "Well, I guess it wouldn't come as much of a surprise to anyone here to know that I'm . . . I'm gay. And I don't believe I've ever said that to anyone before. Whoo. And . . . I guess that's why . . . that's why . . . that's why I'm here. I thought this would be a good place to be accepted for who I am. Whew."

Vinnie put his face in his hands and his shoulders started to quake; he may or may not have been crying. Aaron stepped forward and took Vinnie in his arms, but not before glancing at me, as though to cement his moment of triumph. Then the whole room imploded. David moved forward, sniffling, and put his arms around both Aaron and Vinnie. Then Billy and Ira added another layer to the configuration. Then Barry and Scotty awkwardly joined hands and leaned over the group like it was a football huddle. I was the last one to join the group hug, having to squash my rage at having lost Vinnie to Aaron's embrace.

For a moment there was stillness as nobody knew what to do next. The scene was obviously over, but the director wasn't yelling "Curtain." Finally Scotty broke free of the caterpillar cocoon and announced, "Well, I don't think we're gonna top that tonight!" and the human string ball unraveled twice as quickly as it had formed. "Good work," Aaron said, nodding to all of us in the group, as though Vinnie's revelation had been all in a day's work. "Let's call it a night. But if anybody needs to talk, I'll stay behind. Oh, and I'll need your schedules to set up the next rehearsal."

We all started gathering our things to go. Vinnie immediately stepped into the hall, where he started tying his shoes with extraordinary care. Thank god Billy broke the silence.

"Well, wasn't that thrilling! I must say the suspense was *killing* me." Then, looking mock-lasciviously at Barry, he asked, "Are you going to be next to fly out of the closet?"

"Don't hold your breath," Barry shot back without hesitation.

"Would you hold it for me?" Billy asked.

"Hold this," Barry replied, pointing to his crotch.

But it was all in good fun. Some scary feelings had been stirred up by the group hug, and they now had to be frittered away. Billy and Barry joked. David combed his hair in a window. Ira went over his schedule with Aaron, and only I seemed eager to finish what we'd started. Carefully choosing my moment, I approached Vinnie, who was still lacing up his shoes.

"Are you OK?"

"I feel kind of numb," he said.

"Can I walk you back to your room?"

"Sure. That was pretty weird."

"Yeah. You know . . . I . . . I think I'm gay too," I said.

"I kinda suspected."

"You sure you're OK?" I asked again.

"We really need to talk," Vinnie replied. "There's something I've been meaning to tell you for a long time."

"OK."

As we were leaving, Aaron, looking over Ira's shoulder, caught

Vinnie's eye and mouthed the words "I'll wait for you here." Vinnie waved back, but I couldn't read the look on his face.

"Oh, by the way," I finally said as we got to Vinnie's room and closed the door behind us, "I do like the navy blue shirt. I like it a lot."

"Really?"

"It's a *really* good color for you."

Vinnie sat down on his bed with his back against the wall. I sat down next to him. Vinnie pulled a pillow onto his lap and squeezed it against his chest. For a while he was silent.

"Do you hate me now?"

"No!"

"Oh god. I feel so weird now."

"So what do you need to tell me?" I asked.

"We need better lighting for this." Vinnie reached beside him and lit a candle on his desk. Then he turned off the overhead light, and all I could see now were Vinnie's profile and a corner of a Grateful Dead poster hanging on the wall behind his head. "This is really hard for me to say."

"What a weird night," I said to relieve some of the pressure.

"I'll say," Vinnie replied

Vinnie said. "You know, I think I feel closer to you than anyone. I'm so glad to be getting this out in the open—having feelings for someone and not being able to express them."

"You mean . . . Aaron?"

"Aaron?" Vinnie looked genuinely surprised. "What about him?"

"I thought you liked him."

"Aaron? You thought I liked Aaron?" Vinnie considered the possibility but then laughed at the thought. "No. Somebody else, though. I can't believe I'm finally telling you this."

"You like someone else?" I asked softly.

Vinnie was silent for what seemed like forever.

"Yeah. God, this is so hard to say. I . . . I came to a big realization the night I stayed over at your room. Jaffe, are you shivering?"

Without knowing it I had started to quake with excitement.

"Here," Vinnie said. "Wrap this blanket around you." He lifted an afghan from the foot of his bed and lay it across my shoulders.

"That was a very special night for me too," I said as I leaned on Vinnie's shoulder. "Is this all right?" I asked.

"Yeah. It's great. Taylor and I used to cuddle together."

"Was he gay?"

"No, but he was cool.

I kinda had a crush on Taylor for a while, but it's nothing like what I'm feeling now." Vinnie pulled me closer. I rubbed my face gently against his shoulder. "It's always meant so much to me having you in my life, someone who I thought was gay but not shallow. I . . . I probably shouldn't be judgmental."

"Go right ahead," I murmured sweetly.

"God, I'm so tired of trying to be good all the time. I mean, I can see why all the great saints and spiritual teachers were celibate. Sex is really distracting, but thinking about it all the time and being too afraid to do anything—that's even worse."

"I know what you mean."

"I just want to be happy, and if that means getting off the spiritual path for a couple of years, that's what I'm going to do."

"You know," I whispered as sexily as possible, "doing what makes you happy may be the spiritual path."

"I don't know. I'm still pretty confused."

"No, you're not. You're not fucked up at all."

Vinnie pulled back from me to look deeply in my eyes.

"You know, I almost believe you," he said. "I really love you."

"I love you too." I put my head on Vinnie's chest. "You were saying . . . the night you slept over . . ."

"Oh, yeah . . . god . . . sleeping there in Ira's bed," he continued.

"It really hit me. That's exactly where I wanted to be. I should have said something, that night."

"You didn't have to," I sighed sweetly.

"No, I should have. The smell of his blankets. Knowing that my head was on his pillow. I guess you've already figured it out. I have the biggest crush on your roommate. He's so cute. You think—you think Ira likes me, Jaffe?"

"What?" I finally replied.

"You think he likes me?"

I couldn't answer.

"Are you still there?" Vinnie asked.

"Yeah. I'm still here."

"Did you hear what I said?"

"You have a crush on Ira."

"So what do you think?"

"I don't know. Does Ira know?"

"He must!" Vinnie said. "I mean, how could he not see it in my face?"

The next afternoon I came home and heard laughter coming from the bathroom. Vinnie and Ira were blow-drying each other's hair after showering together. Of course I was devastated, but at dinner in the cafeteria I mumbled something about how thrilled I was for both of them. After dinner they snuck back to Vinnie's room without asking me to come along. I then wandered in a daze to the student union, where I went into the bathroom and looked at myself in the mirror. "How could he not see it in my face?" I wondered. "How did Vinnie not know that I loved him?"

Without thinking, I climbed onto the sink to better examine myself in the mirror. The fluorescence was hideous. I looked like a circus freak. No wonder Vinnie hadn't chosen me. I really was quite repulsive. I'd pursed my lips and sucked in my cheeks to look more like

Marlene Dietrich, but I'd only managed to look like Carol Burnett impersonating Marlene Dietrich. I asked myself again, "How could he not see it in my face?" "Easy," I answered myself. My face wasn't handsome enough. Ira's chin was slightly stronger. His features were slightly more regular. Ira and I had never really looked alike at all. We were sisters, all right, but I was Louise in *Gypsy* and Ira was Dainty June. He was the pretty one, not me.

I got down off the sink and left the bathroom. Outside in the cold, I considered going back to my room but changed my mind. Nothing made sense. Or rather, it all made too much sense. All my life I'd been a serious seeker of truth; was my happiness now to be ruined by a weak chin and crooked teeth? Why hadn't I been born beautiful? There had to be a loophole somewhere. And what was I to do next? Where was I to go? It was clear now that Vinnie would never go to Tucson; the farthest west he'd get would be the West Village. As for me, I was pretty sure I didn't want to hitchhike alone. But I also knew I didn't want to stay in school. And I certainly never wanted to see Vinnie or Ira ever again. I'd be more careful in the future to only hang out with truly spiritual people.

Instinctively I found myself following the trail across campus back to the spot where I'd first landed in this strange new world. Hands in my pocket, I stumbled past the lecture hall, past the chemistry mausoleum, past the humanities tomb, all the way back to Walt Whitman Dormitory, where I'd last said good-bye to my mother on campus. The asphalt glistened in the moonlight. Just then I looked down and saw what I'd come to find, the hole that would lead me out of Wonderland. Actually, it was the oil stain, nearly two years old, left by my mother's car the first day of school. I bent down to touch it. It was dry, barely more than a shadow on the ground. The symbolism was apt; this was where I'd come in, and this was where I would get out. I decided then and there to leave school and travel out west on my own.

The King of Kings and I

On my way back into the dorm, however, I found Scotty sitting on the steps strumming a Grateful Dead tune on his guitar and looking like James Taylor when he still had long hair and a reputation for heroin addiction. Scotty's fingers squeaked as they slid up and down the neck of the guitar, making more noise than the vibrating strings. I sat down beside him.

"Whatcha doing?"

"Just hanging," Scotty said.

"It's three o'clock at night."

"I dropped some acid at midnight."

"Cool."

Then Scotty began to sing. "Truckin', got my chips cashed in." Then he stopped as his fingers struggled to find the right fret.

"Whatcha think of the rehearsal last night?" I asked.

Scotty shook his head without replying.

"So Vinnie's gay," I added.

Scotty shrugged his shoulders. "Looks that way."

"Pretty dramatic," I said.

Scotty shrugged his shoulders.

"I guess some people need drama in their lives." Then Scotty began singing: "Sometimes the lights are shining on me. Other times I can barely see—see—see." Once again his fingers hadn't found the right fret.

"Sounds pretty good," I said, just to be nice.

"Yeah it does." Scotty smiled contentedly. The light from a street lamp shone behind his head, looking like a halo.

"I'm thinking about dropping out next semester," I told him.

"How come?"

"Do some traveling."

"Anyplace would be better than here. I'd leave too if I had somewhere to go. I'd love to see the whole wide world. Every bit of it."

"Every bit of it?"

"Every bit of it."

Scotty's fingers finally found the right fret. He strummed the chord several times, then sang the end of the song.

"Lately it occurs to me-e-e. What a lo-o-ong strange trip it's been."

Suddenly a disembodied voice called out from a window above our heads, "Far out, man. Sing that part again!"

Scotty looked up and smiled angelically.

"The voice of God," he said with a wink.

Then Scotty reapplied his fingers, and the three of us—Scotty, I, and the voice of God—sang together, in perfect harmony, "What a lo-o-ong strange trip it's been." Then we sat quietly listening for a moment.

"Would you really drop out if you had somewhere to go?" I asked.

"Sure!"

I tarried before getting up. Scotty looked up. "Look, there's a falling star. Wow!"

I looked up to see what Scotty had seen, but either I was too late or the acid had kicked in and Scotty had been hallucinating. But Scotty kept looking, his Adam's apple quivering with excitement. I kept looking too, but at my hallmate. I knew so little about him. I wondered if I could ever be attracted to him physically. True, he had a beautiful face, but at six-three, one hundred twenty pounds, the thought of his naked body was not appealing in the least.

"How'd you like to hitchhike to Tucson with me in January?" I finally asked.

"Sure," Scotty said without looking back at me.

"Really?"

"Yup. Look, there goes another one!"

I looked up again, and this time I saw what Scotty was looking at. A brief flash of light illuminated the western sky.

CHAPTER 3

The Aquarian Gospel

The next day I told Aaron that I'd be quitting *Alice in Wonderland* and he'd have to cast a new Tweedledum. In order to deflect any possible opposition, I made my reasons as compelling as possible. "My soul is dying here at school," I told him. "I need more freedom, more sky, more possibilities for adventure!" I hadn't expected much of a reaction, except relief that there'd be one less warm body between him and Vinnie. In fact Aaron seemed to have no reaction at all, nodding thoughtfully, with his fingertips pressed together. "Hmm," he said. "I see it would be useless to try and detain you."

In the meantime, Scotty was my new hero. In those last two

weeks of the semester I inhaled his personality along with about a kilo of his marijuana. I was beyond caring, in a perpetual daze. The day Vinnie and Ira spent the whole afternoon giggling outside my window building a snowman, it didn't bother me. Nor did it bother me the following week when Vinnie slept over every night and I had to listen to him and Ira make out. It didn't even bother me when Vinnie and Ira decided to take advantage of my leaving to become roommates the following semester. None of this was of any concern to me. I was above love. I was on the verge of a brand new life.

The plan was to leave Stony Brook by train on the twenty-second of December, spend the night at my parents' house, and then start hitchhiking on the twenty-third. Just before sunset we boarded the Long Island Railroad, ebullient and eager to hit the road. The westbound train was nearly empty, so Scotty and I hung out on the platform between the cars and smoked another joint. Then, with the wintry wind blowing and me holding on to the door handles for dear life, Scotty managed to strum Neil Young on his guitar while singing in a wobbly falsetto, "Don't let it get you down—it's only castles burning—just find someone who's yearning—and you will come around!" East of Smithtown the ticket taker tried to squeeze past us. At first I thought he was going to use his belly to push us back to our seats; but instead he turned around, pulled off his blue cap to reveal a wild mane of hair, and said, "Sounds good, dude!" Then he whipped out a harmonica and played with us through the next three stations.

The night at my parents' was relatively uneventful. My father picked us up at the train station, and the first thing I noticed was that he'd added to his car several more bumper stickers from the Jewish Chauvinist Series. In addition to an old "Jacob Javitz for Senator" and a royal blue Star of David, he'd recently slapped on "No Land for Peace," "Never Again," two "Hai"s and three "Shalom"s. Then all the way home he complained about the nativity scene that the town council had set up in front of the library. "Haven't they ever heard of

the separation of church and state?" Scotty nodded his head thoughtfully: "Church and state. Definitely!"

My parents' response to my dropping out of school could have
been predicted. Neither one of them was thrilled, but neither of them
tried too hard to prevent me from going. My mother's major concern
was for my safety, so she vowed to quit smoking Kents in a Faustian bar-
gain with God to keep me out of danger. Then, to make sure I wouldn't
starve to death, she pulled two frozen aluminum boulders from the
freezer and informed me that they were meatball sandwiches. "If you
take the northern route they should stay fresh in your backpack."

My father's concerns were for my soul, and his assistance was far
less welcome. My mother had told him that I was on some kind of
spiritual search, so after dinner my father, who had a bad habit of
starting conversations with vague unanswerable questions, cornered
Scotty and me and asked me abruptly, "Have you ever thought about
Judaism?" "In . . . what sense?" I replied. "Spirituality," he answered,
pronouncing all six syllables. "No, not really," I answered as nonchalantly as possible. "Pity," my father said, shaking his head, waiting for
me to ask a question, any question, that would allow him to explicate
further.

Knowing this game, I remained silent, seriously picking at my fingernails and hoping he would go away. When my father saw I wasn't
taking the bait, the old windbag turned toward Scotty and started lecturing him on the benefits of kosher slaughtering. My friend, by virtue
of being a complete stranger, wasn't completely bored with my dad.
On the contrary, he listened attentively, as though he were in the presence of Moses himself. So my father talked and talked; and within minutes he achieved a gaseous state that allowed him to keep expanding
with no further priming. An hour later I finally managed to drag Scotty
out of range, but not before my father got in one last bit of counseling:
"Remind me to send you some cuticle scissors."

Later that night Scotty and I laid out our sleeping bags in the den

and Scotty said something that made me believe he'd been hallucinating.

"Your father, man. He's a seeker."

"For what?" I sighed.

"God."

"I don't think so."

"No, man. There's many paths to the top of the mountain.
Judaism is his path, man. The Tao of righteous eating. Far out."

Now, the thought of Judaism being a spiritual path had never
occurred to me. Judaism was the Belt Parkway at rush hour or the sidewalk in front of Waldbaum's, but hardly a mountain path unless the
mountain happened to be in the Catskills. As usual, Scotty had been
far too generous. "How much pot do we have left?" I asked as I
crawled into my sleeping bag and zipped up the side. "Enough to get
us to Tucson," Scotty replied.

The next morning my mother drove us to exit 41 on the Long
Island Expressway and I stuck out my thumb as Scotty scribbled a sign
reading ARIZONA in black crayons on a piece of corrugated cardboard. Our first ride, a lawn-sprinkler installer from Lake
Ronkonkoma, took us as far as the Valley Stream exit. We got out of
his truck and tried again. Our next ride got us through Manhattan and
as far as Montclair, New Jersey. We got out and tried again. And
again. And again. By nightfall fifteen rides had brought us to within
spitting distance of Pittsburgh, Pennsylvania, where we spent an
eighth of our life savings to purchase a room at the Howard Johnson's.

I'm surprised how unfrightened we were. Partially, we were young.
But mostly it was 1972. We bourgeois kids were still pretty fearless;
we'd been brought up on *Easy Rider*, not *Friday the Thirteenth*—and we
hated the safety of the suburbs. We still believed that somewhere out
there was a better, freer America. Some of us headed into the woods.
Some of us headed into the cities. Urban-freak ghettos sprung up all
over America, and the term *street life* had a very different meaning, not

so much a dead end as an endless Mardi Gras. Homelessness wasn't an issue in 1972; it was an ideal. For Scotty and me, the expectation was that once we dropped out of the Establishment we'd find ourselves in the very best of company—the company of freaks. Unfortunately, as I said earlier, times were already changing. Ideally speaking, Scotty and I were about two years too late for the Hippie Grand Tour, and by the time we hit Ohio it was clear that the number of people willing to stop for two college dropouts had diminished considerably. The Summer of Love had already given way to the Winter of "Who the Fuck Are You!?" and no amount of Scotty's weed could have softened the frustration.

Scotty, on the other hand, never stopped smiling. While I huddled on the guardrail, whimpering and wishing I were back home, Scotty, like the Don Quixote of Route 80, would lean into the icy wind for hours, daring fate to disappoint him. Then he would offer me advice like "You have to beam love at these guys. The trick is to maintain eye contact with the driver of the oncoming car." "Great idea!" I would grumble. "Maintain eye contact. That way, even if they don't stop, at least they'll feel terrible when they drive past." Scotty smiled indulgently, but I do believe we were able to leave a trail of Jewish guilt through three midwestern states.

In Chicago, Scotty made friends with the owner of a gas station and we spent the night curled up on cots, using frozen Jiffy Lube for pillows. The next day we made it as far as Texas, and for the first time the terrain started to look like something other than Long Island. There were now vast stretches of open road where there was nothing but huge rocks piled indiscriminately on the side of the road, as if Mother Nature were having a yard sale.

The people out west were only slightly less craggy than the terrain. I soon formed the opinion that social skills fade exponentially west of St. Louis. With the population density in New York you're never more than a few inches away from somebody who will gladly call you an asshole when you get out of line. Out west, there are scores of psychotics who go for years without being critiqued. One of them was our driver from Fort Worth to El Paso, a seventy-five-year-old cowboy in a white Pontiac and a ten-gallon hat who ate steak for breakfast and drank whiskey from a flask he kept under his seat. He also owned an eight-track cassette of the Jackson Five's greatest hits, which he played repeatedly, singing along in a Texas drawl: "'ABC— It's easy as one, two, three' . . . I jus' love these guys!" he would say over and over again, showing not the least embarrassment about his lack of taste.

We arrived in Tucson the day after Christmas and found our way to Bernie's house on Thirty-third Avenue. It was a small tract house, and it didn't look too bad in the dark. Unfortunately, Bernie had mistaken the day of our arrival, so the living room was filled with his customers, who were laid out on a floor littered with sleeping bags and Zap Comix. Some were awake; some weren't. Most were in a state of consciousness somewhere between the two. After some negotiating Scotty and I scored a place to sleep in an abandoned Volvo parked in the driveway, and we slept soundly until the following morning, when we were awakened early by the Arizona sun and the sounds of dogs barking and children chattering away in Spanish. I picked up my head, with a piece of vinyl broken sticking to my cheek, and got my first good look at the world for which I had sacrificed a college education.

In this *better, freer* America, where middle-class freaks intersected with ghetto culture, there were no well-kept lawns. Bernie's house, like all the other homes on his block, was fronted by a dusty patch of dirt littered with clumps of crabgrass the size of dead artichokes. The house itself had all the decorative detail of an air-raid shelter, and there was considerable confusion about where to put furniture, because the two best couches were outside on the porch while the living room lay as bare as a department store in Moscow.

The inhabitants of this house were an ever-shifting crew of marijuana merchants who, over the next few days, would turn up already stoned and then proceed to consume their entire inventory. There was a constant cannabis cloud in every room, so thick you could have sucked on the keyhole and used the building as a bong. Other than smoking pot, leisure activities at Bernie's included building pipes out of everyday household objects. One guy, Little Red, managed to inhale about three hundred dollars' worth of hashish through a piece of stale pizza crust, with a hole drilled through its center.

The other major time waster was taking care of canines; each freak owned a dog with whom he was far more intimate than any of the humans. There was also a major species reversal in Bernie's household, as these dogs were invariably given the best places to sit and the most expensive vittles, while the humans ran around half naked, were infested with fleas, and caught Frisbees in their teeth. Presiding over this motley crew was Bernie himself, who had finally found a position of power as King of the Gypsies.

I'm happy to say that all this was good for my brother's ego, and my one unadulterated pleasure in Tucson was watching Bernie blossom into a benevolent dictator. As a child he had suffered low self-esteem because of his difficulty with reading—which, in a Jewish household, is a serious condition somewhere between bubonic plague and kidney failure. I, on the other hand, had sucked up books like a brand-new Electrolux. My parents, in an effort to treat us equally, did everything they could to act as though they were thrilled with my brother's other accomplishments, but it would have taken Meryl Streep to convince us that my brother's ashtrays constructed in shop class were equal to my having read *Moby Dick* at the age of nine.

Yet even as a child, Bernie had always been a leader of men, especially when the men were as slow-witted as the crew that had gathered around him in Tucson. In addition, Bernie had a scruffy charm that had won him an "old lady" named Katie, a no-nonsense red-haired girl from Washington State. At first glance she was quite pretty, with large eyes and creamy skin, but there was also something hard about her face: downturned lips, a coldness in her eyes. It was the face of the shiksa pioneer woman. She and Bernie were devoted to each other, and they presided happily over this household of lost boys like a stoned-out Peter Pan and Wendy. Together, they shared a bedroom in which they slept on the one clean mattress in the house, and they screwed all day behind tie-dyed sheets doubling as curtains.

Katie was my salvation those first few weeks in Tucson, and I soon found my place with her in the kitchen, soaking beans and cooking up endless batches of chili. Meanwhile, Scotty found an engine to work on and was covered in black grease for days on end. Neither one of us thought much about our future.

We were too stoned.

In truth, I was blissfully happy. What I lacked in intellectual stimulation I made up for in a lack of intellectual stimulation: there was absolutely nothing to worry about. One day blended into the other. Except for Bernie, none of the guys there showed any interest in sex of any kind, and after all the gay drama of the past few months, it was a relief to hang with guys who wouldn't have gotten a boner if Jane Fonda *and* Warren Beatty had both walked across the lawn stark naked. It's often been said that marijuana reduces sex drive. What's less often said is that this can be a great relief.

One more thing I might mention about Katie: in addition to being stoical and practical, she also threw back LSD like breath mints. It took me a while to realize she was constantly tripping, because her facial expression rarely changed. She was like *American Gothic* on acid. As with Scotty, it was easy to forget with her that she'd just swallowed two hits of windowpane, and this capacity of hers to function normally on drugs always gave me hope. Whenever I felt blue, all I had to do was look at Katie's bland face as she was making flapjacks while tripping her brains out, and I knew that serenity was possible.

The King of Kings and I

One day three weeks after my arrival, Katie offered to split a tab of acid with me. The plan was to drive out of the city to Grant's Pass to watch the sunset, but at the last minute Bernie couldn't find any fixings for a salami sandwich, so Katie and I got in the van and made an impromptu trip to the local Stop and Shop, a supermarket with all the charm of the Sears automotive department. What a bummer! I was hoping to peak surrounded by the mountains, with a great view of the desert. Instead the acid kicked in as I was surrounded by condiments, with a great view of the dairy section.

I knew I was tripping because I was suddenly transfixed by the labels on the frozen sorbet. It was like I'd gone to Switzerland, and I was blissfully happy until a delivery boy with a cracked tooth asked me to close the door to keep the cold air from escaping. That's when I started to lose it. Where was Katie? Where was I? The wall freezers started to buckle; a can of frozen pink lemonade crashed to the floor and rolled beneath my feet. I started to run. I turned a corner. I turned another corner. I kept turning the corner and winding up in the exact same aisle. *Aaaagh!* I was surrounded by cereal boxes that laughed at me from both sides of the aisle. CAPTAIN CRUNCH! TONY THE TIGER! SNAP, CRACKLE, AND POP looked like they were enjoying a threesome and they all hated me.

I had to find Katie. I ran up to the deli counter, but the carnage was terrifying. *All those dead animals!* It was like the city morgue. *Death was everywhere!* The SALAMIS hung from the ceiling like severed limbs. Boar's Head Ham displayed paintings of proud animals who had been *slaughtered* and *stuffed* in cans. I found myself staring into the glassy eye of a WHITEFISH. I wept over the carcasses of some free-range TURKEYS who had sacrificed their breasts so that Oscar Meyer could live. *Aaaagh! I had to get away!* I stumbled into a wall of SARDINES. I wanted to liberate them, but the cans waved back and forth like the windy surf. I thought I would drown in a sea of aluminum. I grabbed for the wall to hold it back. A piece of it fell to the ground, making an awful noise. *Clank! Clank! Clank!* They'd be coming soon to get me. I had to get out of the store! I had to find the exit!

I ran and ran past walls of TOILET PAPER, past bottles of bleach labeled POISON. I found a red-haired girl! I turned her around, but it wasn't Katie. Her mother was a dried-out old woman with the pinched features of a shrunken head. *Dying!* She looked like she was dying. *Everybody around me was dying!* I stumbled past the express lane, past RAZOR BLADES, past SKELETONS in Bermuda shorts. My fellow shoppers were the children and grandchildren of the pioneers who had died in the desert and had been buried in shallow graves. In their faces I saw all the pain, all the *struggle! Life was so sad!* I wanted to scream, *Don't you know you're all going to die?* I stepped out into the parking lot, and the noonday sun burned at my flesh like the nuclear blast over Nagasaki.

A man standing beside me looked like he'd already died. He lit a cigarette. *He was alive!* Maybe he was a cigar-store Indian. *Maybe I was losing my mind.* Maybe Katie was waiting for me by the truck. I started wandering through the parking lot. The hot asphalt buckled beneath me. Then I remembered I wasn't wearing shoes. *Why wasn't I wearing shoes?*

"Hey, man. You cool?" A trippy chick was talking to me. I knew by her peasant blouse that she was a freak just like me. "Hey, man. Smile!"

"It's horrible! It's horrible!" I tried to tell her.

"Hey, man, this dude is having a bad trip!"

"I'm not wearing shoes!" I cried.

Her old man, half naked and wearing nothing but ragged jeans, leaned into me. "Peace," he said. "Just go with it, man. Just go with it."

"We're all gonna die," I said.

The two of them walked past me, the freak turning and proudly pointing to his feet. "I'm not wearing shoes either, man!"

I tumbled forward into the blazing sun and saw two more human creatures walking toward me. One was male and one was female, but it was hard to tell because they were identically dressed and the male didn't have any macho mannerisms. He was sweet and attentive. He put his hand on my shoulder and I felt comforted. He also had this amazing ability to talk and smile at the same time.

"Good morning, brother," he said to me.

"We're all gonna die, man," I responded. "It's horrible!"

The female Earthling stepped forward with a look of grave concern on her face. "I know how you feel," she said. "Would you like us to pray for you?" She held my hand, and I tried to get a better look at my new friends. I noticed that they both had pale blue shirts and white sneakers. The lower parts of their bodies were swathed in beige cloth, although the male wore pants and the female wore a skirt. Even in my disoriented state, they reminded me of creatures from the Osmond Family Christmas special. Even on acid, I knew these weren't the famous Osmonds, but they *could* have been two of the more untalented cousins who always stood in the back of the living room behind the couch and never got a chance to sing.

"Were you ever on TV?" I remember asking them.

The woman ignored my question. "There is someone who loves us," she said, speaking so very seriously that I naturally assumed this person was very close by.

"Where?"

"You can read this."

The female Osmond slipped a pamphlet into my back pocket alongside some wrinkled food stamps and coupons for liquid detergent.

"Thanks," I said.

"May you find peace through Jesus," she said.

Just then Katie came up behind me and pulled on my arm.

"Let's go," she said brusquely.

"Would you like to read this?" the woman asked, offering Katie a pamphlet.

"No thanks," Katie said as she pulled me across the parking lot. "Help me with these packages," she said to me with even less inflection in her voice than usual. In the truck on our way back home, she switched into third gear and lit up a Marlboro at the same time. "You gotta watch those Jesus freaks," Katie said to me sternly. Then, softening her tone, she said, "Looks like I can't leave you by yourself for a minute." As we rounded the corner to our house, she sighed and added, "You're just like your brother. What is it with you guys? You never want to be alone."

The worst part of the acid trip was over. When we got home I lay in a hammock and let the chemical pass through my system. Nearby, Scotty greased a carburetor and Katie planted tomatoes. Later that night after Katie went to sleep, I found myself again with nobody to talk to. The freaks in the living room were passing around a toilet-paper roll that had been turned into a hash pipe, and Scotty had wandered off somewhere. I thought about trying to find him, but, needing to spend some time on my own, I climbed on top of the Volvo, sat cross-legged, and studied the sky.

Outside of Tucson, coyotes perched on mountaintops were howling to the neighborhood dogs, "Head for the hills! Head for the hills!" And their lazy flea-bitten cousins were saying something like, "How's the food up there? How's the food up there?" I listened to their canine conversations, and I knew that some phase of my journey had already ended. In truth, I had only been doing drugs because I was bored, but no amount of weed or LSD would ever lay me back far enough to be a real hippie. Then I thought about what Katie had said to me in the truck, and it occurred to me that when she'd used the term *you guys*, she might have been referring not just to Bernie and me, but to Jewish people in general. Maybe we were chosen to be just a little more needy than everyone else. Maybe we were chosen to think too much, making it impossible for us to really fit in anywhere.

"O God," I said to the millions of stars seeming only a few feet above my head, "what now?" Suddenly I felt a pressure in my back pocket, and I pulled out the pamphlet that the Jesus freaks had given me earlier that afternoon. In the starlight I could make out the picture on the cover—a cartoon, actually—of a scruffy freak like me with a very worried look on his face. He was scratching his head, not knowing where to turn. Above him, in big block letters, was a sentence, as though projected from somewhere high in the sky: DO YOU KNOW WHAT HAPPENS TO YOU AFTER YOU DIE? On the bottom of the cartoon it said, "Turn page and find out!"

This got my attention. I turned the page. High in the right-hand corner of the pamphlet were beams of light and the sentence "You have a choice!" "I do?" asked the scruffy freak. "Yes, you do!" said the voice. "Would you like to know what that choice is?" I did. I turned the page. In burning letters it said, "You could put your faith in the world and wind up in Hell." The scruffy freak was looking into a pit with a man being burned alive like Richard Chamberlain in *The Towering Inferno*. On the next page, however, it said, in lovely script, "Or you could put your faith in—"

I turned the page again and there was a line drawing of Jesus looking very much like the painting on Debbi McDermott's wall, except this Jesus needed to be colored in. "Jesus died for your sins," the caption said, "because He so dearly loves YOU!"

I closed the pamphlet without reading any further. I simply didn't believe that Jesus loved me. If he did, surely I would have known by then. I closed my eyes and prayed, "Jesus, if you dearly love me, what stopped you from telling me? Were you, like me, afraid of rejection? It's not like there were other Gods trying to beat down my door to get to me first. So, Jesus, if you dearly love me, give me some kind of a sign. A Valentine's Day card. A box of chocolates. A complimentary bottle of wine. Anything." I waited another moment and no FTD florist dropped out of the sky, so I ripped the pamphlet in two, climbed off the Volvo, and went back inside to sleep. Meanwhile the coyotes continued to howl in the mountains, from the pain of being left alone in the dark.

*　　*　　*

A few days later Scotty left to transport a shipment of pot from Nogales, Mexico, to San Francisco. He left early in the morning with Little Red, who needed him to manage his marijuana franchise on the south side of Golden Gate Park. As Scotty climbed into Little Red's pickup truck I imagined him spending the rest of his life dispensing joints like hot dogs beneath a colorful Sabrett's umbrella. There'd been some discussion about my going too, but the cab of the truck could hold only three, and the third spot was taken by Big Red, Little Red's enormous Great Dane.

As I handed Scotty his guitar with the two broken strings, I wanted to tell him how much I'd miss him; but I didn't. I'd already learned that among my brother's friends the only righteous attitude was a Zen-like acceptance, a code no less repressive than the one that keeps Buddhist monks in line. The best I could do was ask Scotty, without any inflection in my voice, "Do you think you'll come back?" And the best he could answer was, "Can't say." As the truck pulled away with Scotty squinting into the morning sun, I felt envious of his ability to go wherever the wind blew him. But for the first time, this feeling was stained with pity. As the truck floated down the street, dwarfed by the cobalt sky, I began to think how small Scotty was in relation to the world. He was so tiny; the world was so big. He'd never see every bit of it, and maybe there was no use in trying.

For the next few days I struggled with boredom and depression. It was increasingly clear that I hadn't found spiritual salvation through bong hits. I didn't know where else to turn, and I might have gone back east had it not been for an old acquaintance turning up at our front door. A week after Scotty left, I was rinsing pinto beans when I heard dogs barking and brakes screeching in our front yard. Katie came up behind me and told me that I had a visitor, and then, with a sly wink, she indicated that the visitor was female and *very* anxious to see me. Barely had I stepped out the front door than a woman landed in my arms as though shot from a cannon. Before I could even see who was hugging me I was nearly knocked over by the smell of patchouli oil.

"Janet Eisenberg?" I said, finally recognizing the person hanging off my shoulders like a macramé plant holder.

"Ira gave me your address," Janet said breathlessly.

I stepped back to take an even better look at what had once been a familiar sight. Her hair, like an overgrown vacant lot, had reverted to its natural state. She was now sporting a wild mass of brown curls that could have nested a baby pterodactyl. Gone were the blond highlights. Gone were the arduous nights sitting up straightening her tresses with empty Hi-C cans. Her current massive hairdo would have required an oil drum.

"Look at you," she said. "You look great!" Then, calling to a friend of hers on the lawn, she said, "Lakshmi, this is Ira's roommate, the guy I was telling you about!"

Lakshmi, an unremarkable-looking man in saffron drawstring pants, was already relaxing from the long drive by doing yoga asanas on the lawn. As his feet touched the ground behind his head, two local dogs ran over to curiously sniff his butt, a situation Lakshmi passively accepted and did nothing to discourage. Just then two wide-eyed women exited the van and came up behind Janet with huge smiles on their faces. Janet introduced me to them. "And these are my best friends, Meadow and Forest."

Now, both these gals were dressed in long flowing white dresses. One of them had cymbals on her fingers, and the other carried a tambourine. It seemed that they'd been chanting in the car, and they both radiated an aura of such heavenly insubstantiality that I was shocked when the more forward of the two asked me, "Can we use your bathroom?" "We've been driving straight through from Boulder," Janet explained. "Lakshmi, come say hello to my old friend." But Lakshmi had already found a comfortable position in the transcendent, legs crossed and palms outstretched. He didn't respond to Janet, nor did Janet ask him again. She just smiled and whispered to me, "That's my old man! Isn't he great?" In response to being talked about, Lakshmi just twisted his back and cracked his spine, which was the loudest noise I would ever hear him make.

Lakshmi, I would find out later, had been born Mitchell Glazer in Danbury, Connecticut, and Janet had met him chanting his mantra in Harvard Square. After complimenting her aura, Lakshmi had taken her back to his dorm room at MIT to scrub out her chakras, and the two of them had been having Tantric sex ever since. Outside of bed, however, they rarely seemed to interact. Lakshmi was a cautious soul who could have sucked the fun out of Disneyland, and, as I was beginning to observe, Janet Eisenberg, despite a new wardrobe and a new aesthetic, had not really changed much at all. She'd simply found a new way to be completely ignored by a boyfriend.

Later that night we all went out to dinner at a whole-foods restaurant near the university, called Food for Thought, where, according to Meadow, they seasoned the food with "love." Personally, I would have preferred a little more salt and pepper; and I wasn't thrilled that all the main courses looked like they'd been yanked out of lawn-mower bags. As we daintily chewed dandelions, Janet told me that she and her friends were on their way to a "conscious community" being formed in the desert south of Tucson.

Janet was definitely the talker in the group. Lakshmi hardly spoke throughout the meal; he just noisily sucked the flavor out of some seaweed while Meadow and Forest licked a few twigs and then complained that they were full. Meanwhile, Janet told me that she had no plans to return to the musical-comedy stage and that she didn't miss performing at all. She had traded in her toe shoes for saris, and her greasepaint for sandal paste. The only lyrics she sang now were Om and many names of the Hindu deities.

"That's great!" I said, doing my best to hide my relief that Janet's new belief system had spared the cosmos one more untalented cabaret performer.

"Oh, and I've changed my name!" Janet declared.

"To what?" I asked.

"Well, I wanted something more botanical than Eisenberg—you know, something earthy that would describe where I'm coming from."

"You come from Long Island," I said. "How about 'Front Lawn'?"

Janet laughed, proving she hadn't completely lost her sense of humor.

"Are you ready for this? My new name—Janet Planet."

"That's great!" I told her.

"Oh, Jaffe," she said, "it seems like lifetimes since we hung out!"

Then she shook her head. "I was so fucked up, back then."

"No you weren't," I replied.

"Yes I was," Janet insisted, and this time I let my silence show that maybe, just maybe, I agreed with her. Janet shook her head ruefully, and perhaps it was the light from the scented candle, but bittersweetness looked lovely on her. It made her eyes glisten.

"Ooh! Remember that time we did acid and we climbed that tree?"

"You don't trip anymore, do you?" I asked.

Janet shook her head and pointed silently with her elbow to Lakshmi, who had closed his eyes to avoid distractions while chewing his food. Obviously, Lakshmi didn't approve of drugs.

"No," she sighed. "But that was such a great day. I'll never forget how you climbed to the top. You really inspired me that day."

"I did?"

Meadow and Forest looked at me and smiled in unison.

"No, seriously," Janet said. "This guy is such an old soul!"

Then Janet blew in her tea, creating little ripples moving in my direction. Meadow and Forest nodded their heads thoughtfully, and for a moment I thought I saw a lovely green light about their heads, which may have been their astral bodies—or simply candlelight reflecting off some sprouts at the next table.

That next morning I rolled up my sleeping bag, said good-bye to Bernie and Katie, and crawled into the back of Lakshmi's van. Two hours later, after following Route 19 and an old dirt road, we arrived at a commune ten miles north of the Mexican border. The following day I met some of the community elders and was assigned the job of maintaining the compost heap, which consisted of doing little more than separating the plum pits from the banana peels.

Taking care of organic garbage wasn't the only change in my life; I also resolved to avoid swallowing any drugs stronger than chamomile. While LSD had opened me to a higher level of consciousness, I also knew that one more trip through the "Valley of the Dolls" would land me in a padded cell along with Patty Duke. My new recipe for enlightenment would be communing with nature, surrounding myself with "really high beings," and speaking in platitudes every chance I got. Reading books would be optional. My new home would be a fifty-acre plot of cactus simply referred to as "the Land." The original lease had been shared by several families who had long since pulled up stakes and moved to Albuquerque. The present inhabitants were all friends, cousins of the original settlers who had made a commitment to living peaceably. There was no single guru or teaching on the Land, yet it was everyone's understanding that we would all be doing something to increase our spiritual awareness.

We also worked to maintain several cottage industries that included weaving, jewelry making, and raising organic tomatoes. If all this sounds vague, it may be because my memory has faded, and also because we weren't a practical bunch of people on the Land. In fact, we were *antipractical*. There was, I remember, the fervent hope that the current military industrial complex was on the verge of collapse, so we all lived day to day, hand to mouth, cheerfully awaiting an eco-

nomic apocalypse. Every bit of news about high inflation or a down-
turn in the stock market would thrill us no end.

But what I remember most about the Land was the land itself. In the
center was a valley floor large enough for half a dozen teepees and a veg-
etable garden. Above the valley to the east was a ridge with an old farmhouse, and to the north was a plateau on which were parked several
motorized vehicles including a school bus, a trailer, and an abandoned
Mister Softee truck that had been left there some time ago by a disgruntled ice-cream vendor from Houston. The couples, like Lakshmi and
Janet, lived in teepees down in the valley, where they had "conscious
sex," carefully exploring each other's yin-yangs. The single men like me
slept inside one of the trucks, where we fasted and struggled to live like
peaceful warriors. Carlos Castañeda was our hero. The single women,
like Meadow and Forest, lived in the farmhouse, where they practiced
midwifery and, after a successful birth, would sometimes fry up the pla-
centa with zucchini and onions.

The Mister Softee truck was our unofficial library, kind of like a
Hindu Science Reading Room. This library had been organized by
Lakshmi, a scholar by nature who, when he met Janet, had been writing his Ph.D. thesis on the mythological significance of South Asian
elephant droppings. On my first visit to the library, Lakshmi thought
I might be short on inspiration so he suggested I read biographies of
highly evolved beings, who seemed to fall into one of three cate-
gories: Hindu beggars who lived ninety-seven years on insects and
one side order of rice; medieval Polish nuns who squirted holy water
from their eyeballs; and Navajo wise men who could live in three
states at once without paying income taxes.

Whenever I felt really ambitious I would attempt to read the
Bhagavad Gita or some other arcane Sanskrit text. Under Lakshmi's
guidance I learned that the proper way to read these books was one
syllable at a time. By my third week I'd made it to page two of the
Tibetan Book of the Dead. Meanwhile Lakshmi was reading the *Tibetan*

Book of the Living in the same time it would have taken to crawl up to Mt. Everest. At one point, I leaned over to Lakshmi and suggested that we should combine our own books into the *Tibetan Book of the Bored*, but Lakshmi didn't appreciate the joke, and I suspected that, even when he was Mitchell Glazer, Lakshmi had lacked a sense of humor.

But this never really bothered me. Nor did it bother me that most of my neighbors had taken vows of silence and that, when they did talk, the most scintillating topic of conversation was mung beans. For the first time in my life I was communing with nature. I communed with wildflowers growing, water trickling, and the heat rash spreading across my chest. On most days, I spent most of my time in the hills, hiking with Meadow or stirring the compost heap with Janet Planet. I became like Julie Andrews in *The Sound of Music*, twirling myself dizzy at the joy of being outdoors.

In retrospect, this was a joy I'd never felt before. Like most Jews, I'd never been an outdoors type. My ancestors had clustered in crowded ghettos. As a child I had to be pushed out of the house to get fresh air, and to this day my mother's idea of having fun on a vacation is waiting in the car. Therefore, you won't find many of us Jews doing things like *voluntarily* windsurfing or bungee jumping. For us, cross-country skiing isn't a sport; it's a way of escaping from Austria. On the other hand, Jews have always loved the desert. Maybe it's all those biblical stories we read as kids, but the desert is the one place where Jews *automatically* feel at home, and if we never make it back to Jerusalem, we can buy a condo in Rancho Mirage and live happily with white gravel in our front yards and fig trees outside our windows.

A few weeks after our arrival on the Land, Lakshmi and Janet broke up. The story was that Lakshmi wanted to become celibate in order to become a "rug boy" for Guru Maharaji, a fifteen-year-old chocolate-eating spiritual master who'd recently arrived in the States. I was pretty shocked at first. As far as I could see, Guru Maharaji hadn't mastered anything except the Snickers lever on a vending machine. For another, Lakshmi had gone to MIT, and I was still bourgeois enough to think he should have aspired higher than draping white sheets over a settee every time the Guru needed to take a load off his feet. What would Lakshmi tell his family? That he'd majored in laundry?

Lakshmi, though, was convinced that he should evolve through service to the Guru, and he would have been thrilled to vacuum the corn chips off the floor of his limousine. Meanwhile, I was hurt by his breakup with Janet. Despite a degree of distance between them—or maybe because of it—Lakshmi and Janet reminded me of my own mom and dad. It was like watching my parents getting divorced, the universe dividing; it was like yin breaking up with yang.

Also, despite the official announcement that Lakshmi had made the decision to go, I suspected that Janet had tossed him out on his prayer rug. Lakshmi was too wishy-washy for Janet. In retrospect, Lakshmi, although heterosexual, was probably the most effeminate man I'd ever met, and whenever I start wondering whether or not gayness is physiological, I always think of this guy. Without any apparent testosterone in his body Lakshmi had turned out straight, and any measurement of his hypothalamus would have revealed an organ half the size of a Junior Mint.

The day he left to hitch a ride to Los Angeles to take a job selling Earth Shoes, Lakshmi and I had a nice little talk. He'd already said good-bye to Janet, and he was now putting his eating bowl in his backpack along with his meditation pillow and a small brass bell.

"You know, Jaffe," he whispered, "it's not whether you're gay or straight. The problem is lust."

"I'm sorry that you and Janet broke up."

"I love Janet. I'll always love Janet. But I love God more. I couldn't concentrate on God while I was lusting after Janet."

"Do you think you'll be celibate your whole life now?"

"Probably." Lakshmi shook his head as he packed away a few more sticks of incense for the road. "Women retard our spiritual growth."

"Really?"

Lakshmi leaned into me and whispered very seriously. "Men aspire to higher goals. Women's goals are murky. It's their hormones. It keeps them from evolving on a straight path."

"Oh . . ."

Lakshmi stood and adjusted his backpack. "But I might have a wife someday. Who knows? Take my advice, Jaffe. Never make love to a woman out of lust."

"I promise."

Then he made the peace sign, closed his eyes, and mumbled his mantra several times to himself. When he opened his eyes, I said good-bye.

"See you," I said.

Lakshmi nodded his head, took one last look at the village, and started walking down the road all by himself.

Later that day I went to help Janet pack. Now that she was a single woman she had to leave the teepee and move into the farmhouse, so she was carefully folding her peasant blouses and rolling up the Georgia O'Keeffe prints that she'd pinned to the walls of her wigwam. After piling some boxes onto a wagon we sat down for a cup of tea that Janet had brewed from a few pieces of bark. She was being uncharacteristically quiet.

"Is this supposed to taste like anything?" I finally asked.

"It cleanses the heart chakra."

"Could I get a little tea in this tea?"

"Ha ha," Janet said mournfully.

"So what are you going to do now?" I asked. "Stay here? Go back east?"

"I don't know . . ." Janet bowed her head almost completely, obscuring her face beneath her mass of curls. She looked so sweet and vulnerable, hardly the brash Ethel Merman wannabe I'd met only eighteen months previously. "What about you?" she said.

"I'll stay here until I can figure out the next step. Just let it unfold."

"Oh . . ."

"You think I should have more of a plan?"

"I didn't say that," she sighed. "I don't know anymore."

I felt awkward, not knowing how to comfort her. Outside, a cloud passed overhead. The translucent walls of the teepee magically turned gray, and for a moment I wasn't sure whether I was inside or out. The disorientation was momentarily thrilling.

"I love living here," I said.

"So do I."

Suddenly Janet burst into tears. "Oh, Jaffe—what am I going to do? I want to go back home. I want it to be the way it was!"

"You mean with Lakshmi?"

"No. Before. Before we got so serious. Before we got so spiritual about everything."

We moved toward each other. Janet put her head on my shoulder. I put my arm around my former roommate's former girlfriend and waited for her to finish sobbing.

"Remember the songs we sang that day we tripped?" Then she started humming "Where Is Love?"

"Shh," I said, not wanting her singing to spoil the mood.

"I felt so close to you that day," Janet said. "I was just so glad that Ira made a friend like you!"

Janet continued to cry, and some of her cleansing tears splashed on my arm. I thought about Lakshmi's comment about women's hormones and wondered if he'd been wrong about women being unevolved.

"How come you just didn't stay at Stony Brook and become gay like all the other guys?"

"I—I didn't feel that was right for me."

"You didn't?"

"Not really."

"Did you know Vinnie? The guy he's dating now?"

"A little bit."

"He seems nice," Janet said as she snuggled against me. She'd already stopped crying, but I kept my arm around her.

"Have you . . . have you ever had sex with a woman?" Janet asked when she noticed I wasn't pulling away.

"You mean like . . . well . . . no."

"I was just curious."

"I haven't ruled it out," I said cautiously.

I believe I must have stopped breathing as Janet's fingers started walking up my spine, stopping at the spot behind my heart and digging into me with surprising strength.

So I kissed her. I don't know why. Maybe I felt sorry for her. Maybe I wanted to get revenge on Ira. Maybe it was the only way I could be certain she wouldn't start screeching again. At the time it seemed like it wasn't right to leave her alone and that, since the conversation wasn't going anywhere, sex was our only option. Her lips tasted like strawberry lip gloss, and I remembered, in spite of how far we'd traveled, that we were still just two years out of high school. We made out some more. My mind wandered some more. I remembered Lakshmi's advice about not making love out of lust, and I patted myself on the back for having no trouble following it so thoroughly. Of course, down deep I somehow knew I wasn't being true to myself, but I also knew that people all over the world were probably having sex at that moment for far worse reasons than mine.

It helped, to ease things along, that before Janet pulled off her clothes, she also pulled out a huge chunk of hashish that she'd hidden from Lakshmi, and the two of us got really buzzed. We were so buzzed, in fact, that I can barely remember getting undressed and crawling beneath the quilt that Meadow and Forest had sewed by hand. I just recall Janet saying something like "Do whatever you want" and my flinging the blanket over my head like one of those old-time photographers who need to be covered with cloth in order to focus on their subject.

So Janet and I went all the way. Like two plastic beads on a children's necklace we snapped together, and I even might have enjoyed the linkage had I not been so worried about finishing what I'd started. Fortunately, Janet was much less naive about sex than I. She'd been down this road before with Ira, and she had few illusions about what I might need to get me off. At one point she even squeezed her ample breasts together and laughed, "Doesn't this look like a guy's butt?"

"Almost," I replied. "Almost."

Finally, after what seemed like an eternity, Janet opened her eyes again and looked almost surprised that I was still on top of her working so hard. A look of compassion spread across her face.

"Just let your mind go wherever it wants," she said kindly.

"Are you sure?" I grunted in return.

Janet beamed. "Oh . . . yes. Yes. Yes."

"OK," I said.

Janet smiled and closed her eyes, leaving my mind free to wander through a list of boys' names, many of whom have already been mentioned in this book. Somewhere between Brian and Vinnie my pipes burst. I shot my load. I was finished. Then Janet hugged me and called me baby, got up, shamelessly stark naked, and poked at the logs in the fire. It was chilly, so I knelt beside her and wrapped the blanket around the two of us.

"I'm so glad you're here," she said, looking straight into the fire.

"I am too," I replied.

"I'd be so lonely here without another Jew from Long Island to keep me company."

"I know what you mean," I said.

"I wish Ira were here," she said.

"Yeah, me too."

"Gay guys and celibates," she said ruefully. "At least you take your time. That was great."

"Really?"

Janet nodded her head sweetly, and for the first time that night I regretted that I couldn't love Janet the way she deserved, with my full attention. I didn't even mind when she started singing "Sunrise, Sunset" from *Fiddler on the Roof*.

For the next two weeks I lived in the teepee with Janet Planet and we were fairly happy. We had sex once more, but by the end of the first week we were content to simply cuddle. For the sake of staying in her "couples" teepee we did pretend to be an item to the rest of the commune. Most people assumed that we were soul mates. Meadow, an astrologer, even went so far as to say that she'd never seen two charts so completely compatible. Apparently our Mars and Venus were so closely conjunct that Meadow blushed just thinking about them.

So why did I do it? Did I think having sex with Janet Planet would make me straight? No, I was never *that* naive. In fact, even then I was pretty certain Janet would be my only heterosexual opportunity in this lifetime, so I probably had sex with her the same way a non-Zionist Jew would visit Israel if the airline fares were low enough. In the long run, however, the illusion of heterosexual normalcy wasn't all that rewarding, and within three weeks of Lakshmi's departure I too would leave the Land.

My lack of sexual chemistry with Janet wasn't my only reason for splitting. The New Age was simply getting old fast, and Forest and Meadow were really getting on my nerves. The two of them were always butting into my business, offering me unwanted advice. Forest, who supposedly had the ability to see auras, called me aside one day to tell me that I was very "evolved" because my energy field was a thirty-foot beam of light emanating from the top of my

head. "Great!" I replied. "I'll go back to New York and get a job directing traffic at the airport." Meadow, on the other hand, had become
fascinated with crystals. She'd moved into a hut behind the school-
house and decorated it with more rocks than Howe Caverns. In the
center of her room was a huge hunk of purple granite that doubled as
a coffee table. Having packed on a few pounds baking corn bread,
Meadow swore that this crystal would help her to lose weight. I saw
little hope of this happening unless she used the crystal to block the
pantry door, along with a couple of cinder blocks.

On the other hand, I had not completely lost faith that some
kind of inner bliss was possible, so I started spending even more time
in Lakshmi's library. Day after day I pored through spiritual texts.
Like Goldilocks in the home of the Three Bears, I tried to find the
spiritual path that would be *just* right for me. *Be Here Now* was too soft.
Hermann Hesse was too hard. Krishnamurti was just right, except he
looked a little too much like the Wicked Witch of the West.

Then one day I found this most amazing book. It was called *The
Aquarian Gospel of Jesus the Christ*, and it purported to be the real story of
Jesus of Nazareth as channeled through a Quaker minister named
Levi who lived in the nineteenth century. I hesitated reading this
book because, in spite of how far I'd come since Rabbi Mintz, I was
still enough of a Jew to feel like I'd be doing something really naughty.
Reading about Eastern religions had been perfectly acceptable. In
fact, for many Jews, especially in California, Buddhism is a branch of
Judaism just to the left of Reform. On the other hand, an adoring
account of the Original Goy was definitely *tref*. When I was growing
up in Brooklyn, the only Jesus story we kept in our house was a book
called *The Passover Plot*. According to this historical novel, Jesus was a
Palestinian undercover agent who had held his breath on the cross
and only pretended to be dead. It was like the Gospel according to
Oliver Stone.

Then again, I couldn't *not* read this book. Enough had already

happened in my life—Catholic Mass with Mrs. Potts, the Jesus freaks
in front of the Stop and Shop—that I couldn't ignore Jesus any longer.
So one day I sat down next to the compost heap and read *The Aquarian
Gospel* from cover to cover. What a page turner! It was like reading
Jesus: The Untold Story. Chapter by chapter I learned that Jesus wasn't
just some poor schlepp with shiny hair and moist, delicate eyes. Jesus
had been a learned man, an advanced soul—an Essene, actually—
who'd been through many, many previous incarnations.

The book covered those eighteen years of Jesus' life when the
Bible lost track of him. According to *The Aquarian Gospel* Jesus traveled
the world over and hit all the spiritual hot spots—China, Tibet,
India—and he studied with all the recognized saints and gurus of his
time. Finally, he went back to Egypt, where all the spiritual masters
convened beneath the Great Pyramid and put him through his final
tests, which were like the GEDs for sainthood. Finally they added up
his scores and declared that a new millennium had begun and that
Jesus was "the Avatar"—a new word to me that meant something like
"defining symbol," like Elvis was to the fifties, only bigger.

Then, at the moment of his attaining the Christ position, Jesus'
human soul exited his body and the Infinite Soul of the Universe
moved in and took over. It was kind of like his soul gave up the lease
on his flesh and God got to move into an already furnished apartment.
At this moment—the dawn of the Age of Pisces—the archangels
blew their mighty trumpets. Celestial chimes woke up the neighbor-
ing galaxies. Souls on all levels of creation—the astral plane, the
causal plane, the plain old physical plane—all got together and threw
one huge cosmic coming-out party, and best of all, a great portion of
humankind rejoiced and sang, "The Messiah has come! The Messiah
has come!" And everybody was happy.

Except the Jews.

We just went along pretending that nothing had happened. For
whatever reason, we proceeded to live our lives as though Jesus had never

lived. It was like the story of mankind took a sudden turn while we Jews stayed the course, bumped off the main road, and eventually became a sad sideshow meandering along the treacherous byways and service roads of human history. According to us, there had been no Messiah. As my father would tell you, the lion never lay down with the lamb and no swords were beaten into plowshares. What was the big deal?

And thus my people, this tiny tribe of lawyers, doctors, and stand-up comics, remained blind to what was so clear to everyone else: that the life of Jesus of Nazareth had ushered onto planet Earth a newer and more humane way of picturing God than that of a cranky old man in a striped bathrobe. By the time I finished *The Aquarian Gospel* it seemed to me it was the goyim who had been right all along. We had been wrong.

What now?

Would I become a Christian? Which meant what? Not only was I Jewish and probably gay, I was a hippie! Was I about to give up my torn jeans, get a haircut, and start wearing argyle sweaters and beige slacks? Would I have to start ringing doorbells and annoying people? No way! There had to be a way out of this Jesus thing. Several days in a row I went for long walks in the desert praying that I was suffering from some kind of temporary dementia. If in fact Jesus had been the avatar for the whole planet, what about all those people in China? Could a billion people have missed the boat completely? What about my family? Had their ignorance of Jesus made them inferior to our beer-swilling neighbors? Could all the people who came to my bar mitzvah be complete "heathens"—not counting their table manners?

During this time I almost completely stopped talking to Janet. One morning, a week after reading the gospel, I tried to voice my concerns about Jesus and she told me I was "head-tripping."

"I'm not head-tripping. I'm thinking! What if there aren't many paths to the top of the mountain? What if there is one true way?"

Janet was nonchalantly spreading gooey molasses on a hunk of bread that Meadow had baked in a wood-burning oven.

"What difference does it make who *Jesus* was?" she said. "It's not going to change who *you* are."

"I'm not trying to change who I am!"

"You sure you don't want any bread with molasses?"

"No thanks."

"It will give you iron."

"I already have more iron in me than a Buick!"

"Hmm. Sure you don't want some?" I had to admit, the bread did look good—dripping with sweetness. "No thanks," I said.

"I'm sorry," Janet said, "but the Jesus stuff is the one thing I can't listen to. It gives me the creeps."

I stood up to leave. "Just because it feels weird doesn't mean it's not true!"

Janet shook her head and I walked outside. If there had been a door on the teepee I might even have slammed it. As I stumbled up the hill I remember thinking, "If only Adam in the Garden of Eden had my willpower to turn down food, things would have turned out a whole lot better."

That day I tried to find solace in nature, but—sad to say—nature and I were no longer speaking. Each twist on the path didn't lead me into a Technicolor diorama; the hills were no longer alive with the sound of music. Instead nature just lay there like a sinister lunar landscape so dismal and uninviting that I was almost surprised to be breathing without a space suit. "What a fuckin' unmiraculous piece of rock," I thought to myself. In my two months in the desert the closest I'd come to a Burning Bush was a lit cigarette flicked out of a moving Winnebago.

Meanwhile, I just kept grumbling to myself about the possibility of Jesus' divinity. I remember having trouble with the concept of scale. How could God Junior have squeezed himself into a bag of meat no larger than myself? I found a rock to sit down on and pulled the burrs out of my socks. I listened and watched. An eagle circled a ridge on the distant horizon. Otherwise, there was nothing but silence. "Please, Jesus!" I called into the void. "You see how confused I am. Send me some kind of sign of where I should go next." Nothing happened. I was partially relieved. Then, convinced that I had suffered enough for one day, I started walking back to my teepee with my head hanging so low that if Jesus himself had been walking alongside me, I wouldn't have seen him.

That day, however, something did happen. When I got back to the teepee Janet was waiting there with a letter for me from Katie. It was nothing too informative, but enclosed in it was an unpaid phone bill and a postcard from Scotty in San Francisco. Apparently Scotty had found a cool apartment in Haight-Ashbury, and he thought I might want to come live with him. "The cities are where it's happening now," he said. "It's where the freaks are gathering." He then described the crowd he was living with as a theatrical group kind of like the gang at Stony Brook, guys I "might have a lot in common with." For the first time, the possibility of going to San Francisco and meeting guys with whom I "might have a lot in common" was certainly intriguing. God, I was tired of being spiritual. God, I was tired of living in the desert. There was nothing I wanted more at that moment than to be indoors with somebody I loved, and perhaps—just perhaps—that somebody was living in Haight-Ashbury.

That night I told Janet I'd be hitchhiking up north, and I conveniently neglected to name my city of destination. Janet wasn't very upset; in her mind I was already gone. The next morning she even helped me pack my bags. Then Meadow made buckwheat pancakes, and I began walking up the dirt road toward the highway. For the first time in a while, I knew where I was going. I'd tried drugs. Drugs were OK for some people, but not for me. I'd tried nature. Nature was OK for other people, but not for me. I'd tried loving a woman and I'd even come "this" close to trying Jesus. Now I was going to try loving men, and each step I took was bringing me closer and closer to myself. It was as though the real drama of my life had been playing up in San

Francisco all along, without me. I started to run. I didn't want to miss a second of it.

I did have to make one stop, however, on my way to the highway. High on the ridge, I stopped at Lakshmi's library to return *The Aquarian Gospel* to its rightful place. Christianity, like heterosexuality, was something better practiced by people other than me. "No offense, Mr. Christ, but you're simply not for me." And then I jogged out to Route 19 and stuck out my thumb, fully believing that I'd seen the last of the King of kings.

For me, the sixties ended the same night as my youth—about three years later than it did for everybody else. It was June 3, 1973, the night I slept in a refrigerator box in People's Park. As it turned out, finding Scotty in San Francisco quickly turned into a series of surreal outtakes from *Easy Rider* as directed by Fellini. The address Scotty had given me was a lavender stuccoed structure called the Casa de Carmelita built right above a trolley tunnel. A chubby woman wearing nothing but a boa constrictor answered the door and gave me a forwarding address in the Fillmore district. Across town, nobody answered the door; there was no door. I cautiously entered a dark railroad apartment and found a bearded man, half asleep on the buckled linoleum, who gave me the name of a hotel in Berkeley where Scotty had gone the week before. He told me I could catch the bus downtown and asked me for seven cents to help pay his rent.

My dream of finding romance in San Francisco also vanished quickly, although I did catch a glimpse of several homosexuals on my way out of town, or rather their body parts. It was a bright sunny day, and hundreds of men were squeezed together in the shadowy doorways of leather bars, their shaved skulls, hairy bellies, and tattooed forearms protruding so far onto the sidewalks that one had to step off the curb to get around them. I scurried past. Then at the bus terminal

The King of Kings and I

I bought my ticket, and there was a young collegiate guy who looked at me in the waiting area. I sat down in the seat across the aisle and snuck a glance. He turned away and I looked down. A few moments later I looked up again, praying that he'd be looking. He wasn't, and I assumed I was being rejected. That was it; I got on the bus and left San Francisco forever.

The hotel in Berkeley on Shattuck Avenue was one of the few buildings in that beautiful college town with no charm whatsoever. The ground floor of the hotel boasted several dress shops featuring sun-blanched smocks hanging on faded store dummies more ancient than most Greek statues. Entering the hotel, I gingerly stepped over winos in the lobby and approached the desk clerk, a black man with yellow eyes, who told me that Scotty no longer lived there. "If you don' find him roamin' the hills, you migh' find him in the People' Park." So I ran the few blocks to this world-famous empty lot, covered with enough dog shit to fertilize Montana, where I found a clean refrigerator box and crawled in for the night alongside a few dozen other shell-shocked sixties leftovers with no place else to go.

So the sixties ended and I wasn't sure if I ever got my chance to be free; I certainly hadn't gotten any free love. The next morning I called my mother collect from a noisy street corner beside a taqueria. She accepted the charge, as I knew she would.

"Hello, Mom! It's Jaffe—"

"Hello. Anything the matter?"

"No, everything's great!"

"So how's Arizona?"

"I'm not in Arizona anymore. I'm in Berkeley, California."

There was a pause while my mother ran through several possible ways she could worry herself to death.

"You're in California where they just had the earthquake?"

"There wasn't any earthquake," I replied.

"I read last week there was an earthquake."

"That was in Chile."

"So you're OK then?"

There was a pause while I waited for my mom to start begging me to come back east.

"How's the weather?" she finally asked.

"Fine," I said.

In the background I heard my father yelling. My mother half covered the receiver and yelled to my father that she was talking to me. "Hello, son," my father said as he picked up the phone in the den.

"Hi, Dad."

"Mother tells me you're in California. I read in the paper today you're having a serious drought."

"I don't know. I just got here."

"I'll send you the newspaper article. Do you have an address?"

"I'm sure I can read about it in the papers here."

At the mention of disaster my mother cheerfully reentered the conversation.

"A drought? You didn't tell me you were having a drought."

"It's no big deal," my father tried to reassure her. "He's just not supposed to flush the toilet."

"Why is that?" my mother asked. "Why shouldn't he flush the toilet?"

"It takes up ten gallons of water," my father answered.

"Well, it's worth every drop!"

"I'm still on the line," I tried to inform my parents.

"If you want to flush the toilet," my mother said, "go ahead and flush! Don't let them stop you."

"By the way," my father asked, "who's paying for this phone call?"

"He called collect," my mother sighed.

There was a slight pause while my father calculated the very least that had to be said.

"You OK, son?"

"I'm fine."

"You coming home for the bat mitzvah?"

"Yes . . . yes . . ."

There was another slight pause.

"Roz, the Zimmetbaums are waiting for us at Hunan Pao's. We should get going."

"The Zimmetbaums can wait a few minutes."

"I'm sorry," I said. "I called at a bad time."

"No problem. Just remember my pact with God. I'm not going to smoke a cigarette until you get home safe."

"In that case, don't come home," my father joked. "Bye, son."

"Bye, Dad."

"You sure you're OK?" my mother asked one more time.

"I'm fine." I said. "I just . . ."

"What?"

"I just wanted someone to talk to . . ."

There was a pause while I considered telling her how bad I was really feeling.

"Just get home safe," she finally said.

"Bye."

"Bye."

I hung up the phone feeling like I'd almost got what I wanted.

I walked back to People's Park with the idea that Scotty would eventually come down from the hills. Most of the hippies who'd slept there the night before had rolled up their bags and continued on their journeys. The few who remained looked like wounded veterans from an ancient Matthew Brady photograph. A great civil war had been fought, and these were the stragglers too tired or too confused to leave the front. We were the losers. Even with Nixon already embroiled in Watergate, we knew it was we who had lost the great battle for the soul of America. Our choices now were to go into hiding like MIAs or return to our parents' split-level homes and live like prisoners of war.

Later that day Scotty miraculously appeared; I was still sitting in the park when he came down from the hills behind campus with his new best friend, Otis, a former poli-sci grad student from Oakland with long matted hair who was too crazy to know that the war against the Establishment had already been lost. Otis was in the middle of conducting a bizarre sociological experiment, and he proudly explained to me in a high-pitched stammer that he ate only Wonder Bread. "I want to see how long it will take . . . you see, you see . . . before I fall deathly ill," he said. "I need to disprove . . . you see . . . the theory that Wonder Bread builds strong bodies twelve ways. You see. You see. General Foods is the enemy. He's waging war against the American people!"

As he spoke he rolled a cigarette nervously while Scotty nodded his head in agreement. If anything, Scotty had grown even more silent in the months since we'd traveled together. Sleeping outdoors had not just darkened his skin but hardened it, giving his soft spirit a thick shell. His fingernails were dirty; he'd been doing a lot of chemicals, and he'd forgotten about sending me a postcard in Tucson. That afternoon we dined near a gas-station convenience store where I had a tuna sandwich and Scotty munched on some beef jerky. We sat on a grass road divider while Otis was inside the store stocking up on some soft gooey loaves of bread.

"I'm thinking about going back home," I said.

Scotty didn't reply. His mind was on something else.

"Can I catch Route 80 from here?" I asked.

"Right up the street," Scotty said, pointing west on University Avenue.

"What a long, strange trip it's been," I said, trying to goad Scotty into talking. I was still hoping he'd be able to say something—anything—that would help me not feel so sorry for him.

"Yep," he said.

"Whatever happened to your guitar?" I asked.

The King of Kings and I

"Traded it for these pants," Scotty replied, staring at his jeans.

"Cool," I said.

Scotty continued staring at his pants, a perplexed look clouding his face. "Maybe they weren't these pants." Otis came out of the store and the three of us walked back to People's Park as Scotty's new friend yammered about how Wonder Bread, in conjunction with daylight saving time, was the primary cause of brain cancer—all the while squeezing together several slices of Wonder Bread into a gummy ball the size of a tumor.

The next morning Otis and Scotty slept late, with the sun directly in their eyes. I, however, couldn't sleep. I was too anxious. This was the day I'd be heading home, and nothing could have dispelled the awful feeling that my trip had been a complete failure. Scavenging some change from the bottom of my backpack, I put together enough money for falafel and wandered up Telegraph Avenue onto the Berkeley campus, where I found a water fountain for brushing my teeth and a goldfish pond for cleaning out my armpits. The era when Sproul Hall had been the center of radical protest was long past, and the current crop of students looked like rejects from a casting call for *The Brady Bunch*. The revolution had fizzled; I'd have to find a way to fit in, somehow.

Behind the Theater Department I found a grassy hill where I sat down to close my eyes. The smell of eucalyptus and a sky like a giant blue pearl only made me feel worse. In the few years leading up to this moment I'd made tentative stabs at finding happiness with half a dozen majors, ten ways of getting stoned, a couple of best friends, twenty-four states of the Union, several topographies, two different sexes, and every possible world religion. Still, I had nothing to call my own except a small patch of grass and the pitying smiles of my clean-cut contemporaries. I took a moment to listen to my heart for inner truth, but all I heard was a small still voice telling me to go find a bagel.

I picked myself up off the ground and ambled down Hearst Street to the food co-op, where I found a lovely sesame-seed bialy amid the "exotic delicacies." On my way out I happened to glance to my left and saw the fattest woman I'd ever seen. She was seated in front of some kind of bookstore on what might have been a secondhand sofa. Upon closer inspection, there was no sofa; she was actually standing. She was a short woman—wider than she was tall—and what I'd first thought to be furniture upholstery was actually one of several bolts of wide-wale corduroy swathing this woman from head to toe. The corduroy was pulled tight across her massive bulk, and I found myself imagining that one more meal and her sheath would snap flat out and she'd be wrapped in cloth as smooth as satin.

I tried not to stare, but this woman was impossible to ignore. Besides her unusual girth, she was also laughing raucously at something she'd just said to a delivery man. Her laugh was like music, with clearly distinguished high notes and low notes, and it was the most buoyant sound I'd ever heard. The delivery man referred to her as Sunny, and as I chewed my bialy she exchanged giggles with several more strangers.

"Would you do me a big favor?" she suddenly called to me.

"Me?"

"Yes you. You eating." She laughed as she dug her chubby arms into a large hand-sewn purse made from the same thick red patterned material as her dress.

"I need you to buy me something. Ah, here we go." She pulled a few bills out of her bag. "I can't leave the bookstore. Would you mind going back into the co-op and getting me some corn chips?"

I took her money and started back into the store, but she grabbed me by the arm.

"Listen to me. I'll tell you exactly where they are. They're in aisle eight. The ones that are fried in safflower oil. I can't eat the regular ones."

I looked at her questioningly.

"I see you're shocked that there's something I can't eat." She again burst forth in a symphony of mirth, wiping a tear from her eye and using the back of her hand, like a baby polar bear.

"Sure," I said. "I'll be right back."

I ran back to the co-op, and when I returned with the corn chips Sunny was no longer standing in front of the bookstore. I looked inside and saw that she had somehow managed to waddle back in and had climbed onto a stool behind the cash register. Her feet didn't touch the ground but swung back and forth merrily as she gossiped with a tall, thick-jawed woman with a white pony tail who looked something like George Washington after a sex change. I hesitated at the entrance to the store.

"Come on in. I'm not going to bite you!" Sunny exclaimed, laughing again as I slowly approached the counter, squinting along the way. Because every surface in this bookstore was painted white or beige, it actually seemed brighter inside the store than out. "I know, I know," Sunny laughed. "You need sunglasses in this place. Oh, bless you! Bless you!" she cried as she took the bag of corn chips and hid them below the counter. "These are my dinner."

As Sunny bent over I noticed a line drawing of Jesus Christ on the wall behind her. "Whoo," she said as she righted herself. "Lillian," she said to the white-haired woman, "this is—I didn't catch your name."

"Jaffe."

"Now, Jaffe, what can we do for you?"

"Me?"

I was suddenly struck with an urge to flee, but Sunny's attention on me remained steadfast. Her radiantly happy face was hard to leave.

"I was just—"

"Go ahead. Look around. Look around."

"I need to get going," I said.

"No, you don't!" We both giggled at Sunny's obvious statement of the truth. "Look around," she said. "Go ahead."

I turned my head from side to side without moving my feet. There seemed to be a lovely odor in the store.

"Is that incense?"

"Myrrh," Sunny said smiling. "We also have it in essential oils. Would you like to sample some?"

"No—no thanks."

I started to roam through the bookstore, glancing at titles. There were the usual Bibles: big Bibles, small Bibles, children's Bibles, teenagers' Bibles, and Bibles for the blind. There were the King James Bible, the Good News Bible, and Bibles in foreign tongues. Then there were self-help books labeled things like *What Are You Looking For?*, *Now That You Found Him*, and *Now That You Found Him—You May As Well Stop Looking*. A Hispanic woman reading *El Biblio* glanced at me and then quickly looked away, as did a backpacker carrying a knapsack the size of a tractor trailer who was browsing through a book about angels. I made my way down the aisles, not so much looking for something as avoiding any eye contact with the other people in the store.

One wall caught my eye. It was devoted to the writings of Dale Evans, who had been a star of a Western TV show back in the fifties, kind of like Lucy Ricardo with spurs. I picked up one of her books expecting some juicy show-biz gossip and found myself skimming through pages and pages of endless misery: cancerous children, organ failures, and the untimely death of her horse Buttercup. At the end of every chapter there was the inevitable passage in which she thanked Jesus for every injury and insult that had ever befallen her. Personally, I wasn't impressed, and I was about to flee the store when Sunny snuck up behind me and whispered (as though she could ever be inconspicuous), "I hope you don't mind my saying this, but you seem to be in a *lot* of spiritual pain."

She beamed happily as she sympathized, and I found this odd because the Jewish way of offering help is to make yourself look twice as miserable as the person in distress. Still, I couldn't help answering honestly. "Well . . . yes, I am."

"Could you use a hug?" she asked.

"Umm . . . yeah."

Then Sunny grabbed me tight and pulled me so close that she surrounded me on three sides. I was like a peninsula in a sea of warm milk. I tried to hug her back, but my arms were wedged tight against my sides somewhere between Sunny's oversized liver and her pancreas.

"Don't you feel better now?" Sunny asked.

"Yeah," I mumbled. Sunny let me go and I bounced away from her like a pilot suddenly ejected from a B-52 bomber.

"Would you like us to pray for you?"

"No thanks . . . I . . ."

By this point Lillian and several other patrons had moved closer. Sunny touched my hand reassuringly.

"Are you sure?"

There was something moist and nourishing about her touch. My resistance started to dissolve.

"If it's not too much trouble," I said.

With a nod from Sunny, Lillian quickly closed the venetian blinds on the store and several people crowded together. As well-choreographed as the Rockettes, they all made a circle and sank to their knees on the beige industrial carpet. I did the same.

"O Jesus," Sunny implored, "if you could only show this man just the smallest fraction of the joy you've brought into my life. Please, Jesus, don't let this man be unhappy." Then everyone else said, "Amen!" and one by one they threw in their spiritual two cents, showering me with prayers.

"Bless you, Jesus!" said the old woman.

"We love you, Jesus," said the man with the backpack.

"Dios mío," said the Hispanic woman.

And me? At first I did what every lonely person does when inundated with attention. I felt excruciatingly uncomfortable and patiently waited for it to be over. But then something happened. At first it happened in my body. From a kneeling position, the tension released from my legs and I slowly collapsed to the floor. Then my mind started to relax; my worries settled to the bottom of some vast inland sea, and as they did, the room started to glow. Some organic presence seemed to animate every shelf, every book, and every page of every book. It felt as though the light in the room were thickening into the consistency of golden honey. I closed my eyes and breathed, letting the sweet light pour down my throat.

"Praise Jesus!" Sunny said.

"Praise Jesus!" responded everyone else in the store.

"We're having a prayer meeting tonight at my home," Lillian whispered to me.

"What?" I said, bleary-eyed.

"Would you like to come?" she said.

I nodded my head, and before I left the store I made plans to meet Sunny and a few friends at six o'clock on the corner of Telegraph and Bancroft. She'd be driving me into the Berkeley hills to meet my personal savior.

When Anglos first struck gold in California the first thing they did was build their own personal San Simeons, loosely modeled upon the storybook castles they'd read about as children. That's why the indigenous architecture of California has always been so tacky; it's what you get when cash combines with fairy tales. Nowhere is this more apparent than the Berkeley hills, where you can find, on one block, the witch's cottage from Hansel and Gretel, Zorro's hacienda, and the Tower of London all staring suspiciously at each other from behind eucalyptus trees. Though delightful in themselves, these homes don't even attempt to cohere into anything like a neighborhood, so they leave the visitor feeling like he's arrived at a party where nobody knows anybody else.

At least that was my first impression the night Sunny drove me up there to meet Jesus. At 6:05 P.M. she hadn't arrived at the corner of

The King of Kings and I

Telegraph and Bancroft, and I was more than willing to go back to my cardboard box in People's Park; but at 6:06 a Volkswagen van pulled up beside me generously decorated with scripture. Sunny waved me in and introduced me to her friends Brad and Brent, two men in their thirties with identical thinning blond hair who owned a card shop in San Francisco. Could Brad and Brent have been gay? It was hard to tell, because neither one of them had any gay mannerisms. Actually, neither one of them had any mannerisms at all as long as Sunny dominated the conversation, telling me about all the tourist spots and restaurants in the Bay Area I couldn't afford to go to. Meanwhile the van groaned onward and upward into the hills with Sunny in the backseat for traction and me beside her, my palms sweating so profusely I could have developed stigmata. "Smile!" Sunny said gleefully. "Jesus *really* likes you a lot!"

Our destination was Lillian's house, which, even by Berkeley's standards, was pretty eccentric. Lillian lived in a Greek temple. Her mother, a wealthy heiress, had been a disciple of Isadora Duncan, and she'd built a two-story shrine to Terpsichore, high on a ridge with a view of San Francisco Bay. This impressive marble structure, unfortunately, had never been insulated for twentieth-century habitation, so, like many buildings in Berkeley, it was far colder inside than out. Sunny had warned me to bring a sweater.

We parked the van and walked across a large lawn that, sixty years previously, had hosted modern-dance recitals starring Ms. Duncan and a flock of young girls running around trailing translucent white fabric. Approaching the temple, we walked between two pillars and entered an enclosed courtyard that had been converted into a living room. Though not exactly lit by torches, it had high plaster walls and columns that made it look like a miniature Parthenon or the set for *Quo Vadis*. The furniture had been pushed aside, allowing fifty people to assemble, mostly seated on pillows needlepointed with biblical quotations. One look at this group and I seriously doubted that any chiffon would be flung that night.

This was the palest group of people I'd ever seen; it was like a cousins' meeting in Finland. Everyone there resembled Brad and Brent, with wispy hair, white skin, and pinkish noses. They were like people crossbred with Easter bunnies. Sunny, who seemed to know everyone in sight, walked right up to the front of the room and sat down on a large pillow. Somehow I managed to escape her clutches, found a folding chair, and set it up in the back of the room within sight of the exit. Seated next to me was an older man in a powder blue leisure suit, flipping through a well-worn Bible with his lips moving. On my other side were two blond tykes playing patty-cake to the tune of "Jesus Loves Me, This I Know."

A few minutes later the group leaders arrived, Sheila and Bob, an outgoing husband-and-wife team, a kind of Pentecostal Steve Lawrence and Eydie Gormé. Bob started talking as soon as he entered the room, but he rarely got a chance to finish his sentences because Sheila, who wore a bright blue jump suit, an armload of bracelets, and more makeup than all the other women in the room combined, would inevitably dig her bright red nails into his shoulder, pulling him back and herself forward.

"Sorry we're late!" Bob said as he scurried to his seat in the front of the room. "Sheila's mother called as we left the house."

"Let me tell them!" Sheila exclaimed as she jumped in front of Bob. "Nothing serious. I just couldn't get her off the phone."

"She just doesn't understand. Her problems are not psychological—"

"They are—" Sheila said, yanking the words out of Bob's mouth and then cupping her hand to one ear to better hear the audience's response. "Spiritual!" she and several others concluded. Then the rest of the audience cried, "Amen."

Bob and Sheila settled into their chairs. "Before we get started," Bob asked, "is there anybody new here tonight?"

Sunny twisted her head around to find me. I sunk down into my seat. Luckily a man on the opposite side of the room stood up awkwardly, and the crowd applauded. "Thank you for coming, brother," Bob said. "Now, are there any testimonials?" A young woman sitting next to Sunny wearing pink culottes raised her hand and stood slowly. She'd obviously been struggling hard over the decision to talk in front of the group.

"My name is Andrea," she said, "and I've been a Christian for about three years."

"Amen," said the group.

"And this is my husband, Jim. We've been married six months."

An embarrassed young man on her other side waved his fingers at the group. Andrea giggled, clutched her fist to her bosom, and continued.

"I've always known that you could pray to Jesus for the large things—you know, for world peace and like when my father got sick and . . . well . . . But I never knew that Jesus would help me in little things . . . Well, it wasn't really a little thing to me but—this is so embarrassing!"

Jim reached up and grabbed his wife's hand. Andrea turned to him pleadingly, "Is it OK if I tell them, honey?"

"Praise Jesus," Jim said, nodding his head and smiling.

Andrea continued, "Well, my husband always used to wear this, well—this really ugly baseball hat for the Chicago Cubs because that's where he's from. And me . . . I always hated it. It was this ugly shade of blue and torn in the back and . . . and I always wanted him to take it off, but I never told him because I always felt like . . . you know . . . 'Judge not lest ye yourself be judged,' so I prayed for guidance and . . ." Andrea stopped to catch her breath.

"You could have spoken to me," Jim told her softly.

A tear welled up in Andrea's eye. Jim stroked her forearm gently. Sunny and several other women wept quietly as Andrea turned to Jim and said, "I'm sorry. I just didn't feel I had the right."

"You did," Jim reassured her.

Sunny blew her nose as Andrea finished her story.

"And then one day—praise Jesus—I came home and it was a miracle because . . ." The whole audience leaned in for the punch line. "Jim wasn't wearing the baseball cap!"

The whole audience applauded as if Pavarotti had just concluded an aria or Elizabeth Taylor had just stepped out onstage at the Oscars.

"And he hasn't worn it ever since. Jesus answered my prayers!"

"Aww, honey," Jim said as he stood up and hugged his wife.

"Praise Jesus!" Sunny cried out as she wiped another tear from her eye. "Amen," said scattered individuals in the crowd—quite automatically, like "Gesundheit"s after a sneeze or "L'chaim"s before downing a shot of whiskey. Andrea sat down, and Bob stood up and thanked her. Meanwhile I calculated the distance between myself and the back door and divided it by how fast I could run.

"Anyone else want to give testimony?" Bob asked. From behind him two sets of red fingernails encircled his shoulder.

"Actually, I would like to say something," said Sheila. The crowd oohed. Apparently Sheila had earned quite a reputation as a preacher. At a deliberately slow pace, Sheila took center stage and the audience settled back; they knew they were in for a treat.

"Thank you, Andrea," Sheila began in a whisper that was almost drowned out by the jangling of her bracelets. "No problem is too small that it escapes Jesus' eye, for He truly loves us as you and Jim, no doubt, love each other." Jim put his arm around Andrea and the whole crowd applauded. Sheila, not to be outdone by a mere amateur, reached behind herself and grabbed Bob's hand; he kissed hers sweetly, much to the pleasure of the crowd, which murmured its appreciation.

"You know," Sheila continued, "I was thinking as Bob and I were driving up the hill to this beautiful temple of the Lord—and once again, thank you, Lillian, for opening your house to us this week."

"Praise Jesus," said Lillian.

"Amen," echoed the crowd.

"I was thinking about my mother," Sheila continued, "and why she hasn't found her faith in Jesus. With so much love to give, why can't my mother just reach out and grab it? We all know how powerful the love of God is. What keeps her from coming to Jesus? And—praise the Lord—the answer came to me. Maybe my mother just doesn't want Jesus *badly* enough. Oh, yes, my mother suffers! She has her ex-husbands, she has taxes to pay. But what she doesn't have is that knowledge that life can be *so* much better. And it's that knowledge, the knowledge that life can be better, without a way to make it better—that's what *really* hurts. It's what we all felt before we came to Him."

A smattering of amens inspired Sheila to raise her pitch ever so slightly. "Haven't we all felt that?" she cried. "Who here has felt that agony? Who? Raise your hands." Just about everyone in the room raised their hands. Without thinking I raised one finger. Sheila smiled. She was on a roll now, and her voice got louder and louder. "We are the lucky ones because we felt that pain. We wanted Jesus as badly as we wanted to breathe. We wanted Jesus like our heads were being held underwater and we were gasping for air!" Sheila paused. "Amen," said a man in the back row next to me. Sheila shook her head and lowered her voice to a whisper. "The pain of separation from God. That was the pain that Jesus felt when He was on the cross."

Just then Bob jumped up. He couldn't hold in his feelings any longer. "Before we go any further," he said, "can we just pray for Sheila's mother? Let's bring Sheila's mother to Jesus by praying she feels some of the pain that Christ felt when he was on the cross." Everyone closed their eyes to pray. So I closed my eyes too. I prayed for Sheila's mother to feel some of Jesus' pain. Nothing major—a touch of arthritis, some cramps. But after a few moments I started to feel ridiculous. I was halfway out of my seat when Bob interrupted.

"Thank you all very much," said Bob. "Thank you, Sheila."

Sheila sat back down.

"And now let us all pray together, and when you feel the Holy

Spirit I want you to raise your hand high. Can you all do that? Can you raise your hand high?"

Then everybody closed their eyes to pray again, but I defiantly kept mine open. I felt restless and irritated. I wanted to leave while everyone's eyes were closed, and I might have done so had it not been for a thick wave of sadness that oozed over me like a mud slide, smothering me as it held me in place. I examined the crowd. "Look at them," I thought to myself. "Sunny, Lillian, Sheila, Bob, Andrea, Jim—they may be out of their minds, but at least they have each other. They have homes to return to. They also have the one thing I want most. Faith." I scanned the concrete walls of the room, the pillars and the columns, which all suggested the dramatically stark time of Jesus himself. Would he come if I called him? Would he enter this room so reminiscent of Pontius Pilate's summer house? Maybe he would. I closed my eyes and started singing the Lord's Prayer, barely whispering, like Claudine Longet singing "Silent Night" on some long-forgotten *Andy Williams Show*. "Our father who art in heaven, hallowed be thy name. Thy kingdom come, thy will be done . . ."

And that's when I saw Jesus.

At first he appeared in a blue light somewhere between my mind and the wall in front of me. It was him all right. He was the Jesus from Debbi McDermott's wall, Saint Martin's Church, that brochure in Tucson. He was the Jesus from *The Aquarian Gospel*. He looked just as I'd expected him to look. In that regard, at least, I wasn't surprised. "I've been waiting for you," he said telepathically. I gasped. Then the blue light started getting bigger and bigger. Jesus was coming toward me, getting closer and closer, like a freight train. I panicked. I was being run over by Jesus! I jumped out of my seat and started waving my hand. "I see him! I see him!"

And I thought everyone would be raising their hands too, but I was the only one. Bob yelled out to me, "You, sir. In the back."

"Who, me?" I cried.

"You, sir," Bob repeated. "What's your name?"

"Mine?" I stammered. "I'm . . . I'm . . . I really don't belong here. I'm from New York. I'll just wait in the car. Why don't you all just go back to what you were doing?" I grabbed my sweater and started weaving my way through the parishioners seated on the floor. Just then Sheila opened her eyes and started pulling on her husband's jacket. "Who are you talking to?" she asked.

"You, sir!" Bob yelled again.

"What's he doing?" I heard Sheila ask.

"Would you like us to pray for you, sir?" Bob asked.

"No thanks," I called back. "I'd rather pray by myself. Don't get me wrong!" I cried. "You all seem like very warm people." Near the exit I tripped over a kid. He fell into a man's arms, and a crucifix fell to the floor. Now I was really in trouble. "I'll . . . I'll pay for that tchotchke!" I called over my shoulder as I ran out the door.

Picking up my pace, I stumbled across the lawn. Nobody seemed to be following me. As I reached the street I stopped. "Maybe you should go back in there," I thought. "You're being very rude to these people." I pivoted and started walking back. "Who cares what these people think? Just walk home!" I turned again toward the road. Below me the lights from the Bay Bridge were twinkling, and the air was drenched with the smell of eucalyptus. I was in California! Damn it, I couldn't just walk home! "What should I do?" I asked myself. "Just get your stuff from the van and run to the highway. If you start hitchhiking now, you might get to Utah before sunrise." Through the corner of my eye I could now see Sunny zipping across the lawn toward me, surprisingly quick, like a sofa bed on wheels. "Oh, shit, now I'm in trouble," I thought as I started running toward the van.

"But wait!" I said to myself with one hand on the door handle. "Why are you trying to escape? You saw him! You really saw him! He had the hair and the beard and that Jesus look on his face. Where can you go? If he's real, anyplace else you go for the rest of your life will be a living hell." I suddenly sank to my knees and exclaimed, "I give up!" The next thing I knew Sunny had scooped me up in her arms and once again I was smothered in corduroy.

"I saw him! I saw him!" I cried.

"Well, hallelujah," Sunny laughed.

"No, you don't understand," I whimpered. "I never wanted to be a Christian. I just wanted to be a little less miserable!"

"Blessed are the pure in spirit, for they shall see God!"

By this time Brad, Brent, and Lillian were kneeling beside us. Then Bob came out, followed by Sheila, and everybody seemed to hug everyone else while I sank deeper and deeper into Sunny's bosom.

Eventually someone helped me to my feet and walked me back inside. I apologized for making such a fuss, but Brent assured me, "These psychotic episodes are really quite common around here." I took a seat next to Sunny, who held my hand for the next few hours. The prayer meeting continued uneventfully. I wasn't thrilled by Sheila's reading from Scripture. Nor was I completely bored by the endless discussion of a bake sale to raise money for someone's motorized wheelchair. The truth is, I must have been in complete shock, because the next thing I clearly remember was a few hours later. The prayer group had ended, and Brad and Brent had taken us to the new McDonald's on the corner of Shattuck and Hearst.

Sunny had insisted we stop to eat at the bottom of the hill, and because it was Friday, we all ordered the exact same thing: fish-fillet sandwiches. Brent found a table near the window, and I was just about to rip open my cardboard box when my new friends all bowed their heads and said grace. Then there were hands on the table. There was one to my left and one to my right. I automatically grabbed them both and bowed my head; I'll never forget. There were no fireworks and no startling visuals, but *that* was the moment. It was that second when I very calmly completed the circle that I realized that, sometime that night, I had actually become a Christian. Hallelujah!

CHAPTER 4

Godspell!

A few weeks ago, late at night, I misplaced the keys to my apartment and was forced to wait an hour in the lobby of my building for a locksmith. Even though I was feeling tired and foul, I managed to speak a few perky syllables to the new night doorman, an impeccably dressed young man suffering from his own terminal case of boredom. We quickly unburdened our souls. He told me he was a devout Christian from Missouri, read the Bible daily, and based his core beliefs on the New Testament. I told him I'd been a devout Christian for a total of nineteen days, never read the Bible anymore, and based my core beliefs on Vedic philosophy, Marxist economic theories, and the movie reviews in *Entertainment Weekly*.

He was clever, attentive, and candid; and I think we both felt genuinely at ease with each other—so much so that I had no trouble telling him he was unworldly and a menace to society, and he hadn't the slightest qualm informing me I was being deceived by Satan. In due time the locksmith arrived, jimmied my door open with a credit card, and the doorman and I promised to continue our conversation at a later date. I haven't seen him since and I sincerely hope he's found more congenial employment.

Now there may be many people reading this book—gays and Jews, especially—who have been similarly demonized by well-meaning Christians and now feel creeped out by anything even remotely related to Jesus' name. I know how you feel. I have a similar reaction to the Disney Corporation. You therefore may want to put this book down for a little while, have a cup of coffee and watch a *Seinfeld* re-run. The next few chapters won't be pretty. If, on the other hand, you're not completely horrified by Christianity and have some interest in my perpetual struggle to *not* throw the baby Jesus out with the scriptural bathwater, you'll probably want to forge ahead.

In any event, the morning after my epiphany in the Berkeley hills, I woke up on Sunny's sun porch with the strangest sensation: I wasn't alone anymore. There were two of us now! There were two of us sneaking outside. There were two of us counting our change to buy a corn muffin from a street vendor. There were two of us cutting across campus and waving good morning to the students going off to their classes in chemistry, anthropology, and modern dance. And I wasn't the least bit envious of them as I'd been the day before. I simply wanted to stop them and tell them that they were wasting their time. They didn't need Science. They didn't need Art. All they needed was what I had in my heart. I felt so blessed and pure; I was like Jennifer Jones in *The Song of Bernadette* and I wanted to tell the world, "But I *did* see him. I did! I did!"

That afternoon Lillian drove down the hill to discuss with Sunny the next phase of my life as a Christian. We all agreed that I needed fellowship in order for my faith to grow. Normally I might have stayed at Sunny's house, but Sunny's lease was up in a few days and she was already packing to move to Oakland. Also Lillian might have put me up at the temple, but her grandchildren were coming to visit; so after praying for guidance, we all concluded that Jesus prevailed even on Long Island and it would now be perfectly safe for me to return home. I agreed, believing, without a doubt, that I might bring the Lord to my family and friends.

Was I totally demented? Did I really think I was going to convert my agnostic mother to Christianity, a woman who had never worshiped anything except a good London broil and her collection of Harry Belafonte records? Did I really think that Ira was going to give up singing Sondheim and start belting "Ave Maria"? Once again I have to plead innocence. All this Jesus frenzy was very new to me. I had never met anyone in Brooklyn or Long Island who took the New Testament seriously. Until my first trip out west, I'd believed that literal faith in Christ had gone out with the Spanish Inquisition. Maybe if I'd been raised where Fundamentalists were common I might have developed some immunity. As it was, I was as helpless in Sunny's warmhearted clutches as Pocahontas was the first time she encountered smallpox.

Even more important, something monumental had happened: I'd seen Jesus, and for the first time since leaving Brooklyn I felt at home in the cosmos. In addition, there were the miracles, the chance meetings, the sudden feelings of rapture—which, in retrospect, may have been no more miraculous than Andrea's husband taking off his Chicago Cubs baseball cap. At the time, though, they reinforced a sense of being cared for by the universe, and even today I'm hesitant to deny that my life has never been the same. Something did happen.

The miracles began the day I left. Sunny drove me back to People's Park to say good-bye to Scotty, but he was nowhere to be found. Then we stopped at the bookstore, where Sunny gave me a brand-new Good News Bible. Later, at the entrance ramp to Route 80, we prayed for safe passage, Sunny drove away, and I held up a little sign reading NEW YORK. For several hours nobody stopped, and I began to feel that the fickle universe was done with me. But, just when I was about to lose faith, a dusty old Plymouth stopped with a young couple and a laminated picture of the Lord hanging from the rearview mirror. "Welcome, brother," they said to me as I jumped in the back seat, and then they drove me all the way to Colorado.

In Denver I spent the night off Colfax Avenue, and the next morning I hit the road again. Once again my faith was tested at the entrance ramp, and once again Jesus aced the exam. At first, all the praying in the world couldn't make a car stop. But just as I was about to throw my Bible in front of a truck, a bearded fellow traveler walked up to me and asked, "Are you a Christian?" Hesitantly, I said I was. "Ain't that something," he announced, "'cause so am I!" Then he pulled me down on the ground to pray, and within seconds another car stopped. It was a Mormon driving all the way to Toledo, Ohio, for a gospel competition.

And thus I made it across the country in record time, meeting one true believer after another. Maybe they'd been there all along, but until that week I had no idea how many Christians there were in this great country of ours. All the gas-station attendants, all the waitresses and motel clerks—they all were all servicing Jesus, and so was I! America was *my* country now. I was safe. And as I got closer and closer to New York City, despite the soggy gray heat, I truly believed that I would never again lose that expansive sense of inclusion.

In Hoboken, New Jersey, I called my parents at home, then got on a PATH train to Penn Station, where I changed to the Long Island Railroad. It was a Friday night; the air conditioning in the car had broken down, and there were many tired commuters fanning themselves with their timetables. Jamaica. New Hyde Park. Mineola. Carle Place. Westbury. Hicksville. It was just before sunset when I got to Bethpage. My father wasn't there. "Thank you, Jesus," I whispered to myself, "for giving me this time to collect my thoughts." I scanned the very familiar hometown horizon: the Carvel store, the Esso station, Grumman Aircraft. Across the street, there was a sad row of miniature Cape Cods as plain as the houses on a Monopoly board. These low-cost homes were inhabited by marginal suburbanites, senior citizens like old Mrs. Potts, too frail to walk to church, and lonely drinkers who wanted to live near Doogan's Bar, which catered mostly to wet-eyed commuters who belted down whiskey before going home to face their families. I noticed everything I would have noticed without Jesus in my heart, only now it couldn't hurt me. Bethpage—praise the Lord—wasn't really my home any longer. It was just another town in desperate need of salvation.

I closed my eyes to envision seeing my parents again. My dad I imagined would take one look at me and fall down with amazement. Of the two of them, he seemed the more susceptible to inspiration. I needed only to choose just the right moment. I had to be careful not to blow my spiritual wad indiscriminately, because Sunny had warned me that if one knows about Jesus and still rejects him, one's punishment is twice as severe. I heard a car horn honking and opened my eyes. It wasn't my father but my mother, driving the family Rambler in her usual manner. She lurched to a stop twenty feet from the curb, started moving again, and then halted abruptly ten feet nearer her goal.

As I walked toward the car I noticed my father's bumper stickers; there were even more than I remembered. In fact, the rear fender had more Hebrew lettering than the average Orthodox prayer book, and there was one in particular that I hadn't noticed before: THE NEW TESTAMENT—IT'S NEITHER NEW NOR TRUE! I took a deep breath; I was ready for the challenge.

"Well," my mother said as I threw my knapsack into the trunk, "the prodigal son has returned! Let me look at you."

I climbed into the passenger seat and my mother lurched the car forward. "You look terrible," she said as we started home at seven miles an hour.

"Really?" I thought I looked pretty good.

"The beard," she grimaced. "You look like my father's brother Chaim Meyer." The previous year my mother had begun restoring pictures of her ancestors and displaying them in every room of the house. When she said I looked like her uncle, she was referring to a particularly hideous brown photograph hanging in the laundry room next to the bleach.

"So how was your trip?" she asked, trying to change the subject.

"Amazing!" I said, trying to sound both effusive and vague.

"Amazing?" My mother , like many Jewish women of her generation, had no idea how to respond to such unadulterated positivity. I revised my assessment.

"I mean, interesting."

"Really? Did you meet any interesting people?"

The name of Jesus came to mind. I struggled with the impulse to blurt it out.

"I met . . . one interesting person."

"Really?" my mother asked innocently. "Anyone I know?"

"Well . . ." I said, beginning to broach the subject but not quite sure the timing was right.

"Well, what?" my mother said impatiently. At this point we entered our development and stopped at a stop sign. As sometimes happens, my mother just sat there for a moment with her foot on the brake.

"You can go, by the way," I told her. "The stop sign's not going to turn green."

"Don't be smart," she said as she stepped on the gas, and we lurched forward. Unfortunately, she didn't look where she was going and another car screeched to a halt only a few inches from where I was sitting.

"Watch out!" I cried.

The King of Kings and I

The other driver pulled away, cursing at us vehemently. Luckily our windows were closed and we couldn't hear what he was saying, although a lip reader would surely have blanched from the vulgarity. My mother apologized.

"Sorry about that, kid."

"That's OK," I said, nearly choking on my left ventricle. The near-accident was my sign from God. I would refrain from talking about Jesus for the time being. My mother obviously needed to concentrate on her driving, and much as I wanted to tell her about heaven, I was in no particular rush to get there. We got through the next few stop signs without incident.

"Where's Dad, by the way?" I asked as we turned the corner onto our block.

"Don't ask. He doesn't drive on Shabbos anymore."

"Really . . . Since when?"

"Since he found out it annoyed me. Don't be surprised when he ropes you into lighting Shabbos candles."

"You don't sound thrilled about it."

"We had a big fight last night. It was so ridiculous. Last night we were having dinner again with the Zimmetbaums at Hunan Pao's. Anyway, on top of everything else your father's completely kosher now—well, almost completely—"

We pulled into our driveway. As usual, expressing her opinion was my mother's priority, so she finished her sentence before turning off the ignition.

"So I ordered a lobster," she said, "and he was sitting there with a puss on his face, so I said, 'What's the matter?' and he said, 'God looked down on the Jews in the Sinai and told them not to eat shell-fish.' So I said, 'Jack, you find a lobster in the desert and I'm not going to eat it either.' Anyway, he got very upset."

"Those are his beliefs," I said soothingly.

"Well, I don't want to hear about them," my mother replied. "I've

161

got enough trouble with Rachel's bat mitzvah. I don't need to hear about religion."

With that she unbuckled her seat belt, reached down, and turned off the engine. "Anyway," she said, "it's good to have you home safe. You can tell me later about who you met on your trip."

We both got out of the car and approached the house.

"And by the way," she added as I opened the screen door, "you may want to stay off the subject of Bernie."

"What did he do?"

"He thinks we don't know he's a pothead." At the door my mother screamed inside, "Jack, we're home!"

"What took you so long?" my father screamed back. "It's almost sunset."

My mother looked at me and shook her head: "Oy." At which point I knew that my task would be trickier than I'd thought. It was very important not to cast any pearls before swine—especially if one of the swine was trying to keep kosher.

It's about time you got here," my father said before I even had time to throw my pack on the floor. He pulled me toward him and planted a kiss on my cheek. "It's good to see you, son," he said with all sincerity. My father's eyes always lit up at the sight of any of his children—a good quality in a parent, although I would have preferred he call me by name rather than title.

"Rachel!" he yelled.

"What?" my twelve-year-old sister screamed from her bedroom on the next landing of our split-level house.

"Shabbos candles!" my father yelled. "And come say hello to your brother."

"I'm watching *The Partridge Family*." Then, after a pause, she yelled, "Hello, Jaffe!"

"Hello!" I yelled back.

The King of Kings and I

"Come on," my mother said, clearing off the dining-room table. "Let's get this over with."

My father shook his head with disgust. Then, pulling two yarmulkes out of a drawer in the china cabinet, he gave one to me and placed the other on his own head. My mother then yanked two candle holders from a shelf along with two white candles; she placed them on the table with all the care one might use to stack yesterday's newspapers. "Turn the lights off," my father told her. My mother flicked off the light switch and then slipped into the kitchen to wash a few dishes before Rachel showed up. My father, meanwhile, studied a prayer book.

"When my father died," he said without looking up, "I didn't even know enough Hebrew to say the Mourner's Kaddish. Now I can read most of this. I can't understand a word of it, but I can read it."

"That's great, Dad."

"So how was your trip? Did you find what you were looking for? Did you find inner happiness?" His lips curled downward on the word *happiness*. I decided to ignore his sarcasm.

"Maybe," I said coyly.

"Rachel!" my father yelled just as my sister clumped down the stairs.

"Quit yelling!" she yelled back.

My sister was carrying a food tray on which sat an empty can of Tab, a box of saltines, and a half-eaten Pop-Tart.

"Hurry up," she said as she carried the tray into the kitchen, where my mother was still washing dishes. "It's a commercial."

"How you doing?" I called after her, not expecting much of an answer.

"Shitty," she replied over her shoulder.

"Roz, let's get started." Without missing a beat my mother turned off the faucet and walked up to the table with her arms crossed defiantly, the dish towel hanging from her moist knuckles.

"Aren't you going to cover your head?" my father asked, barely trying to sound polite.

Without saying a word my mother brusquely tossed the damp towel over her head like a shawl. My father didn't pick up on the challenge; he was saving his breath for a battle he was more likely to win.

"Rachel?" he asked coldly.

"What?" she replied sullenly.

"Your head."

Like mother, like daughter. Rachel reached behind her and threw up the hood of her ratty sweatshirt, nearly obscuring her face.

"OK," my father said. "Now we're ready."

My father lit a match and began to recite in English, "Remember the Sabbath day and keep it holy. Six days you shall labor and do all your work; and the seventh day is the Sabbath. You shall not do any work; you, nor your son, nor your daughter . . ."

"Jaffe, where are you sleeping tonight?" Rachel whispered to me.

"My room," I whispered back.

"You can't," she said.

My father continued to drone, ". . . nor your manservant nor your maidservant . . ."

"Why not?" I asked.

"Mom moved your bed into the basement."

". . . nor the stranger within your gates . . ."

"Shh," my mother said. "Maybe he can sleep in your room."

"Would you please shut up!" my father finally hissed.

"I'm not giving up my room!" my sister snarled.

"Shut up! Shut up! Shut!" my father screamed, losing control. Rachel threw down her hood and stomped out of the room.

"This really sucks!" she grumbled.

"Rachel!" my father yelled. Then we were all quiet, listening for her bedroom door to slam shut. Sure enough, the sound reverberated throughout the house like gunshot.

The King of Kings and I

"Let her be," my mother grunted. My father closed his eyes and counted to ten—probably in awkward Hebrew—as my mother explained to me, "She wanted to go roller-skating tonight but . . ." She pointed at my dad, who opened his eyes and announced, "Let's continue." Then he cleared his throat and recited, as though nothing had happened, "For in six days the Lord created the Heaven, the Earth, the Sea, and all that is in them; therefore the Lord blessed the seventh day and made it holy."

Then my father read haltingly, *"Boruch atoh adonai elohenu melech hoolom . . ."* And when he was done with the blessing, he struck a long kitchen match and handed it to my mother, who reluctantly lit the candles, which she nearly extinguished with one of her disgruntled sighs. This done, my father said the blessing over the wine, ending with *"Borei pree hagofen."* My mother said, "Amen," hastily threw back some table wine from a cheap Flintstones glass, and then went back to the kitchen to heat up two leftover skirt steaks. I, too, downed a glass of Manischewitz, hoping to get a nice relaxing buzz and wondering whether the problem with my family was that we didn't drink *nearly* enough.

Parents' ideas of who their children are grow at about one-third the rate of actual earth time. Accordingly, a young man of twenty will be perceived as going on seven. If our parents live to see our sixtieth birthday, they may just be getting the idea that we're not teenagers anymore. Another way to understand this perceptual lag is to think of astronomers looking at stars in distant galaxies. Apparently these celestial orbs burn out light-years before we get a glimpse of them. Similarly, parents look at their children and see little people who no longer exist. The major difference is that astronomers are far away from their objects, whereas parents are way too close to appreciate what they're seeing. In 1973, after having a vision of Jesus, I thought my mother and father would automatically witness the change in me. I see now that this never could have happened.

After we lit the candles Rachel walked to a friend's house, my father went upstairs to relax, and I sat down to plan my strategy. I had forgotten how draining it was to be breathing the same air I breathed as a child, and with each inhalation I seemed to lose an inch of height and a year's worth of hard-earned confidence. "Jesus, don't fail me now," I prayed as I followed my mother into the kitchen; she was standing over the stove with a box of table salt in her hands.

"How do you want your skirt steak done?" she said as she sprinkled enough sodium on the meat to melt the polar ice cap.

"I don't eat meat."

"Since when?"

"I haven't eaten meat since high school."

"So what are you going to eat?"

"I'll find something . . ."

The steaks sizzled in the pan. More than ever I wanted to rescue my mother from the kitchen, from the house she'd never liked, from the neighborhood filled with goyim, from the four walls of her rational mind. I wanted to introduce her to the wonderment of a personal relationship with the creator of the universe.

"Mom?"

"What, dear?"

It was now or never.

"You remember how I used to feel so empty inside?"

"It's because you never got enough protein," she replied sourly. "Look on the second shelf in the refrigerator. I brought home some leftover shrimp and lobster sauce. Eat it quick before your father finds out it's in the house."

"Mom, there's another reason I felt empty."

"What's that?" my mother asked as she flipped the steaks.

"Well—"

The King of Kings and I

Before I could say another word my father called my name from upstairs in his bedroom, where he had gone to relax.

"Go see what your father wants."

"Can we talk later?"

"Where am I going?" she said.

I kissed my mother on the cheek and started up the stairs for my parents' bedroom, where my father, laid out on his overstuffed mattress, generally held court like a medieval pope. I stopped midway to pray for strength and then entered the inner sanctum, where my father was propped up on pillows like Gregory VI, reading *This Is My God* by Herman Wouk and watching *Jeopardy* with the sound turned off. I sat at the foot of the bed, knowing why I was there: my father wanted to get something off his chest and dump it onto mine.

He smiled delightedly when I entered: he had an audience. I'd learned years earlier that one never conversed with Dad, one merely wandered into his interior monologue and hunkered down for the duration. I quickly sized up his mood: his bushy eyebrows were furrowed dramatically; he chuckled sardonically to himself. Tonight my father would start by playing the role of the aggrieved patriarch. "I don't understand Jews like your mother," he said before I'd even settled into position. "They go to services on the High Holy Days but won't keep the Sabbath! Nowhere in the Ten Commandments does it say anything about Rosh Hashanah. But commandment number four—keep the Sabbath!"

There was a slight pause while my father momentarily considered the possibility that his performance wasn't eliciting a response. I was, after all, the dutiful son of the woman he was raking over the coals. Shifting roles, he went from aggrieved patriarch to generous dispenser of wisdom.

"Did you know, of the Ten Commandments, there are only three commands. The rest are prohibitions." My father paused. That was my cue to respond.

"No, Dad, I didn't know that."

"Do you know what they are?"

"No, Dad, I don't."

"Keep the Sabbath, worship one God, and honor thy father and mother—something your sister should learn. It's funny . . ."

My father chuckled to himself and filled his lungs in preparation for an even longer speech. "It doesn't say in the Bible, 'Honor thy children.' Do you know why?"

"No, Dad."

"Because that's natural. Parents automatically love their children. God created us to nurture and feel affection for our offspring. It's good to see you, Bernie."

"Jaffe—"

"Jaffe," my father quickly corrected himself. "Sorry, son." A small light flickered in his eyes. There had been something he'd wanted to tell me personally, and now he was starting to remember what it was.

"So, Jaffe," he said, "you say you found inner happiness out west."

Could it be true? Was my father about to bring up the subject I'd wanted to broach myself? I braced myself for my father's conversion.

"Yes, Dad, I did. I did find happiness."

"Hmm." My father grew thoughtful for a moment.

"I found . . ." I paused for dramatic effect.

"So what did you find?"

"I found—"

But before I could finish my sentence my father interrupted.

"Do you know what *my* definition of happiness is?" he asked. "My definition of happiness is knowing *who* you are."

"Dad, please—"

"And what you are . . . is a Jew."

"Dad, you asked me what I found—"

"And even if you don't believe you're a Jew, they will!"

"Forget it," I said.

The King of Kings and I

"Remember the six million!" my father cried.

I sighed deeply. My cause was now hopeless. I'd been too slow. I hadn't made my case for Christ before he'd gotten onto the subject of Hitler. There'd be no stopping him now. For the next few minutes my father lectured me about atrocities, none of which I wasn't aware of. In 1973 my father's obsession with the Holocaust was still relatively new. In the years to come, it would only grow, until the physical survival of the Jews would become his *only* concern. He would read every book, patronize every exhibit, and devour every documentary he could find on the subject. In some strange way it would become his only joy in life. In the meantime, I had to retreat and recoup my energies. I checked my wrist as though I were wearing a watch.

"Dad, I'm going to go lie down for a while. I feel like I have jet lag."

My father looked at me, confused.

"I thought you came home by car."

"Culture shock—something—I don't know."

"We'll continue talking later." He smiled as he reburied himself in his book.

I went to my bedroom to lie down and restrategize. Unfortunately, Rachel had been correct. My mother had converted my old room into a "sewing room," which is suburbanese for any bedroom from where a child has gone to college and the bed's been yanked out. I lay down on the floor and turned off the lights. I tried to figure out why I'd come home. Closing my eyes, I wanted to feel Christ's presence. There was a slight breeze from the window and the delightful smell of freshly mowed lawn. Could that have been him? Within moments I was asleep on the shag rug.

I woke up in the middle of the night disoriented and thinking for a moment that I was still in Berkeley. Again I felt like there were two of us. I looked around me and recognized my physical surroundings, but I couldn't actually feel like I was home. I was merely lying on the floor in a house where I'd spent a good deal of time as a child. This feeling of dislocation was strangely liberating. I got up. Realizing how late it was, I tiptoed down to the kitchen like a hunter stalking his prey. I was going after big game, and I found her at the dining-room table playing solitaire in the middle of the night. Having no desire to sleep, she'd been lingering over her game, playing it the slow way: dealing three cards at a time and only using the third. I sat down beside her, put my arm on the back of her chair, and looked over her shoulder.

"I thought you were sleeping," my mother said.

"I woke up. Red queen," I said.

My mother peered over her glasses to see what I'd seen.

"Where?" she asked.

I picked the card from the pile and moved it to where it would do the most good.

"Thank you."

"Can I ask you a question?"

"Sure."

"Were you angry at me before?"

"When?"

"Before. In the kitchen. You didn't want to talk."

"I was angry at the world. You just happened to be there."

"Black eight," I suggested.

Without having to ask, my mother knew which card I meant and where it had to go. Now we were in synch. I might have brought up the subject of Jesus, but I still wasn't ready for such a direct approach.

"Why does it bother you that Dad wants to light Shabbos candles?"

My mother continued to play without looking up.

"Why does it bother me? It bothers me because—" She stopped, stretched her neck, and looked at the ceiling.

"It doesn't bother me he wants to light candles. If you want to light candles, light candles. It bothers me that he's not happy unless I want to light candles also. It bothers me he doesn't leave me alone. That's what bothers me."

"Oh."

She was in a tough mood. I would need to soften her up a bit.

"You looking forward to the bat mitzvah?"

"Looking forward? No. Happy to get it over with? Yes."

"You're a bundle of joy," I said sarcastically.

"Do you have any idea how hard it is to bat mitzvah a girl who doesn't want to?"

"So it was all Dad's idea?"

"Who else? And guess who gets stuck doing all the work?"

"So, don't do it."

My mother looked me in the eyes as if to say, "You must be joking." I gave her a look back saying, "Why not?" She sighed. My last question, even without being spoken, was too difficult to answer.

"Red seven," I said.

My mother continued to play solitaire. Again I watched her carefully, mesmerized by her total concentration. Of all the people in our family, she was the only one who had the power to do one thing at a time without being bored. When she sliced cucumbers, she sliced cucumbers. When she put in a wash, she put in a wash. She was a woman of action who, in her best moments, really enjoyed the simple things in life like cloud formations or sucking on a chicken bone until it dissolved in her mouth. It's not that she never asked herself the big questions, it's just that these philosophical inquiries sounded in her mind like a radio playing next door or a bluebird tweeting in a distant tree; and if you asked my mother what she was doing while she was wondering about the existence of God, she'd always answer that she was making a salad or doing laundry. Those were her priorities.

"Mom," I asked, "do you believe in God?"

"In the traditional sense, I'd have to say it depends on what day you asked me."

"Would you like to believe in God more often?"

"Sure, and I've always been envious of people who could."

"You could if you wanted. Black nine."

My mother looked where I was pointing and shifted a column of cards. She said, "You know the real reason I'm angry at Dad for lighting Shabbos candles? I'm angry because your father is a person who all his life has wanted to find easy answers. There are *no* easy answers in life. I don't see the sense of ritual and I never will."

"Never?"

"I shouldn't exaggerate. Probably never."

My mother surveyed the table. She'd been dealt a hard hand, but she'd done the best she could. Now it was time for her to go to sleep. She shrugged, folded her cards, and put her palms facedown on the table. She was about to leave, and I still hadn't told her about Jesus.

"Stay. You can win," I protested. "All you have to do is go through the cards one at a time."

"But that would be cheating," my mother replied.

"You can't cheat yourself."

"Don't be so sure. In the meantime, let's try to be generous with your crazy father. Grandpa Hershel's death hasn't been easy for him."

With that she pushed back her chair and slowly raised herself muscle by muscle and ligament by ligament. She groaned as her overworked pulley system pulled together to do the job, and I watched her stand as I sometimes watched steam shovels repairing city streets. She was larger than life, superhumanly strong, and seemingly capable of crushing me if I got between her and her work. I instinctively got out of her way.

"I'll see you in the morning," she said when she achieved her full height of just over five enormous feet.

"Good night, Mom."

As soon as she was gone I moved into her seat and surveyed the unfinished game of solitaire. The situation wasn't at all hopeless. My mother had already laid out three aces, and not that many cards were buried. Against my mother's creed, I started playing her hand one card at a time, and after a few minutes the game opened up. A few minutes later something clicked and I knew that I'd won. With Jesus as my partner the cards flew out of my hand. Hearts fell on hearts. Clubs on clubs. A few minutes later I had all my cards on the table, and I went to sleep knowing that I was still on the right path.

Despite my best intentions, for the next few days I did what most young adults would have done in their parents' houses: I brought a mattress up from the basement and lay down for about a week. I quickly settled on a schedule. I woke up every day at about 8:30 and pulled the Good News Bible out from underneath my pillow. I kept it beneath my pillow, because for my parents, finding the New Testament in their house would not have been such good news. I would then try to read the Bible, but I'd be distracted by noises coming from the bathroom adjacent to my room.

From 8:15 to 8:20 my father would shave, and I'd hear him wincing as he continually cut himself with his old single-edged razor. At 8:45 he would then leave for work with enough strips of bloody Kleenex hanging off his face to make him look like he'd been run over by a ticker-tape parade. As soon as he was gone my sister would sneak into the bathroom and start coughing up phlegm. Apparently she had just started sneaking cigarettes from my mother. Her voice was deepening and was well on her way to sounding like Lauren Bacall with emphysema. When she was finished she'd get on her bike and ride off to the community pool, leaving me alone in the house with my mother.

Mom's schedule would vary. Some mornings she would wash clothes. Other mornings she'd pay bills or vacuum. At noon she'd invariably yell upstairs that she was leaving and then usually go shopping at Waldbaum's. There were usually a few hours in the middle of the day when I could count on the house being empty. At this point I hid my Bible and wafted outside to the backyard to get some fresh air and pray. When my mother returned in the late afternoon she would usually find me lying beneath the willow tree. Sometimes she needed me to help her carry in packages. Sometimes she didn't.

My mother's late afternoons were spent preparing for the bat mitzvah. The RSVPs were coming in, and her main job was creating a seating plan that wouldn't upset any of our large and contentious family; a diplomatic task no less daunting than the partition of Poland. For hours she'd arrange and rearrange place cards, and she'd usually be struggling at the dining-room table when my father came home from work. In order not to disturb my mother's concentration, my dad would dutifully start the barbecue outside on the patio, and my mother would yell things like, "Jack, is your cousin Miriam still not talking to your aunt Florence?"

"Miriam's not talking to anyone!"

"Good!" my mother would yell. "In that case she'll be miserable wherever she sits."

"Where's our number-two son?" my father would sometimes yell back.

"Under the tree."

At this point my father would call, "Bernie—I mean, Jaffe—how do you want your hamburger done?" and I would say to him for the umpteenth time, "Dad, I don't eat meat!" Then I'd get up and go to the refrigerator to rummage for food. On a typical evening, I'd make a tuna-fish sandwich, go back to my room, and try to get through a few more verses of Matthew, Luke, or Peter. Amazingly, neither one of my parents ever asked me what I was reading.

By the second week, however, I was starting to lose my mind and my mother was starting to notice bits and pieces of it lying around the house. Maybe she'd found the Bible while fluffing up my pillow. Maybe I had said something flattering about Billy Graham. Or maybe my mother had simply begun to wonder about my dismal lack of financial prospects. My only income at this time was pocketing the loose change every time my mother sent me on an errand; I suspect she was getting tired of paying twenty bucks for a pack of Kent King Size whenever I went to the store.

My second week home, she said to me that I should go back to work at the Tupperware distributor. I was horrified. I needed more time to read the Bible, and I probably quoted her something really stupid like, "The lilies of the field never had to work and yet they were clothed and fed." In any event, the following day my mother stayed home all afternoon. She said she was doing an extra load of wash, but I knew she had stayed home to spy on me. All afternoon, while I lay in the backyard, the house ticked, a suburban time bomb just waiting to explode.

Around two o'clock the front door flew open and she came into the yard to hang her brassieres on the line, which had been strung between two aluminum crucifixes in the side yard facing the McDermotts'. She lugged a large laundry basket, and in her mouth she clenched about two dozen clothespins; she looked like she could have snapped them in two with her jaw. At the ominous sight of her, a flock of birds squawked and fled the clothesline for a safer perch. High in the sky, the sun seemed to hide behind a cloud. Somewhere else on our planet, the earth opened and swallowed a few thousand innocent lives. The battle commenced immediately.

"Do you have shoes to wear to the bat mitzvah?" she asked me, spitting out the clothespins like so many bullets.

"I don't think so," I replied as cheerfully as possible.

My mother groaned. "What about those shoes you wore to your cousin Norman's wedding?"

"They're too small."

"Then do me a favor. They're having a sale at Gertz. I will loan you the money; you can go out and buy yourself a new pair of shoes."

"I'd rather not have to borrow your money," I said diplomatically.

"Oh yeah?" My mother shrugged. "Then what do you want for dinner?" Before I could answer she added sadistically, "We're out of tuna fish."

"Pizza would be OK," I said.

"With whose money?" my mother demanded with a bitter smile.

Was she denying me money for food? This was a serious breach of the Geneva Convention. According to the unwritten rules of familial warfare, once a Jewish mother bears a child, she's technically responsible for feeding it the rest of its life. She was obviously out to draw blood, and I may have put a bitter spin on the verb in my next response.

"Can I *borrow* five dollars?"

"Until *when*?" my mother countered icily.

"Until I get a job," I answered, stating what she wanted to hear, but with enough disdain in my voice to dissolve lead.

"Ehh!" My mother shook her head with disgust and said, "Until the Messiah comes is more like it!"

A light went on in my brain. This was it! This was my sign from God! She'd said the magic word, and it now became obvious where this conversation was taking us. I went in for the kill. "Mom!" I said. "The Messiah! He's already come!"

My mother turned on me. "What?"

There was no stopping me now. I would either convert her to Christianity or be destroyed making the attempt. "Mom, remember as a child I used to be worried about what happened to us after we die. Well, I'm not worried anymore."

"Good," my mother said and went back to pinning up her brassieres. I moved in closer, like an early Christian martyr feeding himself to the lions.

"Don't you want to know why?" I asked.

"Not particularly."

"Don't you even care?" I said, my pitch rising.

"No."

"Mom?!"

"We told you a long time ago. The purpose of a good life is a good life."

"No, Mom!" I interrupted. "The purpose of a good life is to be uplifted by the Holy Spirit."

My mother swatted away that concept like a mosquito. I ran around to her other side hoping to find an ear that was still open.

"Just think about it, Mom. A bat mitzvah. It's a spiritual event—"

"It's not a spiritual event!" she countered. "It's a family event!"

"No, Mom. I've been thinking about this. The reason you're so resentful. You're just not appreciating the role of spirit in all this. A bat mitzvah is when the Jewish child is welcomed into his kingdom."

"*Whose* kingdom?"

"*His* kingdom!"

"I don't want to hear about it." My mother bent down to pick up her laundry basket. I made one last-ditch attempt.

"Mom, just listen to what I'm saying. Is *this* all there is?"

"What?"

"This," I repeated, gesturing grandly to our unimpressive quarter-acre plot. "Don't you want to know about God? Don't you care about the eternal soul that lives on after we die?"

Her back against the wall, my mother counterattacked using every last ounce of her physical and rhetorical powers. The sky seemed to grow darker. The maelstrom increased, building to a violent crescendo.

"After we die?" my mother yelled back. "Who the hell has time to live on *after* we die? Jaffe, you know what I have to do today? After I finish the table arrangement, I have the temple to deal with, the hall to deal with, who eats kosher, who doesn't eat kosher. I've got to figure out how to pay the cantor, the rabbi, the florist. I've got a husband working two jobs so I can pay the cantor the rabbi and the florist. I've got a daughter going through puberty and I've got a son lying around my backyard who won't lift a goddamn finger! So whatever Bible you've been reading up in your room—if there's not a chapter about helping your mother in it, *I don't want to hear about it!*"

Round one was over. Several hedges had burst into flames. The grass lay scorched around my feet. A saner man might have kept his mouth shut, but I couldn't resist my genetic predisposition for getting the last word in. I threw back my shoulders and announced my conditions for surrender.

"If that's your attitude, I'm not going to the bat mitzvah."

Unfortunately, I'd miscalculated. I was, after all, addressing half of my gene pool—the deeper end, actually—and my mother wasn't about to make any concessions.

"Good!" she said. "Just stay out of my way!"

I was momentarily taken aback by the quickness of her response and had no time to counter before she added, "Jaffe, you are twenty years old. Personally I don't give a shit what you do. But, financially, if you're going to be living under this roof, you're going to have to look for work!"

She had said the *w* word. There was nothing more to say. She bent down to pick up her laundry basket, and was halfway through the door before reconsidering her Pyrrhic victory. She couldn't quite leave me without asking, "So, what did you say you wanted for dinner?"

"Nothing," I replied as nonchalantly as I could.

Smoke poured from my mother's nostrils. She'd won the battle, but guilt would always prevent her from winning the war. As much as she wanted to, she could never completely devastate one of her children.

"OK," she said, shaking her battle-scarred head. "I'm leaving five bucks on the kitchen table." Then she lifted her basket and strode back into the house. I graciously rushed to hold open the screen door for her. "But don't think I'm not serious. You either find work or you live somewhere else." She disappeared into the dark interior; the door slammed shut behind her.

What was I going to do now? For a brief moment I saw myself through my mother's eyes, a twenty-year-old college dropout with no future, no filial devotion, and no propensity for employment. It was too horrible to contemplate. I dropped to my knees. "Jesus, please! You've brought me this far. You've got to help me!" Jesus' response was a subtle shifting in the light. Then a warm breeze blew through the yard, inspiring me with a modicum of hope while effectively drying my mother's brassieres.

Later that night I found five dollars left for me on the kitchen counter and snuck off to Raffaele's Pizzeria. On the way home, sated with extra cheese, I noticed my attitude begin to soften a bit. "I don't actually have to take a job," I thought. "I just need to show her that I'm looking." I would also help out with the bat mitzvah, so when I got home I went straight to the attic to find the dress shoes I'd worn to my cousin Norman's wedding.

God works in mysterious ways, however. Just when you think you know his will, he changes his mind completely. While snooping around the dusty crawl space in the dark I tripped over some rolled-up canvas and shined my flashlight on what turned out to be my father's old army tent. Could this have been a sign from Jesus? I carried it outside and set it up in the backyard. Perfect! Then I dragged out a few blankets, and by the time my mother woke up the next morning I had moved out of her house. I'd show her! I had a new plan. Because my parents were not capable of being saved, I simply would forsake them, live in the backyard, read the Bible, and grow stronger in the eyes of the One True God.

My father's main concern was that I not ruin the lawn, so the next day he asked that I move the tent to a patch of ground where the grass wasn't growing anyway. The new spot was beneath

Jaffe Cohen

the mimosa tree, in the shade of the McDermotts' hedges, and the major drawback was that I now had a root going through my floor, making it uncomfortable to sleep. My mother, as far as I know, never expressed an opinion about my living in the backyard until years later, when she confessed, "With everything else going on that summer, you were the least of my problems." She was far more concerned about the imminent arrival of Bernie, who had recently been busted by the pigs in Tucson and was in danger of having a criminal record. "With you," she said, "we knew it was just a phase. You didn't even like the Cub Scouts. How long were you going to sleep outside on the lawn?"

This never stopped her from leaving me terse notes on the kitchen table suggesting there were errands I *might* run *if* I wanted to be of use. Otherwise we didn't communicate, except I always suspected she was watching me through the curtains. I also noticed that, whenever I snuck inside the house for food, there was usually a can of Chicken of the Sea, my favorite brand of tuna, sitting out on the kitchen counter. And there was always that moment when she'd get in the car to go to Waldbaum's; she'd open the door and pause—listen for just one second—and then slam the car door shut.

My mental state, at this time, was somewhere between Robinson Crusoe and Job with an agonizing skin condition. Of course I was lonely and miserable, but I kept reminding myself that Jesus had spent forty days in the wilderness, so this little ordeal was the least I could do. Not that my wilderness was particularly remote. It was just a side lawn with a mimosa tree, a pussy willow, a four-foot wooden fence, and a rusty swing set. In fact, because we were a corner plot, there wasn't even a spot in our yard that couldn't be seen from the sidewalk.

That's *if* there had been anyone on the sidewalk. Since most of the neighborhood kids were the same age when we moved in, the development was now completely void of my contemporaries. Anyone I'd known as a child either was away at college or had opted for early alcoholism at Doogan's Bar. With the possible exception of Ira, who was spending the summer at his parents' a few towns away in Wantagh, I hadn't a friend for miles around. Every now and then I thought of seeking out a Christian prayer group, but in order to get there I would have needed my parents' car. Needless to say, I didn't want to tell them where I was going. Nor did I want to lie to them, so day after day I hung around the yard. My only fun was decorating my tent with two pictures of the Sea of Galilee, posters that my father had received in the mail from El Al Airlines.

At the risk of sounding redundant, I read the Bible religiously. I started from the beginning: Genesis and the Garden of Eden. This story was familiar to me from my days with Rabbi Mintz, and I had girded myself for the inconsistencies. In truth, the story of Adam and Eve went down well. I was living in a weedy garden myself, so I identified with the characters. I also got through the Tower of Babel and Noah's Ark feeling charmed and inspired; it wasn't until Abraham and Isaac that I began to feel seriously disturbed. "Where was this poor boy's mother?" I kept asking myself. If my father had walked any of *my* mother's kids into the woods to play human sacrifice she would have called the police and gotten a court order against the schmuck.

It only got worse after that. I questioned some of God's choices. Why should Esau have lost his birthright to his sneaky brother? Why did Joseph's brothers have to put up with their father's favoritism? I skipped ahead to Exodus and I began to doubt the miracles. No matter how hard I tried, I couldn't imagine thousands of Jews staying dry as they walked through the Red Sea. The closest I could picture was my mother and her friends doing the sidestroke across the community pool without getting their hair wet.

It got even more frightening once we entered the Promised Land. God was vengeful, mean, and didn't mind slaughtering thousands of noncombatant populations. I felt sorry for all those poor Moabites and Amekalites who had the misfortune of living on land God had intended for other purposes. They reminded me of those people across town who had lost their homes when they built the Long Island Expressway. I didn't understand God's intentions. In many cases I didn't understand his methods. It was years before I found a definition of *murraine,* one of the plagues God visited upon the Egyptians; and I'm still not sure what brimstone is, as in "fire and brimstone." It sounded like some kind of tacky outdoor siding one might purchase at a Home Garden Center. However, I doubted that God was punishing people in 3000 B.C. by making them look like they lived in New Jersey.

At best, my mind—hardwired for irony—skimmed across the surface of the Bible like oil on holy water. Nothing penetrated. When I read a sentence like "Blessed be He who brought forth Bread from the Earth," I didn't feel grateful. All I thought was, back in Brooklyn, if you found bread on the earth, you left it there. Even worse, the Bible started getting nightmares. On a muggy summer day I should have been reading *Heidi* or *The Call of the Wild,* something to cool me off, not endless stories of slaughter and battles over dusty plots of land where nobody would want to live anyway. I'd also seen far too many bad biblical epics on television; it was hard enough being uplifted by the story of David and Bathsheba without having to imagine Gregory Peck and Susan Hayward in the worst performances of their careers.

I finally gave up and skipped ahead to the New Testament, but the gloom only thickened. Whereas *The Aquarian Gospel* had concentrated on Jesus' life, Matthew, Mark, and Luke all fast-forwarded to Jesus' grisly death. Even with the Resurrection, this was not a happy tale—and a very questionable basis for a religion. With all that miserable cleaving of tongues and mingling of wine with gall, it was enough to make me nauseous. I soon found myself reading less and less and just staring off into space. I wrestled with the queer turns my mind inevitably took; there was, after all, something so romantic about Jesus' life among his disciples. Down deep I still wanted just one guy to call my own, and Jesus had twelve.

One morning I lay back in my tent and fell asleep. I'd been day-dreaming about how Jesus got his tresses so shiny and clean before the invention of hair conditioner. (Did his halo burn off the grime like a self-cleaning oven?) Anyway, I probably slept for only a few minutes, but it seemed longer because I had a vivid and complex dream about the crucifixion. Maybe it was all those "saint" pictures in Debbi McDermott's house, because I somehow mixed up two historical assassinations. In my dream, it was Dallas in 1963, and Jesus and Mary Magdalene, who was wearing a pillbox hat, were being driven through the city in the back of a limousine. They were both waving to the crowd when, suddenly, somebody threw a spike from a window and hit Jesus right in his hand; his palm began to bleed.

The next thing I knew, the accused attacker was surrounded by reporters and policemen. To make matters more intense, upon closer inspection, the suspect was none other than me! As a Jew, it was me who was being accused of the murder of Christ. I was being led from my cell—Lee Harvey Berkowitz—when someone came rushing toward me wearing a raincoat and carrying what looked like a gun. It was Brian McDermott. He opened his raincoat and exposed his erection. He ran into me and pushed his hard dick against my midsection. He knocked me to the ground and I writhed under the pressure.

And I writhed—

And I writhed—

And I writhed—

As I writhed, I heard somebody call my name. I woke up. My whole face and body were pressed up against the hard root of the mimosa tree.

"Jaffe!"

I heard somebody calling my name again.

"Jaffe! Where are you?"

The voice sounded familiar. I got up and left my tent. A little unsure of myself, I snuck up to the garage wall and peeked around toward the front yard.

"Jaffe! Anybody home?"

"Oh my god!" It was Ira backing away from the front door, looking peeved, with his hand on his hip. His father's Pontiac was parked in our driveway and he was wearing tight short shorts and a pink tank top and carrying an oversize wicker beach bag on which had been stitched an orange daisy molded out of pastel-colored straw. I prayed it belonged to his mother and not to him.

"Ira! I'm in the backyard!"

I certainly didn't want the neighbors to see him like that.

"Where?"

Ira spun around and saw me. A look of delight came over his face.

"Oh, there you are! Your mother told me you were napping, so I told her not to wake you. Oh my god!"

Ira flew toward me and was about to throw his arms around my neck. "Let me look at you first." He stepped back to examine me from head to foot. He made no attempt to hide his disappointment.

"You grew a beard?"

"I just haven't shaved."

"You look like one of those Smith Brothers on the box of cough drops," he said. "But we can deal with that later." Then he hugged me and squealed, "I have *so* much to tell you!"

Ira followed me into the backyard. He was in a hypertheatrical mood; in the half year we'd been apart, his inner queen had obviously been coronated and placed upon her throne.

"You know, I shouldn't even be talking to you," he pouted. "Why didn't you call me as soon as you got home?"

"I don't know."

I walked Ira into the yard and we plopped down on the grass. I sat cross-legged like Siddhartha while Ira languished on his side like Scheherazade.

"What's this?" he asked, pointing at my tent.

"It's where I live."

"You live in a tent?" Ira scrunched up his face and decided not to pursue his next thought. Myself, I had no idea what to say, so I nodded my head awkwardly, letting my end of the dialogue come crashing to the ground. Luckily, Ira—who would have preferred me to be more voluble—was also perfectly willing to launch into a monologue. "So," he said, "*why* didn't you call me?"

"I've been going through a lot of changes," I confessed.

"Nu? You're the only one?" Ira sputtered breathlessly. "You missed a great semester! I don't even know where to begin. OK. David Albright. She has all these new friends from the Dance Department at Nassau Community College—" Ira stopped himself. "Oops, did I say 'she'? That's how we talk now. *Everyone* is a 'she.' I haven't used a masculine pronoun since February. Oooh. You want to hear something funny? Yesterday my aunt Enid asked me about my father, and it just slipped out: 'She's retired now!' Not that I really care. I am just so 'out' to everybody! It's fabulous!"

Ira paused to gauge my reaction to his unfettered flamboyance. Responding to his look, I carefully raised an eyebrow to indicate my precise degree of difficulty. Ira quickly counted the wrinkles on my forehead, decided I wasn't hopelessly resistant, and steamed ahead breathlessly. "Changes!" he continued. "*Everybody's* been going through changes. Mental changes. Physical changes. Oooh, get this. Billy Quintana put lemon juice in his hair to bring out the blond. He's so sour now. We think the citric acid might have seeped into his brain—"

Ira stopped to again measure my response. "I know what you're thinking," he said musically. "You think I've turned into a big JAP! Well, I am a JAP and I love it!"

Ira threw his wrist heavenward and snapped his fingers. I smiled as tolerantly as I could.

"So how was your trip?" Ira asked, shifting his weight in preparation for what he hoped would be a long series of hilarious western anecdotes.

"Umm . . . fine," I said.

The next pause was truly uncomfortable.

"So . . ." Ira said hesitantly. "I don't suppose you'd want to come to the beach today?"

"I don't know . . . I . . ."

"Oh, please come!" Ira quickly changed his tune back to unbridled enthusiasm. "David found this amazing spot! You go to Field Six at Jones Beach and walk another mile east and the men there are gorgeous and, best of all, they're *all* gay!"

"All of them?"

"Yeah. Well, ninety-nine percent—"

"No thanks," I said.

Ira looked me in the eyes and chose his words very carefully. "Would you want to go—maybe—at another time?"

And I chose my response just as carefully. If the unspoken subtext of our conversation had been any more distinct it would have been carved into our foreheads.

"Yeah. Maybe," I said as noncommittally as possible. There was another long pause while Ira looked at my pathetic little tent and avoided stating the obvious—that he was feeling terribly sorry for me because I had been missing out on all the fun that year.

"I better get going," Ira said. But he didn't move. Silence. Somewhere down the street a neighbor was trying to start his lawn mower. A bee landed on a dandelion. Ira had said everything he'd rehearsed in the car on the way over. Now it was time to really talk.

"So," Ira finally confessed, "I thought maybe you'd write?"

"I'm sorry," I said.

"Maybe you didn't feel like staying in touch."

"That's not it."

"Or you were angry with me."

I didn't respond, and Ira rocked back and forth, trying to regain some comfort.

"How's Vinnie?" I asked.

Ira grimaced. "Uggh. I don't want to talk about that!"

"Why? What happened?"

"I don't know," Ira said, pulling out clumps of grass and scattering them thoughtlessly.

"Are you two still . . . you know . . ."

"You really want to hear this? OK. We broke up. For good this time."

"Oh. I'm sorry to hear that."

Ira threw some grass in the air and let it land on his head. "*Que sera sera.* We fought all the time. He's so uptight, and I was just way too gay for him. One day he told me that he wanted a boyfriend more straight acting and straight appearing. So I looked him straight in the eyes and told him Ernest Borgnine was still available."

"So . . . is he dating somebody else now?"

"Are you kidding? The ink wasn't even dry on the divorce papers, he met this little blond queen from the Dance Department named Chad. Now Vinnie's the biggest queen of us all. Seriously. They dress exactly alike; they bought some stupid little poodle."

"You're kidding!"

"They have all these rich friends from Manhattan. It's weird."

"Wow!"

Ira noticed my heightened level of interest and made the decision to be perfectly blunt.

"So you *were* mad at me last winter."

"I was never mad at you."

"You loved Vinnie. Didn't you?"

"No!"

"Vinnie thought *maybe* you did. We both felt so terrible when you just dropped out of school. I just wanted us all to be together, like a family."

"I know, but—"

"If only you had told me—"

"I didn't love Vinnie."

"Then did you think I didn't need you anymore as a friend just because I had a lover?"

"No."

"And just because you grew a beard and we don't dress alike anymore doesn't mean that we still can't be close. I missed you."

"I'm sorry. It was just a really weird trip. I'll . . . I'll tell you about it some other time." Ira gave me a quizzical look that threatened to break my heart. "I guess you better get going," I said, "if you want to get to the beach."

Ira must have realized I wouldn't be any more candid that day, so he quickly changed the subject. Sitting up suddenly, he looked at the sky, and jumped to his feet, alarmed.

"Oh, my God! I'm missing the best tanning hours."

Then he pulled down his shirt to cover his midriff. I stood as well, relieved the conversation had ended.

"Are you meeting anyone there?" I asked.

"The usual queens. David and Billy," Ira replied, snapping back into fun mode as he brushed some grass off his rear end. "Oh, I didn't even tell you about Aaron Grossman. After he canceled *Alice and Wonderland* he decided to direct an all-male version of García Lorca's *Blood Wedding* and he became lovers with his leading man!"

"Really?"

"José Rubens—an Upward Bound student from East Harlem. Cute. Cute. Cute. So, if Aaron can get a boyfriend, there's hope for us all . . . Jaffe, if you ever need to talk . . ."

"I'm fine," I said.

"OK . . ."

Just then Ira reached into his wicker beach bag and pulled out a
Kodak Instamatic.

"Can I at least take your picture? Stand next to your tent."

"Now? I look horrible!"

"That's true, but twenty years from now when you look back,
you'll look even worse."

I grinned ruefully. Ira snapped the picture, flicked the camera
back into his beach bag, and quickly slung the bag over his shoulder.

"Are you *sure* you don't want to come?" he said as he scurried
across the lawn.

"No . . . I mean, I am sure . . . but . . . not today."

Ira sensed the uncertainty in my voice and turned to me one last
time. "Well, we are going to be there every day this week if you
change your mind."

Then he trotted to his car and I scurried after him like a baby
goose. Part of me was just starting to realize how much I had missed
him.

As Ira got into the car he had one last thought. "Oh, I didn't even
tell you the best news. I got cast in *Godspell!* You know . . . the Jesus
musical! I play Judas, the villain. Well, he's not really the villain. Not
the way that I play him. Do you know the story?"

"Umm . . . a little," I said.

"Judas is the best part in the whole show. OK, OK, so I betray
Christ at the end. Who cares? I get all the best songs!"

Ira slid behind the wheel, started the engine, then pulled the
rearview mirror toward him to check out his tan.

"Ucch. I'm so pale."

"No, you're not," I said weakly.

"I'll call you tomorrow," he said without thinking. Then he
paused and rephrased himself. "Better yet, you call me. Please."

"I'll call you," I promised.

"I still love you," Ira mouthed silently as he pressed a button on his armrest and a plate of glass heartlessly slid between us; Ira's face disappeared, replaced by my own reflection. "Bye, Ira!" I said again, knowing he couldn't hear me. "I will phone you! I promise!" The over-size Pontiac then floated down the driveway as Ira struggled manfully with the manual steering. I kept waving, feeling vaguely sick, as Ira turned the corner and disappeared from sight. Then I walked slowly back to my tent, pausing to break a dry branch off an evergreen tree. The block seemed even quieter now. A few houses away the lawn mower ground slowly to a halt. I struggled to listen. There was no sound anywhere.

I reached into my tent, pulled out my Bible, and opened it. I had a sudden urge to close it again. I did this several times until I was quite sure that I was incapable of reading. Then I lay on my back. More silence. The lawn mower started again. There were no other sounds, and I became frightened that there were no longer two of us. I got into a kneeling position on the lawn and pressed the palms of my hands together in prayer. "Jesus," I said out loud, "if you're still around, please don't punish Ira! He means well. And this gay thing he's going through, I'm sure it's just a phase. Once he finds you the way that I have he'll see the error of his ways and—"

It suddenly occurred to me that I had absolutely no idea whether or not Jesus disapproved of gays. Like most people, I had only assumed homosexuality was verboten. I needed to see it in black and white, so I grabbed my Bible and quickly turned to the index. What did it say on the subject of homosexuality? I flipped to "H." The sub-ject wasn't listed there, so I tried *sodomy* and, finally, *sexual immorality*. I turned to the first reference I could find, in Leviticus.

"Thou shalt not lie down with men the way you lie down with women."

Suddenly—*vroooom!*—a lawn mower started up next door at the

The King of Kings and I

McDermotts', and some cut grass shot under the hedges. I tried to ignore it until a flurry of twigs landed on me and my Bible. "Hey!" I yelled, running to the hedge. "Put on a lawn-mower bag!" I stood on my tippy toes to look into my neighbors' yard, fully expecting to see Mrs. McDermott or one of her homely daughters. But instead I saw a boy, a very handsome blond boy no older than sixteen. At first I thought it was Brian and that time had stood still. I waved my arms to catch his attention; he turned, smiled, and flicked off his machine. "The grass," I complained. "It's . . . umm . . . shooting through the hedge."

"Jaffe! Hey!" the boy said with a strangely familiar grin on his face.

I was momentarily confused.

"Don't you remember me? Eddie. I'm Eddie!"

He came up to his side of the hedge to shake my hand.

"Oh my god!" I said. "Eddie!"

It *was* Eddie, the youngest of the McDermotts. The last time I'd seen this kid he had been eleven. Now he was a teenager with broad shoulders and a deepening voice.

"Hey!" he said. "My sisters told me you were home! How's it going?"

"Great!" I said.

And he was stunning, even more conventionally handsome than Brian had ever been, and possibly just as dumb. I was in dangerous territory.

Eddie was the youngest of the McDermotts. Seventeen years ago his absurdly fertile mother had gone to the hospital for a long-overdue hysterectomy and discovered she was pregnant; Eddie popped out three months later. The handsome fifteen-year-old standing in front of me had been Mrs. McDermott's "change of life" baby, and now, simply by running his fingers through his thick blond hair, he was about to change my life as well.

"I didn't know you were home," I said.

"I go back and forth," Eddie said. "Between my dad's and here."

"Where does your dad live now?"

"Westbury," Eddie said, pointing east.

"You mean Westbury?" I said, pointing west, where I knew Westbury to be. Eddie stopped to think and pivoted on his heel in the direction I had pointed.

"Oh, yeah . . . Westbury. You're right. Westbury."

"So, how you doing?" I asked as quickly as possible to keep him from feeling too stupid.

"Great!" Eddie smiled. (God, he was gorgeous!) "I got a job in the bowling alley."

"Helping your mother out?"

"Yeah. My sisters don't do this shit, and Brian's——"

"Where is Brian?" I asked eagerly.

"He's still living with Theresa. They got an apartment above the bar in town."

"Really?"

"Oh yeah. They're doing great! It's a great place."

Eddie's broad smile indicated no suspicion that his older brother may have made some less than inspiring choices in his life. I quickly decided not to challenge his fraternal admiration.

"Good! Good!" I said, nodding like an idiot.

"Phew! It's hot." Eddie reached down and pulled up the hem of his T-shirt to fan his face, giving me a great view of what we now call abs. They were as white and tight as a bongo drum. I tried not to stare. I even tried not to stare when Eddie pulled off his shirt to wipe the sweat off the back of his neck. But it was hopeless; I was fighting a natural attraction no less powerful than the gravitational force on Jupiter. My eyes started plummeting toward his heavenly body like a broken space ship. Surely there must have been a square inch of his flesh somewhere that didn't exert an inexorable erotic attraction—but no.

The King of Kings and I

It was a lost cause. Even his clavicle was gorgeous. My mind crash-landed on his chest. I simply *had* to have him.

"Whatcha got there?" he said, pointing over the hedge to my tent.

"That? That's my home."

"You're kidding."

"No. I'm living in the tent."

"How come?"

"I like . . . I like being outdoors."

"Cool."

"You want to see?"

"Yeah!"

With that Eddie simply walked through the hedges. It was a miracle! He didn't walk around the hedges. He didn't even part the hedges with his hand. He simply stepped into my yard as though the hedges weren't there, and the hedges magically closed up behind him.

"You sleep out here too?" Eddie questioned as he pulled aside the flap and bent over to look inside.

"Yeah, sure," I said, trying not to let him hear that my teeth were chattering with lust. Eddie stooped down and slipped inside.

"What's this?" he asked, looking at my Israeli posters. I crawled inside after him and sat down on my sleeping bag.

"The Holy Land," I answered.

"Like Europe somewhere?"

"Umm . . . yeah. Technically, Asia . . . but . . ."

I was talking to a kid who didn't even know where Westbury was. It didn't seem worth pressing the issue.

"It's in the same general direction," I concluded. Eddie sat down on the ground across from me and pulled his legs up to his chest. I couldn't get over how much he looked and spoke like Brian.

"This would be a great place to get high!" he said. "You get high?"

I hadn't smoked weed since that awful day in Tucson when I'd almost lost my mind on acid. I hadn't even thought of smoking pot since then.

"Yeah, sure I do," I said without a moment's hesitation.

"You want to get high now?"

"Yeah, sure!" I said.

"Bernie sent me a stash in the mail from Tucson. I got it over at my dad's house."

"Go get it!" I said.

"You want me to get it?"

"Yeah. That's a great idea! Go—go get your stash . . ." I started stammering helplessly. The fervent hope that history might repeat itself with this McDermott was setting my brain on fire. My words tumbled out of my skull like terrified children fleeing an orphanage about to burn to the ground. "That's a great idea! Great idea!" I sputtered. "Go to your father's house and go get your stash and then come right back!"

"I'll hurry," Eddie said smiling. "I got my bike here." As he exited the tent, he bent down, his pants slipped, and I caught a glimpse of his butt crack. That may have been the moment when the last retaining wall in my brain crashed to the ground in a blizzard of burning embers. "Great!" I babbled. "I can expect you when?—fifteen minutes? Great—go get your stash! Right. Go get your stash and come right back! Come back! I'll wait for you here!"

As soon as Eddie disappeared through the hedges I fell to my knees and clasped my hands together.

"Oh, Jesus, please! Can I have him? I know. I know it says in the Bible that you're not supposed to lie down with a man the way you lie down with a woman. But . . . but . . . we can do it standing up! Whaddya say? Please! Please! Please!"

But I didn't even wait for an answer. Mumbling something to myself like, "If it's meant to be, it's meant to be," I threw back the flap of my tent to air out my living quarters. I needed to convert my home into the proper setting for seduction. Every variable had to be accounted for. I experimented with lighting by opening and closing the canvas window flap. Then I rearranged my furniture by moving the sleeping bag from one side of the root to the other. Then I ran around the yard to make sure that we'd be alone. I looked both ways down the deserted driveway, and for the first time ever, the complete silence of suburbia filled me with bliss. It was 1:15 P.M.

By two o'clock Eddie still hadn't returned from Westbury, so I set about removing every dandelion and twig from the pathway between the gate and my tent. At three o'clock I ran inside and brushed my teeth. At four o'clock my sister returned from the community pool and turned on the TV set to watch *The Mike Douglas Show*. At 4:30 my mother got back from her meeting with the caterers and set herself up at the dining-room table to finish the seating arrangements. Life went on.

At 5:30 my father came home and started the barbecue. For the first time in weeks the smell of charred flesh was irresistible. At seven I went into the kitchen and made myself a plate of food including an extra-large helping of shrimp salad from the deli counter at Foodtown. Then I brushed my teeth and waited some more. It wasn't until five after midnight that I finally admitted to myself that Eddie wasn't coming back that day. "He'll be here tomorrow," I cheerfully told myself as I lay down and closed my eyes.

But that night I couldn't sleep. I listened for the sound of Eddie creeping across the lawn in the dark. I practiced the many shades of nonchalance I would use when I told him, "That's OK. I forgot you were coming back." Then I tried to figure out all the different ways in which I still might trick him into taking off his clothes. I might spill a beverage on him and offer to do his laundry.. I could tell him he looked fat, take off his pants, and weigh him on the bathroom scale. I could tell him he looked feverish and then offer to take his temperature with a rectal thermometer. I could . . .

The birds started singing just before sunrise. I hadn't slept a wink, and I now had an awful headache. Eight o'clock. Nine o'clock. I knew I was out of control, so I got up and prayed. I fell to my knees and begged—begged—Jesus to release me from temptation. But it didn't work. Temptation felt too good. I started scheming again. There may have been a perfectly good explanation for why he hadn't come back to me. I simply needed more information. Information. Yes! That's what I needed. So I went into the house to find my sister. She gossiped with the McDermott girls; maybe she knew something useful.

"Rachel," I called as I entered the house. There was no answer, but the theme from *I Love Lucy* could be heard coming from the den. I skipped downstairs, where I found her on the couch, surrounded by throw pillows, teen magazines, and a breakfast tray covered with cake crumbs and a banana peel. I sat down beside her and pulled a piece of afghan over my feet.

"What are you doing inside?" she asked me during the commercial.

"Nothing. Where's Mom?"

"Went shopping."

"Her car's still in the driveway."

"Natalie picked her up. She'll be gone all day."

We watched another commercial; I now had about thirty seconds to retrieve any vital information.

"I saw Eddie McDermott yesterday," I said casually. "He was mowing the lawn."

"He's fucked up," Rachel replied.

"Whaddya mean?"

"Yesterday his father threw him out of the house."

"Really. He seems like a nice kid."

"Whaddya kidding? He kicked a teacher in the balls. Mr. Frankelman the drama teacher."

"He musta had a good reason," I suggested.

The King of Kings and I

"Eddie thought he was a homo."

"Really?"

"The poor guy's in Mid-Island Hospital with a bleeding kidney."

The commercial was over. I stood up unsteadily to leave the room.

"If you're going upstairs," Rachel asked me, "would you drop these in the sink?" Rachel handed me her tray, picked a scab off her knee, and went back to watching television. I stumbled up the steps and staggered to the kitchen sink. It was all too horrible to contemplate. Mr. Frankelman?

My life had hit rock bottom, and the thought of spending one more day keeping my feelings to myself was unbearable. Whom could I talk to? I paced the kitchen. I considered walking over to Saint Martin's and making an appointment to confess to a priest, but I wasn't sure what the office hours were. "Besides," I asked myself innocently, "what would a priest know about gay sex?"

No, there was only one person to whom I could unburden my sins. Yesterday, Ira had told me he'd be at the beach.

"Rachel!" I yelled downstairs. "When Mom gets back, tell her I borrowed her car."

"You better not!" Rachel yelled back.

She was right. Taking my mother's car was a gamble.

"Tell her . . ." I said. "Tell her I went to look for a job!"

There was silence from below; that was all the encouragement I needed. I grabbed the extra set of car keys from the kitchen cabinet behind the punch bowl, jumped into my mom's Rambler, and then ran through four red lights on my way to Field Six at Jones Beach.

CHAPTER 5

The Promised Land

A few years ago, I was wasting time at Grand Central Station when I stopped to browse at a small shop selling Catholic religious icons. One item in particular caught my eye. It was a brightly colored 3-D rendering of Jesus suffering on the cross that seemed to open and close its eyes depending on how you looked at it. Tilt to the right and Jesus closed his eyes; tilt to the left and he opened his baby blues heavenward. For the low low price of $14.95 you got not one but two Sons of God: one peaceful, the other imploring. Peaceful. Imploring. Peaceful. Imploring. What amazed me most was that these two views were existing simultaneously within one picture. Now, that was a miracle!

The King of Kings and I

A few weeks ago I read in the Science Times section of the *New York Times* that physicists are speculating that the universe itself is constructed like that picture in that it consists of an infinite number of parallel worlds that overlap. According to this theory two items *can* occupy the same space at the same time; it all depends on how you look at it. There are many straight people who have a hard time wrapping their imaginations around this concept, but as a gay man, I know this model of the universe to be correct.

After all, for twenty years I lived on the earth and completely didn't see how much of it had been claimed by queer folk. All it took was the decision to notice, and a parallel universe opened to me, occupying the same area as the world in which I had been raised. It was a brave new world consisting of whole towns like Provincetown and Key West, as well as neighborhoods like Greenwich Village and West Hollywood. It includes thousands of hotels, millions of motels, and countless acres of parkland, parking lots, and card shops. One could add up the gay bathroom stalls alone and have a continent twice the size of Australia. It was all right under my nose, but until I tilted ever so slightly to the left I never saw that it was there.

How else can I explain why I'd never noticed the steady stream of well-built men who, for decades, had been getting off the bus from Manhattan at Field Four and marching east past Fields Five and Six to a distant stretch of sand known only to them? As a suburban teenager I'd often sat in the path of these pilgrims; I may have even lusted after one or two, but I'd never thought to ask where they were going. Today, while looking for Ira, I decided to follow two of them who stumbled along the wet sand managing to look elegant while holding a cooler between them, upon which had been stacked several pastel-colored beach chairs. Like Manya and Fanya these two guys were obviously coming to the beach prepared. Later I would discover that gay men often bring furniture to the beach—even in the most remote locations—as part of an instinctual drive to boldly decorate where no gay man has decorated before.

How else did I know these two were homos? Simple. They were

enjoying each other's conversation, something straight men rarely do. Unselfconsciously, they gossiped and giggled as they floated past adolescent girls in bikinis with nary a glance. There was also something about the way they flung off their muscle shirts as soon as they hit the sand and desperately applied tanning lotion as though the sun would *not* come out tomorrow. I scrutinized these guys as an understudy might watch an actor he might one day need to replace. Before we even got to the gay section I was already wishing I'd shaved and worn a slightly more revealing outfit than my raggy cutoffs and baggy T-shirt.

At some point we started trekking through the Neutral Zone that separated the gay section from the "World Federation of Straights." This is the area of beach generally populated by lesbians, who come to the ocean carrying even more furniture and more food than the gay men. In this transitional area one might also find the gay men who have recently broken up with their lovers and are spending the afternoon avoiding the all-male section, drinking white wine with their "fag hags," and crying on their shoulders.

As one continues to walk, however, the estrogen disappears completely and one arrives in a densely populated stretch of real estate inhabited exclusively by testosterone-driven men who have come to the beach to see one another and to be seen. Some gay men have described this experience as crossing over into paradise. My reaction was decidedly mixed. Like Alice entering Wonderland, I was terrified but I couldn't turn back. I also couldn't stop ogling. "Look at all these poor sinners!" I thought to myself. "With great bodies." Then, as with most guys coming out, the issue quickly changed from "Do I dare?" to "How do I look?" With every step I grew paler, flabbier, and more hopelessly out of style.

In every way imaginable—spiritually, physically, sartorially—I was completely lost. How would I find Ira among all these great-looking guys crowded together, as indistinguishable from one another as seals wearing Speedos? The beach was as packed as the D train at rush hour. Most of the men had arrived in groups of three and four, but, as in urban neighborhoods that originally had been separate villages, they'd long since melded together into one huge thriving metropolis. It was a greasy city. Half the men were lying down. Half were standing next to their towels for no other reason than that their bodies happened to look great that day.

Like plants bending toward the light, the vast majority of the beach towels had been slowly turning all day in order to be in a direct line with the sun. There was much loud laughter, throwing back of heads, and high-pitched cries of delight. I passed by two nude men discussing Angela Lansbury. There were two couples playing in the surf who had wrapped their bathing suits around their heads like turbans. Several others—set designers, perhaps—had built an elaborate sand castle in the shape of a Chinese pagoda. There were large radios playing disco. There were *Vanity Fairs* and *GQs* half buried in the sand. There were long-stemmed glasses, roasted macadamia nuts, kiwifruit, and Finnish crackers covered with Brie. There were colorful flags and tie-dyed parachutes being used for shade. There were designer poodles, and one man had a macaw on his shoulder who could sing "Here's to the Ladies Who Lunch" from *Company*. This was, in fact, my first exposure to the "gay lifestyle" circa 1973—which looked a hell of a lot more expensive than merely having homosexual desires.

Even if I wanted to fit in, could I afford it? Was I witty enough? Sufficiently cosmopolitan and well groomed? Some mysterious force had made me homosexual; becoming gay would require a lot of hard work and cold cash. I stopped dead in my tracks. Hoping to feel rooted, I let my bare feet sink into the sand deeper and deeper with each wave that pounded away at my ankles. "O Jesus, what am I going to do?"

"Ja-fay!"

One of the naked swimmers was working his way out of the water and coming toward me through the surf. He had removed his red bathing suit from his head and was using it to dry his chest.

"Ja-fay, I thought that was you! *Bonjour, ma petite!*"

"Is that him?" yelled another queen bobbing up and down in the waves. I recognized the throaty show voice of Billy Quintana, and the man approaching me was a very naked David Albright speaking to me in his usual affected mixture of English and French.

"Ira informed us you might turn up this week. Well, *comment allez-vous?*"

"Is Ira here? I haven't seen him."

"I saw him walking—which way am I facing?—that way." David pointed east in the direction I'd been heading. "*Mon chéri*, you look wonderful. How was your trip? *Bon, j'espère.*"

Billy yelled, "Tell him to come in the water! We need another synchronized swimmer!"

"She's having her Esther Williams moment!"

"This place is really something," I offered.

"Heaven!" David closed his eyes to savor the thought of where he was. I instinctively glanced at his penis, which was much larger than I thought it would be on such an effeminate man. "Heaven, *absolument!*" David concluded.

"You look good," I commented.

"When you feel good, you look good."

"Come back in the water!" Billy screamed again.

"So tell me all about the Wild Wild West!" David demanded.

I began babbling something about the scenery in Arizona, but all I could think about was how handsome my old hallmate looked. In fact, if I hadn't known it was David Albright I might even have supposed I was attracted to him. He'd been working out. His arms and neck were thicker; he'd grown some stubble and had cut his hair like a Marine's. Whereas Ira had grown more fey while I was out west, David's coming out gay had produced the surprising result of making

him seem more masculine. Or maybe my standards of manliness, after
fifteen minutes on Field Six, had already been changed forever.

"Are you going back to school in the fall?" I asked him.

"Ira didn't tell you? I'm going to be studying at the Sorbonne."

"That's great!" I said. "You mean in Paris?"

"No, the Sorbonne in Schenectady. Oh, Ja-fay, I wish you'd been
here this last semester. I've never been so happy. Look at me!" David
stepped back and pointed to himself with all the fingers on both
hands. "I'm young. I'm gorgeous. I have a lover *and* a big dick. Every
day I say, '*Merci dieu!*' for finding this place. My only fear is I'll never be
this happy again."

Billy called from the water, "Honey, get back in here!"

"What about Billy—if you go to Paris?"

"Oh." David suddenly turned sad. "*Que sera sera.*"

Then, throwing his bathing suit around his neck, David started
backing his way into the surf. "Love you!" Then he turned and dove
into a wave that was just about to break on his back. He surfaced a few
moments later beneath Billy, whom he lifted high up on his shoulders.
The two of them gleefully charged into another couple, creating an
explosion of wrists, ankles, overturned legs, and bare buttocks. "God!"
I wondered to myself. Had I been wasting my time that year searching for happiness *within?*

I pulled my own ankles out of the wet sand and started walking
farther east. I was so confused. I tried to fit in. I tried to stand out. I
tried to look my fellow humans in the eye. I tried not to stare. I tried
to believe that whatever sin I was committing, Jesus would forgive
me. I kept walking until the crowd began to thin, along with my
hopes of finding Ira. At the same time that the crowd thinned it also
began to darken; like other American metropolises, this city by the
sea had its own ghetto. Though more integrated than most, it seemed
to consign its people of color to a less desirable location farther from
the concession stand.

On this beach, however, the blacks and Puerto Ricans didn't

inhabit the inner city. They lived on a suburban stretch of beach where each towel had an eighth of an acre. I walked past the last blanket, beyond which was a wilderness inhabited only by a handful of straight nudists who all had as little use for mainstream opinion as queer folk. The only other warm-blooded creatures were a few lonely fishermen casting their lines into the waves and their faithful dogs, dizzy with smells from the sea.

I walked even farther—to a point, marked by a sandbar, where two joggers were turning on their heels and starting back in the other direction. I was just about to do this myself when a white baby poodle wearing a red kerchief around its neck ran yelping through my legs, closely followed by a black Lab who looked like he was ready for some French cuisine.

"Bijou!" a voice called out. "Bad dog!"

I bent down to pick up the puppy, who gladly leaped into my arms for safety.

"Bijou! Hold him!"

One of the joggers started running toward me as I tried to lift the puppy away from its canine pursuer. Once in my arms, however, the stupid little animal turned on the black Lab and did her best to growl ferociously. The larger dog responded with a large sloppy bark, as wet as it was loud.

"Bijou!" Two nervous hands reached for the puppy while the other jogger grabbed the larger dog by its collar and started walking it down the beach toward a fisherman who had started calling for his pet.

"Oh, thank you!" the first jogger said breathily with a slight southern accent. "Bad dog, Bijou. Bad dog!"

I found myself looking into the bluest eyes and most perfect teeth I'd ever seen. The jogger was gorgeous, and I would have hated him immediately if he hadn't been so genuinely friendly.

"Oh, thank you!" he repeated. "You saved my little puppy's life."

I also noticed that this guy was wearing a red kerchief around his neck to match Bijou's, an affectation that might have looked ridiculous on anyone else; but on him it only complemented the unreal quality of his beauty. It was a beauty that, in real life, goes unadored for only very brief moments; and, sure enough, before another word was spoken, his boyfriend came up behind him and wrapped his dark muscular arms around his waist. Not surprisingly, he too had tied a red kerchief around his neck. The family portrait was complete.

"How's baby?" he asked in a deeper voice than his partner's, with just a trace of a New Yawk accent. Then he reached out to shake my hand. I recognized who it was, and I couldn't have been more over-joyed; it wasn't Ira, the friend I'd been looking for, but Vinnie, the friend I feared I'd never see again.

Looking back, I see that the reason I hadn't recognized Vinnie immediately was that his appearance, like David Albright's, had changed dramatically. It wasn't just that he was bronzed or that he'd been building up his biceps and toning his stomach. It wasn't that his hair had been cut stylishly. It was something else—perhaps the way he held himself so stiffly as we walked. For me, Vinnie's appearance, unlike David's, had not improved; the Vinnie I had known couldn't have become more beautiful. There was something else about him, though, that was dulling his luster even more than the dark suntan he'd been slavishly working on since April: Vinnie now knew that he was beautiful. That was the difference.

Paradoxically, he'd also grown more insecure. As the three of us strolled west along the shoreline, it was as if he were keeping score. I could see in his eyes some newly inflamed section of brain. He was doing the math, calculating who was cruising his blond boyfriend and who was cruising his own swarthy Mediterranean looks. All in all, this made him seem less generous and, oddly, less happy than the boy I'd left behind. At the age of twenty Vinnie's beauty had already started to curdle and curl in on itself.

"So where are you living this summer?" I asked him.

"We're subletting in the Village."

"Wow! How'd you afford an apartment?"

"Chad met a guy who owns an exclusive restaurant. You wouldn't believe how much money I'm making!"

"You're waiting on tables?" I asked incredulously. "You can do that?"

"It's not hard work!" Chad interjected. "If you're young and pretty."

"*And* I've got my honey to come home to," Vinnie added.

Vinnie reached out and put his arm around Chad, who lay his head on Vinnie's shoulder. Just then two men brushed past us going in the opposite direction. Chad turned to catch their eyes and smile.

"Do you know them?" Vinnie asked suspiciously.

"Not yet," Chad teased.

"You're gonna get it when we get home," Vinnie warned him.

"Promises, promises," Chad retorted.

Vinnie playfully pushed Chad away. Bijou, who had been trotting behind us trying to keep up, started yipping madly. "Oh, look, he's protecting Mommy," Chad squealed. Then he scooped up Bijou and covered his face with kisses as I strenuously resisted the urge to vomit.

When we got to their blanket Vinnie introduced me to his new friends from the city, all gorgeous men, and one elderly gentleman who sat in the middle of the group like a wrinkled Nero, running his fingers through several heads of dirty blond hair. The rest of the sunbathers languished on their blankets like the Roman slaves in *Fellini Satyricon*, with their faces perpetually three-quarters toward the sun, as though they were waiting for Bruce Weber to arrive at any moment to take their pictures.

I tried to be friendly, but the concentration of bored beauty was so dense that I had a hard time breathing. I also had a hard time talk-ing, because most of them preferred to let their cheekbones speak for themselves. I really tried my best not to hate these guys merely because they were gorgeous, but I was soon defeated by their relent-lessly shallow comments about pop culture, which they pronounced so slowly that I soon realized that most of them had taken some kind of horse tranquilizer—which, combined with narcissism, is almost always socially fatal.

Their self-consciousness was contagious; I pulled my feet into my chest to cover as much of my body as possible. Vinnie realized my discomfort, because as soon as Chad skipped away to play paddleball, he turned to me and concurred, "It's a pretty weird scene."

"No, your friends seem very nice," I lied.

"They're mostly guys that Chad met." Vinnie sighed, and for the first time that day, he looked like the lonely seeker I'd met standing in front of the bulletin board trying to choose a course in philosophy.

"Remember," Vinnie asked, "how back in school we used to think that everyone was beautiful in their own way?"

"Yeah," I said.

"Well, now only two or three of us are really beautiful, and the rest of us want to kill ourselves."

"*You* look great!" I said.

"Me? No. These guys are beautiful. Me. Forget it." Vinnie pointed to Chad playing paddleball near the water with one of the models and winning. "Look at him. I can't believe that somebody that incredible would ever love me."

"You're better looking than he is," I protested.

Vinnie squinted, giving me an incredulous goombah look. "Yeah, right!"

"No, you are," I repeated.

Vinnie examined my face to see if I was telling the truth. Then he shook his head. "Like, why should I care? It's all an illusion."

"Ego," I agreed.

"But what an illusion!" Vinnie's eyes scanned the beach looking at all the beautiful gay men, some of whom were already packing up to catch the train back to the city. Then he looked at me and seemed to finally understand how truly unhappy I'd been. "Hey, Jaffe!" he said, patting my knee. "You gotta learn to live it up more. Remember what I told you: quantum physics—this all could disappear just like that!" Then he snapped his fingers. "Just like that!" he repeated.

We sat quietly for a few moments as I scooped up handfuls of dry sand and sprinkled them onto my feet.

"I didn't tell you," I said, "I've really been thinking a lot about Jesus lately . . ."

"Really?" Vinnie asked, sincerely curious.

Just then Chad, who may have been jealous because Vinnie was giving me so much attention, came running back and grabbed Vinnie's hand, followed by Bijou, who was yapping mercilessly.

"Vinnie, c'mere. We have to go meet someone."

"Who?"

"Remember I told you about the dentist who has the house on Fire Island? I think I can get us an invitation. He's dating an old boyfriend of mine."

"Where is he?" Vinnie stood up, more interested than I wanted him to be.

"Two blankets south-southwest. See that guy over there in the white bathing suit? The one standing up? Oh, look! He sees us. He's waving!" Chad blew a kiss across the beach with all the subtlety of a Rose Bowl Queen riding through Pasadena. "Let's go over there!" he cried.

Chad started dragging away Vinnie, who turned to me and apologized: "I have to go . . ."

"If I don't see you again," Chad interjected breathlessly, "it was *really* nice meeting you."

Then across the beach they both skipped away from me, the

perfect gay couple, one dark, one light, both heartbreakingly hand-some and somewhat shallow. For the first time that afternoon, it occurred to me that the gay scene wasn't just distracting, it was downright evil. What should I do? I closed my eyes to pray, leaning back on my elbows, head upturned, so I might look like I was merely tanning.

"O Jesus, what do you want from me? I know I don't belong here, but where else can I go? If you love me, you're going to have to change me. O Jesus, I need a miracle. Nothing major. I don't have lep-rosy. I don't need to be raised from the dead. I just need some kind of sign. Something to help me put the pieces together!"

I opened my eyes to see if anyone had overheard my plea. The beach towels next to me were now empty except for that one elderly gentleman, who was staring between my legs. "How dare he?" I glanced down to see that my left testicle had been exposed. I quickly tucked myself away, which brought an exclamation of regret from my unwanted admirer.

"Ah!" he exclaimed in a cultured voice. "Your scrotum looked so lovely *in flagrante*."

"Thanks," I replied sheepishly. "I hope you don't mind. I was med-itating."

"And why shouldn't you?" the man replied. "I too was meditating."

"You were?"

"Oh yes!" he said enthusiastically. "Just now I was meditating on the sunshine, the ocean, and yourself."

"Me?"

"Ah-men," the old gentleman sighed, but I wasn't sure if he'd said "Amen" or "Ah! Men!" and I had no intention of finding out.

"If you don't mind," I said hesitantly, "I'm going for a walk."

The old man smiled graciously as I stood up, brushed the sand off my legs, and started strolling toward the shore. Vinnie and Chad were nowhere in sight, probably blanket-hopping. The rest of the beach was starting to empty out. Again I thought to look for Ira, but I had no idea where to turn. Finally I started walking east, for no other reason than that everybody else was walking west. The stream of men exiting the beach had now grown to a river of tired queens, played out, sunburned, and reluctant to return home to the Straight Federation. Many of them were men of color and biracial couples who had been camping out in the nether regions. As I walked I listened for guidance, but every time I might have heard Jesus' voice, another thunderous wave crashed against the shore and another burst of gay laughter exploded from a passing stranger.

I lowered my head and tried to block out the distractions, but as soon as I did, I heard my name being called in a distinctly human tone of voice.

"Jaffe!"

At first I thought it was Ira; who else could it have been? I looked up hopefully.

"Jaffe? Is that you?" Twenty yards ahead of me the lighter half of a biracial couple had stopped dead in his tracks. "Well. Well. Well," he said, walking toward me, and before he said another word I could see that it was Aaron Grossman. "Jaffe," he said, with a sly hint of scolding in his voice, "I just knew you'd turn up here sooner or later."

An auxiliary of Murphy's Law states that the people you'd least like to see generally turn up when you least want to see them. That being the case, I wasn't surprised to see Aaron Grossman walking toward me. I was, however, angry at the New York Parks Department for not supplying the shoreline with any large boulders to hide behind. I also considered drowning myself, but death wouldn't have come quickly enough.

"Aaron Grossman!" I said. "I thought that was you."

Aaron trotted up to me, closely followed by his boyfriend José, more pretty than handsome and wearing nothing but an orange bathing suit cut high in the thigh and a ludicrously small knapsack no larger than a Chanel makeup kit.

"I had a feeling we'd run into each other today," Aaron said as he pressed his palms together with delight. "When did you get back?"

"Just few days ago," I lied.

Aaron nodded thoughtfully. José hung back a few steps and looked less than thrilled as Aaron cheated on him spiritually by fucking with my mind.

"Ira tells me you're living in a tent in your parents' backyard."

"Have you seen him?" I asked.

"He had to leave early. You didn't see him go by?"

"No. I—"

"He just walked past a few minutes ago. You must have had your eyes closed."

"I must have been napping."

"So, fill me in," Aaron said as he put one of his caterpillar claws on my shoulder. "How are you, really?"

Because José was already starting to shift his weight impatiently, I attempted to give the shortest possible account of my trip. I did my best to leave out any detail that would have been of the slightest interest; but the more vague and general I became, the more intensely Aaron leaned forward to decipher the subtext of my every syllable. Meanwhile, José certainly made no attempt to disguise his displeasure. He began pursing his lips with a loud squeaking noise, wiggling his fingers, and snorting through his nose. There was obviously a lot of tension between him and Aaron, but I wasn't sure whether I'd caught this couple in the middle of an argument or at the beginning of a new one.

Finally José coughed dramatically into his fist and Aaron simply couldn't ignore him any longer.

"Excuse me. I'm afraid I haven't introduced you. Jaffe Cohen, José Rubens."

José held out his hand daintily. "With Aaron, it's like I'm not here sometimes."

"I've told you about Jaffe," Aaron said sweetly. "From last semester."

"Yes, you did. I know *all* about him," Jose replied with enough edge in his voice to sharpen a steak knife. "How nice to *finally* meet you."

"You're an actor?" I asked politely.

"Yes, I am. And a damn good one, too."

With that José snapped his fingers and announced, "Now *I* have to meet some of *my* friends. So when you two are done reminiscing . . ."

"Wait for me at the concession stand!" Aaron called after him.

"Don't be long," José yelled over his shoulder as he strutted away. "I'll be sucking on a Twizzler!"

Then he started sashaying down the beach with only slightly less tidal motion than the ocean itself.

"Is he OK?" I asked.

"He's just jealous."

"Why?"

Aaron squinted, shook his head, and looked me in the eye.

"You really have no idea, do you?"

"Idea about what?"

"Last semester. The day you came to tell me you were dropping out of the show, it occurred to me that—despite what I thought had been obvious overtures . . ." Aaron shrugged his shoulders and chuckled at an irony known only to him.

"What?" I asked.

"I never expected to be playing this scene on the beach."

"What?" I repeated.

"Do I have to say it?"

I shook my head and looked away. Aaron studied me one last time before taking a step back, and then, with his big toe, he drew a heart in the moist sand. Then, just to make sure I got the point, he very laboriously etched our initials in the heart. JC and AG. I couldn't believe my eyes. Was Aaron telling me that he liked me? I couldn't have been more stunned if Aaron had just revealed he was my grand-mother. Overhead a seagull squawked maniacally.

"Who, me?" I asked.

Aaron nodded his head.

"You like me?"

"Like? Liked? I thought I was over you, but seeing you here now . . ." Aaron laughed to himself. "Oh, boy."

"Since when?" I asked.

"Since last semester."

I stared at Aaron incredulously.

"You mean like . . . during *Alice*?"

"You really had *no* idea, did you? Ira never told you? I told him not to say anything. I never dreamed he would take me seriously."

"You liked me like a boyfriend?"

Aaron took my face in his hands like a sadistic old aunt and squeezed my cheeks while he looked me straight in the eyes. "Yes," he said emphatically.

"I'm . . . I'm sorry."

"For what?"

"For not knowing."

Aaron stepped back and raised his hands in defeat.

"No harm done. I may have been a little too subtle for my own good. I foolishly thought my actions would have spoken for them-selves."

"What actions?"

"Let me count the ways," Aaron announced poetically as he counted off on his fingers. "I chose the project so you could be in it. I cast your best friends as a way to lure you to me. I used Vinnie to demonstrate the type of attention that I was hoping to lavish on you.

Couldn't you see it in my face each time I glanced your way at rehearsals?"

My blank expression was all the answer that Aaron needed.

"Well, the good news," he said, "is that you didn't consciously reject me."

"Not yet," I joked.

Aaron chuckled. Then, maybe it was my general state of disorientation, but all of a sudden he didn't look *too* bad. In fact, if I had squinted my eyes and looked sideways, Aaron wouldn't have been totally unattractive. "So should we get together sometime and talk?" I asked.

Aaron shrugged his shoulders as he backed away in the direction of the concession stand. "It's a little late for that now," he said. "As you can see, I'm a married man."

"Yeah, you better go." I let him take a few more awkward steps before blurting out a question I'd always wanted to be able to ask someone. "Aaron!" I called. "Why—why me?"

Aaron stopped to consider. He was finally in a position where he had something I wanted passionately. I needed to know if I was attractive.

"Because," he finally responded, "you're so delightfully innocent."

"Me? Innocent?"

"Oh, Jaffe," he said shaking his head. "You really don't know how lovable you are, do you?"

Having spoken his exit line, he turned on his heels and quickly disappeared into the crowd of men leaving the beach. My knees buckled and I sat down in the wet sand. For some reason I was enraged. Had I just been rejected by a man I didn't want? "Aaron Grossman!?" I said to myself. Was that the best God had to offer?

"Jesus, why? Why don't I ever get what I *really* want?" Not wasting a moment, I took off my glasses and buried them under a loose mound of sand where I could find them later. Then I galloped into the ocean, raising my knees high, knowing that the cold water would hurt when I hit the waves. I wanted to feel the sting of something—anything—against my body. I wanted to smash against the water. I wanted to exert myself. I wanted to swim as far as I could and make the ocean my home, to be accepted by her like she'd accepted all the other gay men without spitting us out or drowning us as the Red Sea had destroyed Pharaoh's men. I swam under the water as far as I could. Then I surfaced and lay on my back out where the ocean rolled gently, my arms outstretched as if I were on a cross, my head tilted back as if I were being baptized. I floated with the sun in my eyes. I floated until I got bored.

Then I laboriously swam back to shore; there was a strong undertow. I wanted to dry off and find my glasses, but when I got out of the water, the loose mound of sand wasn't where I thought it would be. Starting to panic, I studied the topography of the dunes. I wasn't at the same spot where I'd entered the surf. While I'd been floating, the current had pulled me dozens of yards to the west. Not only that, but the tide had come in a few feet, and for all I knew, my spectacles had been washed away and were halfway to France. "Oh, fuck!" I mumbled to myself as I started stumbling east searching for some kind of marker and praying that some nearsighted jellyfish hadn't absconded with my eyewear.

Several times I stopped to dig, and several times I found nothing but more sand and an occasional Styrofoam cup. "Oh, fuck. Oh, fuck. Oh, fuck" became the mantra I used to block out any thought of calling my parents and having them pick me up because I was too nearsighted to drive home in the car I'd taken without asking. With luck, they'd believe Rachel's story about my looking for a job, but would they ever believe I'd been seeking employment as a lifeguard on a gay beach? "Oh, fuck. Oh, fuck. Fuck you, God!" I finally screamed as I plowed through the moist sand like a hungry dog digging for a bone. "Fuck you! Fuck you! Fuck you!"

"Are you planting a garden?"

The voice was only slightly familiar. I looked up to see the fuzzy outline of the lascivious old gentleman, and from the tone of his voice, I guessed that he was smiling. Just what I needed!

"I lost my glasses. I buried them around here somewhere."

"Is that what you were doing before?"

"I'm really dumb."

"Perhaps I can be of assistance."

"I don't think I'm going to find them."

"Which doesn't mean we still can't enjoy the search."

With more quickness than I thought him capable of, the old man dropped to his knees. Before digging, however, he used all of his senses to survey the terrain and figure out where I'd been. "You told me before that you were going for a walk," he said, pointing to his ear. "And I believe this is the longitude where you entered the water," he said, pointing to his eye. "Let me see. You left me and traveled in a straight line. Now, latitude? Hmm." He pointed to his nose and sniffed the air. "The tide has come in a few yards, which means the ridge into which you probably dug is now this moist lump. Aha!" He reached into the wet sand and dug with an almost orgasmic sense of appreciation. "Lovely! And . . . here they are!" From beneath the earth he pulled on a piece of metal and out came my glasses, muddied and bent, but seemingly salvageable.

"Only slightly the worse for wear," he said.

"Thank you."

"Let me readjust them."

With professional skill, the old man twisted my spectacles back into shape and gently placed them on my face. I stood there grateful.

"This is the first good thing that's happened to me all day."

"I find that hard to believe. To me, you look truly blessed."

"Thank you," I said, awkwardly standing. The old man nodded. I didn't know what else to say. "I better get my towel now and go home."

I slowly walked back to where I'd left my stuff and looked longingly at the gay beach one last time. I wasn't sure if I'd ever return, and I wanted to know exactly what I'd be missing. It was only five o'clock, but the greasy city had already torn itself down like a circus carnival that had moved on to the next town. In its place were a few squatters reading books or napping, separated by yards and yards of wilderness. The sun had turned bright orange, almost radioactive, and purple shadows were starting to form behind miniature dunes and half-buried planks. It was the time of day when Mother Nature whispers her secrets. I wanted to stay longer, but I needed to find a pay phone and call Mother Cohen to tell her that her car was safe.

Before leaving, however, I decided to say one last good-bye to the old man, who had turned his weathered profile to the sea. He looked just like Christopher Isherwood.

"Thanks again," I said awkwardly.

"My pleasure," he replied in the cultured voice of a more well-mannered time and place.

"Your friends left?" I asked.

"Oh, yes. Charming young men. Friends of friends."

The old man looked into my eyes and sighed with complete delight.

"What are you looking at?"

The old man shook his head gently as if to tell me that the answer should have been obvious. "I'm meditating again," he whispered play-fully.

"So you keep your eyes open when you meditate? You don't need to close them?"

"Close my eyes? Oh, no. Heavens!" The elderly gentleman shook his head. "I imagine there'll be plenty of time for that soon enough." The old man turned his face again toward the sea.

"Do you live around here?" I asked.

"Not really. Most of the year I live in Florida."

"Florida?" I questioned. "You don't look Jewish."

"Excuse me?" he asked.

"I thought only old Jews lived in Florida."

"There are some old queens who live there as well."

"So where are you going later? I mean when you go home."

"Oh, yes," he said, as though the thought had not yet crossed his mind. "Where am I going? I'm currently staying in Bay Shore with my mother."

"His mother?" I wondered. "This old guy has a mother? Who? Lillian Gish?"

"Are you going to stay to watch the sunset?" I asked.

"No. I may have seen all the beauty I can possibly take for one day."

"You have a car?"

"The bus," the old man answered somewhat mournfully.

"Oh," I said, quickly calculating where Bay Shore was on the map. "Can I offer you a ride home?"

In the car the old man told me that his name was Herman and not much more. It wasn't that Herman wanted to keep any secrets from me. Rather, for all his apparent eccentricity, he still practiced a gentle restraint that was almost Victorian. I figured he'd been brought up in some kind of exotic Protestant sect—like Presbyterianism—wherein one doesn't burden strangers with too much personal information. Paradoxically, these rules of behavior that may have evolved to make Presbyterians feel more comfortable among themselves tend to make Jews feel quite the opposite. Polite Protestants make us paranoid. Whenever the goyim grow silent we assume we've done something awful and we're about to be kicked out of the country. That's one of the reasons Jews are so loudly inquisitive; we *need* to know what they're hiding from us.

With Herman, however, I didn't feel he would ever pass a law against me, throw a brick through my store window, or toss me from my shtetl. He was a good goy, a man of peace. As he sat next to me in the passenger seat smiling at familiar streets, I was reminded of Scotty and me peacefully hitchhiking out west. As we floated past bowling alleys and fast-food places, Long Island's Sunrise Highway looked less like a tired suburb and more like a land I'd never seen. Later, as the evening wore on, I would ask Herman many questions, less out of paranoia and more because I was fascinated with how Herman had managed to grow so wrinkled on the outside while remaining so youthful in spirit. He had the most radiantly youthful eyes I'd ever seen, like a happy jack-o'-lantern with a candle beaming generously from within.

When we got to his mother's house, Herman graciously asked me inside for tea. I gratefully accepted—there was no harm in keeping the old gentleman company—and I followed him into a brick home shaded by maple trees and set off from the street. The house was older than the others on the block; it had probably been a farmhouse when Long Island still had resplendent views and its inhabitants were still Dutchmen, potatoes, and ducks. When we got inside I dialed my mother and I lied. I told her that I was at the Mid-Island Shopping Center dragging myself from shoe store to shoe store and looking for a job in retail. Luckily, I caught her at either a very good time or a very bad one, because she didn't bother to question me any further. When I hung up the phone Herman asked me, "How will you explain your suntan?"

"Am I tan? Oh, no!"

"As a nut," he said as he gently touched my cheek. "Would you like to come upstairs and apply some ointment?"

A little shyly, I followed Herman up a narrow stairway that brought us into a dark room that spread the whole length of the house. As old as Herman was, this cluttered attic was older still, and it was covered from floor to ceiling with the most interesting artifacts and furniture. It looked like it hadn't been furnished, but rather that furniture had grown out of the walls like knots on an enchanted tree. There was a full-length mirror in a mahogany frame such as Greta Garbo might have used in *Camille*. The walls were lined with bookcases upon which rested dusty landscape paintings peeking out of thick gilded frames. There was an extensive butterfly collection and an old brown army photograph wherein all the men looked like General Custer.

There were also three small beds tucked into gables, which reminded me that, more than anything else, this attic had once been a haven for children. I could almost hear the laughter of bloomered youngsters who had snuck away from the oppressive nightmares of their parents. "This has always been my room," Herman announced gaily as he handed me some aloe vera lotion. "And it always will be," he smiled as a halo of dust danced around his head. Outside the sun was setting, but Herman didn't turn on the lights. He preferred to let his face disappear into the romantic atmosphere of the room.

There was a chair next to Herman's, but for the moment I preferred to flit from tchotchke to tchotchke, rubbing salve into my hands and examining as many objects as possible.

"That's my cavalry regiment," Herman said as he saw me staring at the old brown photograph.

"Cavalry regiment?" I thought to myself.

"Beautiful, beautiful men!" Herman added somewhat mournfully, and I noticed again what a lovely voice he had. Its vibration tickled my spine, and if I just listened to it without looking at his face, he didn't sound a day over . . . sixty . . . seventy . . .

"Can I ask you a question?" I said aloud. "How old are you?"

For the first time that day, Herman seemed at a loss for words.

"Older than God," he finally managed to say.

"Oh."

It was getting too dark to see much of anything in the attic, so I joined Herman in the sitting area. We sat quietly for a moment while I tried to think of polite conversation. Herman finally broke the silence.

"On the beach," he asked, "were you meditating on any particular deity?"

"Jesus," I announced, surprised by how easily I could say the word.

"Ahh!" Herman said. "He's one of my favorites!"

"Really? So are you a—"

"A Christian." Herman finished my sentence. "Among other things."

"Do you . . . do you follow the Bible?"

"Do I follow the Bible?" Herman pondered. "I would say, at my age, the Bible follows me. Would you like your tea now?"

Then Herman went down to the kitchen while I made myself comfortable on the couch, getting into a lotus position in order to feel more spiritual. Nervously, I started thumbing through a photo album Herman had left lying on a coffee table. Inside were pictures of many handsome men photographed against backgrounds of tropical plants and flowers. These guys, when they weren't leaning on each other, were leaning on rakes or watering lawns. They also had something else in common; they were all dark and strangely Semitic, like Sal Mineo in the movie *Exodus*. There wasn't a blond among them.

When Herman returned with a tray, he cheerfully announced that the men in the album were his employees. I hadn't bothered to ask him what he did for a living; apparently he owned a thriving landscape company on one of the Florida keys.

"If you decide not to go back to school," he said as he poured me a cup of tea, "you might want to think of coming down south. I could put you to work."

"It looks like you've already hired the whole Israeli army," I said as I carefully took the saucer into my own hands. Taking a sip, I couldn't resist adding, "You must really like Jewish men."

"Oh, yes!" Herman said as he took a surprisingly manly gulp of Earl Grey. "I've been accused of being a kosher queen."

Suddenly I felt like a slab of salami on a fat man's plate. What I was doing wasn't right! Who was this guy? What new form of temptation had the devil thought of now? I gulped my tea quickly until I could feel the tea leaves tickle the back of my throat. Then I carefully placed my cup in the saucer, stood up, and tried to keep my knees from shaking.

"I better get going," I said.

"So soon?" Herman inquired.

"Yeah. I'm really nervous."

"I'm sorry. Was I making you nervous?"

"No," I said. "You seem very nice. It's just that . . ." My mind considered several lies it could tell before settling on what it believed was the truth. "It's just that I don't want to have sex with you."

"That's quite all right," Herman assured me.

"I mean, that is the reason why you brought me up here."

"Yes," Herman nodded as he stood up. "I suppose that's true." Then he extended his palm to shake mine. "Well," he said, "good day." I shook Herman's hand and started backing away toward the staircase when, suddenly, I was halted by a voice. It sounded familiar, something like the voice I'd heard at the prayer meeting back in Berkeley. Whoever it was, it was much more authoritative than was usual for the inside my head. It neither stammered nor whined. "You have someplace better to go?" it asked me calmly. "Stay."

At that moment I didn't fall to my knees, but I did turn to my host and state as politely as possible, "Well, I don't have to leave *right* away."

"I'm so glad!" Herman responded.

"I mean, it's not like I haven't had an erection for the past fifteen minutes!"

Before I lay down on one of the children's beds, Herman had one request: that I put on a pair of blue jeans that he kept in the bottom drawer of an antique bureau. I thought this request odd, but I'd given up all resistance and I was glad to be guided. I struggled with the zipper; the pants were tight. Then Herman watched me as I modeled theatrically in front of the full-length mirror. His appreciation of me was unconditional as I practiced different expressions like I'd seen in the movie *Blow-Up*. I was coy, pouty, seductive, aloof, and yet somehow available. I was a luscious kaleidoscope of contradictions. Herman chuckled until I finally relaxed and simply looked directly in the looking glass at the kid I'd once been and the man I was about to become.

I was different. For the first time in my life I didn't feel like a buck-toothed bar mitzvah boy struggling to get through grade Gimmel. No, I was a Hebrew warrior. I was Judah Maccabeus with a touch of Queen Esther. I was every Jewish hero and heroine, Samson and Ruth, Paul Newman and Barbra Streisand, all rolled into one. Herman came up behind me and led me to the bed; I lay down and he lay on top of me. I was frightened, yet alert—very Joey Heatherton. I closed my eyes, but when he kissed me the pressure of his head against mine felt like a penetration and I opened them again. I had never been so close to such an old face before.

I stared into his eyes, and they were deep and cluttered, like the room. There was lust in his eyes. That was a little scary. But there was also fatigue—old men do get tired even when they're lusting—and something else that I would only describe as love. Herman loved me. And I loved Herman. It wasn't romantic love. There were no illusions of a future together. I mean, I wasn't about to move to Florida to do yard work. For my part, I was grateful for his hospitality; I had never felt so welcome. For his part, perhaps he was thinking, "I love you for being here. I love you for being so beautiful. I love you because I'm old and I may die soon and only you, my dear, can take this awful horror and turn it into a fabulous mystery."

And now that I'm more than twice as old as I was back then, I realize that Herman loved me as only someone very old can love someone much younger than himself. Twenty-four years later, I certainly have no regrets. It says in the Bible, "Do unto others as you would have them do unto you." Even then, it occurred to me that having sex with Herman was preparing me for my future as a dirty—yet kindly—old man. "It's the wheel of karma," I told myself. "What goes around, comes around." And someday when I'm "older than God" I fully expect to meet somebody every bit as lovely as I was when I was twenty.

The next hour passed like a dream. I remember being completely naked. I remember Herman's mouth exploring my body like Livingston searching for the source of the Nile. I remember coming. I don't remember Herman's coming. (Some things never change.) I remember Herman turning on a table lamp, and noticing that it had a plaster base in the shape of whaling ship. I could have stayed there all evening, but then Herman's mother came home in her Ford Fairlane and honked the horn in the driveway. Herman and I jumped out of bed, got dressed, and skipped down the stairs to help her carry some packages into the kitchen.

Like old Mrs. Potts from Bethpage, Grace was ancient, happy, and slow. Herman was delightfully patient with her as he helped her stack cans in the pantry. Grace asked me to stay for dinner, but, unfortunately, the old woman ate foods so startlingly unkosher that even Joseph Mengele would have turned his head away in disgust. That night she was planning to make "sandwich loaf," a conceptual food sculpture consisting of white bread, deviled ham, and pimiento pork spread frosted with cream cheese. I declined her generous offer, but when it turned out that she had forgotten to buy liverwurst at the store ("I'm such a silly goose!" she said), I volunteered to accompany Herman back to the local Waldbaum's.

We took Grace's car, and Herman drove. The two of us held hands in the front seat like young lovers in a beach-blanket movie. In some strange way, doing errands for his mother had transformed him into one of my contemporaries. For the first time he appeared vulnerable, and I wanted to hold him and pass my strength on to him. I did this by touching him every chance I could, hooking my pinkie finger into his belt loop when I thought the other shoppers weren't looking.

"Do you think about religion a lot?" I asked him as we waited our turn at the deli counter.

"In my weaker moments," he smiled. "Fortunately, now isn't one of them."

"But you seem so spiritually aware," I said.

"Spiritually aware? Oh, no!" he replied. " I'm just old and I don't want to miss anything."

Just then the deli worker, a slightly overweight man named Manuel, passed a greasy bag over the counter. Herman thanked him by name and winked flirtatiously. Surprisingly, Manuel winked back, making me wonder if Herman had ever been manual with Manuel.

"Is he a friend of yours?" I asked as we got back in the car.

Herman nodded without saying anything, and I didn't pursue the topic any further. My day with Herman was coming to an end, and there was no need to spoil it with jealousy.

On our way back to his mother's house we made one short detour down to the seashore because Herman wanted to show me his favorite place in the world. He didn't say so, but I imagined it was where he played as a child. We got out of the car and walked down a dock past a row of motorboats tied up for the night. At the end of the pier we sat down and looked out into the Great South Bay. The sky was bursting with stars, and the air was so thick with the smell of brine we could have feasted on the smells.

"So what is it that you like about Jewish men?" I asked, gently leaning into his shoulder.

"You have such a marvelous sense of history," he replied.

"So do you," I said.

"Darling, I'm nearly history myself."

Herman leaned back on his hands. I mimicked his pose so that our fingers touched behind us. Time was running out, and I could only ask one more question. "Are you ever afraid to die?" I heard myself say.

Herman looked at me as if I had just belched really loud.

"Heavens, what a question!" Then he thought for a moment. "I would have to say . . . no."

"I'm glad," I said, genuinely relieved.

"I might have been when I was younger. But at a certain point death stops looking like such a great mystery. I've had too many friends pass on. Far too many. And they all died heroically, and no two of them had the same religion. Isn't this lovely?" Herman rhapsodized, looking at the bay in front of us. "What a joy!"

"Yeah," I said.

"My whole life, I've always taken pleasure in finding beautiful places where few other people think to come. I'm such a queer old thing."

A ferry passed by on its way out to sea.

"Where's that boat going?" I asked.

"You see that, my dear? It's Fire Island." Herman pointed at a row of lights on the horizon. I had heard something about the place.

"It's looks so close," I said. "Can we swim there from here?"

"I used to think so," Herman said. "Shall we make the attempt?"

Without another word we both jumped off the low pier onto some soft wet sand. Then, stripping naked behind some reeds, we skipped into the water. The tide was so low it actually seemed we could walk all the way across. At some points the bay was so shallow that it was nothing more than a wet film. Then the water would become deeper and we had to step high over ripples catching the light from the shore. I couldn't see the baby fish, but I knew they were there, fleeing from us as we pushed forward. Nor could I see the baby crabs, but I knew they were in the sand beneath our toes, digging their way to China. I don't know how we did it, but we walked for a long long way, and the warm water got no deeper than our knees. We just kept walking until the pier was far behind us and the summer land sounds of TVs, engines, and crickets were absorbed by the more gentle lapping sounds of the water.

To this day I don't know how Herman and I managed to walk so far into the Great South Bay. Maybe we were walking on a sandbar. Maybe we were like Moses, and the water was opening up to let us pass. Maybe, like Jesus, we were walking on the water itself. In any event, when the bay reached our waists we didn't turn back. We submerged ourselves and started doing a gentle breaststroke. We swam for a good long distance—halfway to Fire Island, perhaps—until it finally made sense to stop.

"Looks like we might have to turn back," Herman admitted.

"This is far enough," I agreed.

I paddled over to Herman and dove beneath the surface to see what he felt like under the water. I hugged his torso. His skin, without gravity, was buoyant and smooth. In the water my mate was simply another sea mammal wiggling his limbs in order to stay afloat. He was without age. He was without gender. I stayed beneath the water as long as I could, sliding my hands up and down his body. Then I came up for air. Thinking I might find some in Herman's mouth, I kissed him passionately and my head filled with light.

On my way back from Herman's I found an open shoe store in Massapequa and bought a pair of shoes for Rachel's bat mitzvah. Having just come of age myself, I was feeling very generous. Then when I got home, my mother was in a particularly mellow mood. She told me that Ira had been trying to phone me all evening. When I returned his call, he apologized for having missed me at Field Six and suggested that it might be fun to meet at a place in Bellmore called Pal Joey's. Once again, I had to borrow my mother's car, so I told her I wanted to go over to Ira's.

Now, my mother had never liked Ira very much; he was always a little too theatrical for her taste. Strangely enough, though, she happily gave her permission and told me, "Have fun! Knock yourself out." Maybe she was just relieved that my bizarre mood of the last few weeks had definitely lifted. On the other hand, I've always suspected she knew exactly what was going on and, by loaning me her car, was giving her tacit approval. She probably figured that, if I was going to be "sleeping outside with people I hardly knew," at least I should have some friends who were Jewish.

I couldn't wait to get to Pal Joey's. On my way out of the development, however, I passed by Saint Martin's and had a sudden urge to stop. Parking the car at the curb, I climbed the steps of the church where Brian had once taken me to confession. Nothing much had changed. The aluminum Gates of Paradise had tarnished a bit, but across Central Avenue the twenty-foot stainless-steel cross atop the parochial school was just like I remembered it. With nobody around, I got down on my knees and made my first and last confession.

"Jesus," I said, choosing my words carefully, "today I had sex with a man—although I suspect you already know this. I think you were there when I decided to go through with it. Anyway, it was pretty good. And I'm probably going to want to do it again, every now and then, so if you don't like this—and I'm not sure that you don't, but if you don't like this—could you . . . could you just turn that antenna around and watch someone on another channel?"

Then I stood up and brushed the dirt off my knees. "Thank you," I said. Only later in the car did I begin to reflect. "Just think," I told myself, "all these years I thought I needed to be saved by Jesus when almost any man would have done just as well."

EPILOGUE:
LOS ANGELES, 1997

I hadn't seen Ira and Joshua for a year, and, spotting them at the airport, my worst fears were realized. There they were beneath the American Airlines sign, wearing identical reflective sunglasses and dragging identical powder blue luggage. They'd now had over three years for their styles to meld, and Murphy's Law of gay relationships states that the queen with the tackier taste generally winds up shopping for the two of them. Resolving not to mock, I pulled my dusty old Plymouth over to the curb and jumped out to lift up the back.

"Is this your car?" Ira asked.

"Of course it is! You can't live in L.A. without a car."

"It's great!" Joshua said, apparently as unimpressed with my vehicle as I was with his eyewear. "You got a clutch in this car?" he said as he climbed into the backseat.

"No, but I have a lovely handbag under the seat."

"Let me look at you!" Ira said, sliding in beside me. "How come you're not dark?"

"Who has time to get tan? In twelve months I've seen the Pacific Ocean three times."

"Is it always sunny like this?" Joshua asked as we exited the airport and turned onto Lincoln Boulevard.

"Oh, god. Yes. Every morning I close the shades and pray for clouds. I feel like Morticia Addams. 'Oh, Gomez, I wish it would it rain!'"

"I thought you liked it out here," Joshua said, looking out the window.

"Uggh. The phoniness and materialism are so repulsive."

"And that's just you!" Ira quipped, anticipating the punch line.

"Have you made any friends out here?" Joshua asked.

"Sure, but they're mostly from San Francisco or New York, and all we do is get together and bitch about L.A."

"So basically your life is going great," Ira said knowingly.

"I can't complain," I said.

It just so happened that Ira was right. Shortly after our conversation on the steps of Saint Anthony's in 1995, I was walking down Eighth Avenue—like Paul on the road to Damascus—when I was suddenly struck by an urgent desire to go to Hollywood. Arriving in L.A., determined to focus on my career, I was soon hired by an old friend to write for TV and could thus replenish my bank account. Better still, I found Los Angeles so uninteresting that I also found time to write the book Ira had suggested: the history of our coming out in the heady spiritual times of the early seventies. So, once again, the Wild West had opened up a world of possibilities. Meanwhile, Ira and Joshua had continued to thrive in their new house in upstate New York, deepening their commitment to each other with every room they wallpapered.

Now Joshua's software company had sent him out on a trip to L.A., and Ira had come along to visit. When we got to the Marriott Courtyard in Marina del Rey, Joshua discovered that their room was situated right next to the ice machine and went down to argue with the desk clerk about moving elsewhere. This left Ira and me alone to flop on the beds, lie head to head, and gossip.

"You go first," I said. "Who have you seen lately?"

"Remember Janet Eisenberg?"

"Of course I do! Janet Planet."

"I ran into her at the half-price ticket booth buying tickets to *Miss Saigon*."

"Is that still running!? The war didn't last so long!"

"She lives in Cedarhurst. Married a gynecologist. She's very happy. Looks great. And get this! She was with her nineteen-year-old son—gorgeous, by the way—who has two pierced ears, platinum blond hair, and he wants to study ballet."

"Really!"

"You think he might be gay?"

"You mean like every other man in Janet's life? What were the earrings like?"

"They were an old pair of Janet's."

"No taste! He could be straight. Who else have you seen?"

"Aaron Grossman."

I was almost afraid to ask. "What's *she* up to?"

"You would not believe how much money he's making now. He just directed *The Color Me Elmo Easter Pageant* at Madison Square Garden. He and Raheem are still together, by the way. Oh . . ."

Ira took a deep breath. I expected the worse. "Well, you know Billy Quintana died?"

"Yeah," I said.

"How did you know?"

"Actually, I ran into David at the Sports Connection and he told me."

"David Albright? He lives out here now?"

"He's in casting. He works on *Frasier*."

"Billy." Ira shook his head sadly.

"Billy Quintana," I repeated. "I thought he might make it."

We were silent for a moment while we both stared at the ceiling as if it were the bottom rung of heaven.

"You know who I still miss sometimes?" Ira said.

"Who?"

"Vinnie," Ira said.

"Me too," I whispered as we snuggled closer on the bed. "I've actually been thinking about him a lot lately. God, he was right. Everything pops out of nothing, and it could all disappear again just like that." I rolled even closer to Ira and put my head on his chest.

"We've known so many," Ira said.

"And they all died heroically, and no two of them had the same religion."

Then, as happens so often with Ira, the specific moment seemed to drift away and we really didn't know, or care, if we were eighteen or eighty or whether we were experiencing our future or our past.

"How's your book coming?" Ira asked.

"OK," I said hesitantly.

"But?"

"OK, here's the problem. Obviously at the end of the story I don't become a Christian, because I decide that my real life is more important than some idea of who God might be. And of all the people I've known you are the most real. My most devoted friend. You *are* my real life."

"So?"

"So, how do I describe you? At different points in my life, you've been my confidante, my rival, my substitute spouse, my touchstone. No matter what I say about us, it always sounds either hokey or trivial."

Ira couldn't answer my question.

"Why didn't we ever become lovers?" I asked.

"It never seemed necessary," Ira said, pulling me toward him as we

both sat up to stare out the window. We continued to lie there holding hands, both of us feeling like ocean liners refueling before once
again heading out to sea. Outside, the sun was setting over the Pacific,
and I realized that one of the reasons I rarely went to the beach in
California was that I had never fallen in love with this particular
ocean. It didn't smell like the ocean I'd grown up with in Brooklyn.
The Atlantic was sweeter, more manageable, and it bordered coun-
tries like England, France, and Israel—places where my imagination
had lived. The Pacific just seemed to border on more Pacific. The
Atlantic was every place I'd been and still wanted to recall. The Pacific
was every place I hadn't gone and wasn't ready to think about yet. It
frightened me, but it frightened me less with Ira seated beside me.

"You know," Ira whispered, "Joshua is still asking me about
whether or not you actually saw Jesus."

"He is?"

"So, once and for all. Do you really think it was Jesus you saw in
Berkeley?"

I lay my head on the pillow and thought long and hard. With Ira,
there was no need to be glib.

"Yes."

Ira furrowed his brow and leaned in closer.

"So you *really* took Jesus into your life?"

"Absolutely," I said. "In fact, there are still scary moments—like
on an airplane and we're experiencing turbulence—when I feel sorry
I didn't work harder to *keep* Jesus in my life."

"So you still have a relationship with Jesus?"

"Oh, yeah," I said. "But like most of my relationships, it was hot
for three weeks and I've been talking about it for twenty years. You
and me, on the other hand . . ."

The room was nearly dark now. The dark ocean had blended into
the night sky, and some of the moist darkness seemed to enter the
room.

"When I die, Ira, will you promise to be there, so it won't be so scary?"

"You mean like Susan Sarandon in *Dead Man Walking*? The face of love'?"

"Yeah."

"Of course I will," Ira said. "Of course I will."